Gender, Sexualities and Culture in Asia

The Gender, Sexualities and Culture in Asia book series provides a welcome new forum for monographs and anthologies focusing on the intersections between gender, sexuality and culture across Asia. Titles in the series include multi- and interdisciplinary research by scholars within Asia as well as in North American, European and Australian academic contexts. It offers a distinctive space for the exploration of topics of growing academic concern, from non-normative cultures of sexuality in Asia, to studies of gendered identities cross the region, and expands the field of Asian genders and sexualities by applying a cultural lens to current debates, including rural lives, migration patterns, religion, transgender identities, sex industry and family.

More information about this series at
http://www.palgrave.com/gp/series/15191

Joseph N. Goh

Becoming a Malaysian Trans Man

Gender, Society, Body and Faith

palgrave
macmillan

Joseph N. Goh
School of Arts and Social Sciences
Monash University Malaysia
Bandar Sunway, Selangor, Malaysia

Gender, Sexualities and Culture in Asia
ISBN 978-981-15-4533-7 ISBN 978-981-15-4534-4 (eBook)
https://doi.org/10.1007/978-981-15-4534-4

Cover illustration: Contributor: Cultura RM/Alamy Stock Photo

This Palgrave Macmillan imprint is published by the registered company Springer Nature Singapore Pte Ltd.
The registered company address is: 152 Beach Road, #21-01/04 Gateway East, Singapore 189721, Singapore

To my parents, sister and niece, the Hallims, EQARS, SASS and Monash colleagues, all transgender, nonbinary, gender nonconforming and queer Malaysians and our allies, all who fight for gender and sexuality rights, and the eternal memory of my husband R.

Foreword

In the rapidly growing field of, loosely defined, scholarly works on transgender people, Joseph N. Goh's contribution distinguishes itself by its multiple layers of contributions. First and foremost, *Becoming a Malaysian Trans Man: Gender, Society, Body and Faith* documents, situates and examines the experiences of 15 Malaysian self-identified trans men. By working closely with the community organization Transmen of Malaysia and a highly visible trans activist in Malaysia, Goh was able to listen closely to the ways in which Malaysian trans men construct their subjectivities on a spectrum of transmasculinity. His discussion reflects political, sociocultural and faith discourses specific to Malaysian constructions of masculinity.

The participants in Goh's study shared their life stories, allowing him to construct vignettes of how Malaysian trans men become trans men, transmasculine or simply men. His grounded theory analysis delicately avoids essentializing and over-generalizing but still succeeds in situating the knowledge he is documenting and co-creating in a global context of transdisciplinary gender and sexuality studies.

Goh's explicit goal of unsilencing studies on Malaysian trans men is a driving force throughout the text and lives up to the authorial intent of bringing into visibility both scholarly work and lived experiences of transgender men in Malaysia.

In five engaging chapters, Goh analyzes the ways in which the participants in his study construct their identities, engage with society, grapple with gender dysphoria, embark on medical transitioning and perform their faiths. By offering interview excerpts and conversational summaries, Goh portrays the ways in which social interactions with families, friends and coworkers as much as intrapersonal communication about one's place in a gendered world shape his participants' life experiences. Each participant's individuality as *one* human experiencing *one* life in a shared cultural context clearly emerges from the interviews, and Goh's respect for each individual's self-location manifests in his writing.

These analyses of the interviews are bracketed by a prologue and an epilogue that position Goh's observations and findings in widening fields of literature: scholarship on Asian queer subjectivities, scholarship on trans and nonbinary identities, and scholarship on the philosophical relationships between being, becoming and gender. Goh's discussion of the role of faith and religion in the becomings of Malaysian trans men is particularly meaningful because this constitutes an understudied and silenced topic within transgender scholarship and activism at large.

Goh's self-location is multi-faceted and complex. He describes his multiple identities as 'a masculine-presenting cis gay man, trans ally, educator and research in gender and sexuality studies, activist, ordained minister and Malaysian citizen of mostly Chinese heritage who is more spiritual than religious'. In addition, Goh's work is clearly marked by nuanced, self-reflexive awareness of linguistic registers and language use, which brings a cultural depth to his work that is often absent in work of researchers who are dominantly monolingual.

A highly accessible and clearly written book, *Becoming a Malaysian Trans Man* beautifully illustrates that 'to *become* a trans man is precisely to become, and never to *be* as fait accompli even if *being* is an aspiration'. By transcending oversimplified or deterministic identity models and categorization, Goh moves forward a theoretical discussion that has been taking shape within transgender literatures, a discussion that has applied consequences for the self-understanding of those who are seeking sustainable self-locations in quickly shifting, highly localized yet globally informed gender discourses. It makes a remarkable contribution to the field and has the potential to bring the comfort of self-avowal, self-recognition and knowledge of shared experiences to Malaysian trans men.

matthew heinz
Vice-Provost, Graduate and Interdisciplinary Studies
Professor, School of Communication and Culture
Royal Roads University, Victoria, BC, Canada

Acknowledgments I would like to express my gratitude to the *Illahi* who breathed life into this project; Aarone, Adam, Alco, Axman, Bottle, Braveheart, Hadi, Jon, Michael, Pokerface, Ray, Schulz, SR, Superman and Warp, for sharing their stories with me; Dorian Wilde and Transmen of Malaysia (ToM), my gatekeepers; the Series Editors Stevi Jackson, Olivia Khoo and Denise Tse-Shang Tang; the peer reviewers; collaborators at Palgrave Macmillan and Springer, especially Connie Li and Zobariya Jidda; and the School of Arts and Social Sciences, Monash University Malaysia for its support towards this project.

Contents

CHAPTER 1

Prologue

Meeting Dorian Wilde

Germinal ideas for this monograph had sprung from a plethora of questions that swirled in my mind soon after I was first acquainted with a Malaysian trans man, Dorian Wilde,[1] in 2010. I had just returned to Malaysia in that same year after completing graduate studies in the United States and commenced employment with PT Foundation, a community-based organisation in Kuala Lumpur that aims to promote greater awareness of issues connected to gender, sexuality and sexual health. At that time, the financial support that came primarily from the Ministry of Health and the Ministry of Women, Family and Community Development enabled the organisation to operationalise various departments or Programmes that corresponded with population groups which were most at risk of contracting and spreading HIV. Such groups included Men who have Sex with Men (MSM), male-to-female transgender (TG) or *mak nyah*[2] sex workers, female sex workers, injecting

[1] Dorian Wilde's assigned name at birth as it appears in his *MyKad* or Malaysian Identity Card is adequately androgynous-sounding to elude gender policing. Nonetheless, he has indicated his preference to use, and be addressed and referred to as 'Dorian Wilde'. See also 'Appendix 2: Interviewing Dorian Wilde'.

[2] The precise etymology of '*mak nyah*' remains obscure, but Thaatchaayini Kananatu and I suggest the following: ""*[M]ak*" is a Malay honorific used for senior women. "*Nyah*" is an abbreviation of "*nyonya*", a term used for Malaysian ladies of mixed parentage. It is

J. N. Goh, *Becoming a Malaysian Trans Man*,
Gender, Sexualities and Culture in Asia,
https://doi.org/10.1007/978-981-15-4534-4_1

drug users and People Living with HIV (PLHIV). As the new Voluntary HIV Counselling and Testing Programme manager, I felt privileged to work alongside colleagues who shared a similar vision of empowering marginalised communities from physical, medical, legal and spiritual perspectives.

Wilde and I met for the first time at an event organised by the Mak Nyah Programme in which a non-Malaysian trans woman activist was invited to share on her work. I soon learned that Wilde was in his mid-twenties, of Indian descent, self-employed, a pioneering Malaysian trans activist and an advocate for gender and sexuality rights (Fong 2015b). He was also the founder and co-leader of the online support group Transmen of Malaysia (ToM) founded in 2011, and a key member of several transgender networks such as MyNetra and Justice for Sisters (Khor 2014). Our subsequent encounters were mostly unpremeditated, sporadic and brief, but proved to be no obstacle to quality conversations on the vicissitudes of lesbian, gay, bisexual, transgender, intersex and queer (LGBTIQ) Malaysians, whom I also refer to in this volume as transgender and queer people.[3]

When the day finally drew to a close, I found myself inevitably given to contemplation. Who was this courageous person? Why did a Malaysian who was assigned female and woman at birth decide to become a man in a country that was unequivocally intolerant of gender and sexual diversity? When did he come to realise his gender identity? Had he undergone Gender Affirmation Surgery? Had he started Gender-Affirming Hormone Therapy? If so, where did he go to for such medical support? How was he treated by his family, friends and society in morally conservative Malaysia?

often used in reference to effeminate male-bodied subjects. Taken together, "*mak nyah*" can be understoodas a respectful term for effeminate, lady-like men' (2018, n. 1). Trans activist Khartini Slamah (2005) states that the term was chosen and appropriated by trans women in Peninsular Malaysia themselves in 1987 in order to create a unique group identity that would simultaneously confer a sense of dignity.

[3]There are three matters I wish to bring up here. First, Western-groomed categories that make up the LGBTIQ acronym continue to gain traction among Malaysians. The imaginaries of self-empowerment and self-actualisation that 'LGBTIQ' harbour are far more appealing than mostly derogatory local terms. Second, 'LGBTIQ' is my extension of the term 'LGBT' which is gaining popularity in 'newspaper articles without parenthetical explanation' (Ferrarese et al. 2015, 54) and is used in a disparaging manner by Malaysian politicians and religious leaders. Gay men and trans women arguably command greater prominence as compared to other communities in the country.

How did religion play a role in his journey if he was a person of faith? What did he have to retain and relinquish in order to live out his gender identity? What were the complex arrangements of his joys and sorrows, triumphs and failures? And many more questions.

In 2011, I left PT Foundation to pursue doctoral studies. I also found myself collaborating with Patrick S. Cheng of the United States as the co-editor of the *Queer Asian Spirit* e-magazine (2012). Between 2012 and 2014, this online platform sought to publish religious, theological and spiritual perspectives by LGBTIQ people of Asian descent around the world. Upon my request, Wilde graciously contributed a short article in which he divulged his identity as 'a pansexual transman with drag queen tendencies' (2012a). In that short piece, he also described his spirituality as being 'part of the endless energy of this universe, and [that he was] here in this human form to experience the experiences assigned to [him]'. I was attracted to his acute self-awareness and the strong material grounding of his sense of the sacred that informed his self-affirmed gender identity.

Over time, I learned more about Wilde from mutual friends, the news media and subsequently an elite interview. As one of the most significant activists for Malaysian trans men, he is highly respected by fellow trans men, Malaysian LGBTIQ communities and allies. Wilde began chronicling his gender-affirming transitioning on YouTube in 2010 (2010), and these videos continue to be a source of inspiration for many local trans men. They have also been instrumental in connecting hidden and isolated trans men to Wilde and eventually to ToM, at which point they are provided with opportunities for fraternal support in addition to relevant information on physical, mental and emotional health (Appendix 2: Interviewing Dorian Wilde, paras. 8, 45–46). Wilde has spoken publicly about his life as a Malaysian trans man in Malaysia to various media portals. Aside from the aforementioned YouTube videos, he has appeared in international and local online videos that touch on diverse aspects of transgender life (I Am the T 2014; Justice for Sisters 2014).

Wilde believes that his gender identity as a man began from the womb (quoted in Uthaya 2013)[4] even as his corporeality does not totally reflect

[4]Owing to the fact that a majority of Malay-Muslim, Indian and indigenous Malaysians use patronymic names, I will refer to most of them by their first names. However, it must be noted that while some do adopt surnames, its use is arbitrary, inconsistent and undetermined.

his 'real' gender identity (Fong 2015b; Khor 2014; Minderjeet 2017). He has also reiterated that his basic identity as a human being transcends all other labels (Wilde 2012a, b), which I understand as a strategy on his part to underscore the basic commonality of humanity irrespective of gender and sexual identities. In response to a news reporter who wanted to know what his answer would be 'if someone asked him about what to do as a transgender', Wilde replied that 'he would say: "Accept yourself and don't be afraid"' (quoted in Fong 2015b). Despite living in a country that continues to persecute its LGBTIQ citizens, Wilde has publicly expressed his optimism that LGBTIQ rights are imminent (Malaysian Digest 2017). He admits that he constantly meets with personal challenges but continues to be at the forefront of LGBTIQ activism—particularly for the sake of trans men—as his personal mission is 'to help others, who are like [him], to brave their way through life' (quoted in Fong 2015b).

The questions I had posed myself when Wilde and I first met were in gestation until some six years later, when he conceded to an elite interview. His warm affability, gender and sexual self-assuredness, pragmatic approach to spirituality, unshakeable optimism, indomitable spirit and indefatigable zeal to help others disclosed an interiority which refused to be crushed and vanquished by transnegative discourses in Malaysia. I sensed a similar openness, forthrightness, passion, inner strength and resilience in 'Aarone', 'Adam', 'Alco', 'Axman', 'Bottle', 'Braveheart', 'Hadi', 'Jon', 'Michael', 'Pokerface', 'Ray', 'Schulz', 'SR', 'Superman' and 'Warp',[5] fifteen trans men who agreed to tell me their life stories for my research project and whose narratives have become the bedrock of this volume.[6]

This monograph does not embark on a mission to suggest new labels, types, categories or classifications of identity among trans men in the Malaysian context, or to connect the contemporary trans men with autochthonous subjectivities for historical justification, even though such approaches can be extremely helpful to locate and understand the self-positionalities of contemporary trans men. Instead, this book offers glimpses of *how Malaysian trans men become trans men*—or for some,

[5] See 'Appendix 1: Designing the Research Project' for a fuller description of each research participant.

[6] These names are all self-selected pseudonyms. In 'Appendix 1: Designing the Research Project', I provide more information on the research design and research participants.

become transmasculine, and for others, simply men—through multifaceted *becomings* that involve active performances of gender, society, body and faith within political, cultural and socio-economic particularities. Such becomings accentuate the fact that 'gender infuses all our identities so that race, age, class, ethnicity, ability and nationality are also gender specific identities' (Peterson and True 1998, 16).

In this volume, I borrow Noreen Giffney's interpretation of 'becoming' as inspired by Gilles Deleuze and Félix Guattari:

> Becoming signifies not the movement through identification from one category to another – being via becoming to being – but the understanding that change is all there is. Becoming involves the shedding of the chimera of stability and certainty wrought through our attachments to objects towards an awareness and acceptance of the unrelenting dynamism that underpins the act of living itself. (2009, 6)

Becoming is exceedingly helpful in contemplating the subjective production of trans men. As I see it, the becomings of trans men do not imply that they 'have migrated from one ontological state of gendered and sexualized existence to another' (J. N. Goh 2014a, 128). Nor am I suggesting that becoming even has precise points of departure and arrival. As I see it, to become a trans man is precisely to *become*, and never to *be* as fait accompli even if *being* is an aspiration of 'successful' ontological achievement. Becoming is inextricably linked to identities as it galvanises, mobilises, shifts and upends any fixity or permanence in identity. Logically therefore, the processes of self-actualisation and self-determination towards self-affirmed gender identities must not be understood as the solidification of identity, but as an interminable, unruly, oscillating, unpredictable and ambiguous unravelling of meanings.

I use 'trans' and 'transgender' in this volume to refer to individuals 'who have "crossed" genders' [, in which 'trans' means] 'cross', 'across', 'beyond' or 'through' (Brown 2016, 7), often resulting in some of definitive self-affirming gender identity rather than gender fluidity or ambiguity. In this Chapter, I reserve the use of 'gender nonconformity', 'gender variance', 'gender diversity' and their cognates for individuals who straddle or reject definitive gender identities and expressions. In the same vein, my use of 'cisgender' or 'cis' allies itself with matthew heinz's observation that 'the Latin prefix *cis* denotes "on the same side" and has come to be understood as an antonym to *trans*' (2016,

8; original italics). My use of 'transgender' or 'trans' *men* throughout these pages refers specifically to individuals who were assigned female at birth but live as men in the particularities of their everyday existence, irrespective of surgical and endocrinal interventions. While 'transgender*ed*' (Cromwell 1999; Tanis 2003), 'transgender*ism*' (Winter 2006) and 'transsexual*ism*' (Chong 1990; Devor 2016; Watts 2002) are also widely circulated terms, I deliberately eschew them because of their tacit 'medico-psychiatry' (Cromwell 1999, 23) connotations and turn instead to the notion of subjectivity.[7] I am also fully cognisant of numerous Malaysian studies on transgender people that simplistically conflate transgender, transsexual and transvestite subjectivities (DeAlwis and David 2010; Samsul Draman et al. 2016).

My use of 'subject' and 'subjectivity' echoes Tom Boellstorff's 'social constructionist theory' of sexual subjectivity as '*the various senses of self* – erotics, assumptions about one's life course, and so forth – that obtain when occupying a subject position, whether partially or completely, temporarily or permanently' (2005, 10; added emphasis). His understanding of subjectivity draws on the Bahasa Indonesia[8] concepts of '*pribadi* or *jati diri*, both of which mean approximately "self-conception"' (2005, 10). He argues that 'it is not possible to have subjectivities without subject positions' because subjects occupy subject positions, or 'extant social categories of selfhood' (2005, 10) within spatial and temporal boundaries. Subjectivities do not adopt ahistorical identities, or remain in eternal subjective permanence. Subjectivities are socioculturally and politically contingent, malleable, permeable and capacious just as subject positions 'are shaped by their embedded notions of their own history and what counts as history' (2005, 35).

Pribadi bears a striking similarity to the Bahasa Malaysia[9] term *keperibadian*, which translates as 'personality', 'personhood' or 'individuality' and thus still falls within the ambit of self-conception. Here, I also look

[7] During a face-to-face conversation on 4th June 2016, Wilde expressed his discomfort with the term 'transgenderism' and insisted vehemently that Malaysian trans men are not 'isms'. Since then I have avoided the term in favour of 'subjectivity', 'self-affirmed gender identity', 'gender identity', 'personhood' and other similar terms. See 'Epilogue'.

[8] The national language of Indonesia which is similar to the national language of Malaysia.

[9] *Bahasa Malaysia* or Malay, sometimes referred to as *Bahasa Melayu*, is the national language of Malaysia.

to Katherine Johnson's concept of embodied subjectivity, namely 'how the self is *lived* through embodied practices … particularly … for those who undergo radical body modification' (2016, 55; original emphasis).

By proposing trans man subjectivities as dynamic projects of self-reflexivity and self-realisation within a historical ethos, I am able to articulate the becoming of a trans man as the pursuit of a self-affirmed gender identity that is perpetually in progress, the embodiment of an 'unrelenting dynamism that underpins the act of living itself' (Giffney 2009, 6) and a profound sense of the material-self-in-society that is constantly decentred, negotiated and evolving. As the ensuing chapters will reveal, Malaysian trans men vary in their understandings of, and the need for a gendered telos.

Transdiscourses: The Vocabulary of Becoming

Jason Cromwell explains that transdiscourses diverge from the pathologising and hegemonising discourses of 'medico-psychological practitioners' (1999, 19). Transdiscourses constitute the apposite language of transgender communities which are 'adapted out of (or created from) trans experiences' and thus 'affirming, empowering, positive, and reflective of trans experiences and the lives people choose to live' (Cromwell 1999, 19). Transdiscourses provide an alternative to violent narratives, hateful rhetoric and ignorant speech. They enable transgender people to live and flourish according to their own terms, to speak on behalf of themselves rather than to be spoken *at*, *about* and *against*. As this book will show, transdiscourses accord to trans men the vocabulary of becoming trans men.

Terminologies of self-identity are examples of transdiscourses. They reveal how indispensable transdiscourses are to transgender people because they restore autonomy, agency and dignity to transgender people. In this regard, the efforts of trans men in the United States is particularly noteworthy. In addition to accepting affirming descriptors from other transgender communities, they have developed an impressive array of terminologies to define both to themselves and to society what they believe in, feel and experience inside. Griffin Hansbury lists 'Man … Transsexual Man, Man of Transsexual Experience, New Man, Transman, Transfag, Transqueer, GenderQueer, Guy, Boi, Trans-Butch, Tomboy, Boy-Chick, Gender Outlaw, Drag King, Passing Woman, Bearded Female, Two-Spirit, Ungendered, Gender Trash, Questioning,

Just Curious [and] Woodworkers' (2005, 245–46) as some examples. matthew heinz furnishes a litany that includes 'affirmed male, bi-gender, boi, boy ... guy ... male, male-identified, male of centre ... man of transgendered experience, man with transsexual history, new man, non-binary guy, trannyboi, transboy, transfag, transguy, transmale, transman, transmasculine, or transmasculine-leaning' (2016, 3).

Cromwell observes that trans men have also created '"native", insider, or emic' acronyms for themselves such as 'FTM (female-to-male) or F2M; MTM (male-to-men, based on some FTMs'/transmen's belief that they have always been men in spite of being born with female bodies)' (1999, 24). To this repertoire, heinz adds 'AFAB (Assigned female at birth) ... FAAB (female assigned at birth), f2m, F2M, female-bodied man [and] M2M' (2016, 3). The gendering of genitalia and the de-naturalisation of biological immutabilities have been well argued (Butler 1999, 1993), but the pervasive and persistent intermingling of gender and anatomy in these terminologies and acronyms tells of an irresistible and ineradicable mutuality between categories of embodiment, relationality and emotion within the gendered subject's lived realities.

The magnitude of self-descriptors as devised by North American trans men or favourably assigned to trans men by other transgender communities implies *a drive for meaningful self-expression that emanates from substantive agency*, even if this agency is conditioned, interpreted and curtailed by existing cultural semiotics. In many cases, purposeful self-description lends itself heterogeneously yet effectively to self-empowerment and self-realisation. At the same time, the astounding variety of these appellations and their meanings lay bare the instability, fluidity and evolution of becoming a trans man. A significant self-designated name for one trans man 'may be another's Gender Trash' (Hansbury 2005, 245). It could hold significance only for a specific period of time before other more compelling labels emerge and take its place. Contrastingly, Malaysian trans men may not necessarily possess the cultural capital, legal and political resources, or religious liberty to engage in similarly diverse pursuits of self-description.

Miriam J. Abelson's recent study unearths the negotiations of trans men with dominant manifestations of American masculinities such as 'hypermasculine men, regular guys, progressive men, and faggy men' (2019, 26) as conditioned by issues of ethnicity, class and geographical space. Malaysian trans men also encounter such negotiations, although issues of ethnicity, class and space often do not seem to be at the forefront of their consciousness in such deliberations.[10] Instead, issues of identity, social engagement, dysphoria, transitioning and religion appear to take centre stage in their subjectivities. Admittedly, any denotation of what it means to be a man in Malaysia—or any part of the world—is always a precarious project, given that each man is socialised into, and consequently self-polices and self-defines 'man' in accordance with the specificities of his lived realities. Yet it is possible to locate the political, sociocultural and religious rhetoric that determines and shapes notions of 'manness', 'manhood', 'manliness', 'maleness' and 'masculinity'.[11]

Malaysian studies on men indicate that male masculinities are conditioned by class, ethnic and religious factors. For instance, traits such as crudeness, boisterousness, physical strength and disputatiousness among Malaysian Chinese male truck drivers stand in contrast with the dignity, authority and self-restraint among male truck owners (Nonini 1999). Moreover, machines figure largely in cultural interpretations of a technology-driven masculinity among Malaysian Chinese working-class men (Mellström 2003). Financial stability, job security, good physical health, sexual virility and male-designated genitalia are prized as 'manly' traits (Felix 2014; J. N. Goh 2018; Low et al. 2006; Ng et al. 2008). Patriarchal practices also serve to corroborate both ethnic, sociocultural and Malay-Muslim dictates of masculinity (Morrison 1995; Noritah 2006). Same-sex attractions between men—often erroneously ascribed to trans women (Ismail 2001)—is unanimously condemned as illicit in largely conservative Malaysia, mostly due to the convergence of ethnic (read Malay-Muslim), Islamic and nationalistic ideologies (Chua 2014; J. N. Goh 2014b; Jerome 2011; Shah 2018; Shamsul and Mohamad Fauzi 2006). There is also an uncontested and steadfast belief that masculinity is superior to femininity in Malaysia (J. N. Goh 2014b). These contributory elements of masculinity impact heavily on formations of gender identity among trans men.

[10] My research participants provided sparse feedback on class, ethnicity and spatial issues, even when persistently prompted. I am inclined to believe that these issues are ordinarily more implicitly than explicitly experienced and articulated.

[11] Throughout this book, I use such terms, as well as 'womanness', 'womanhood', 'womanliness', 'femaleness' and 'femininity' without inverted commas not in an ontological sense, but to denote a performance of traits that convincingly portray a desired gender identity.

Wilde advises that there is a lack of cohesiveness in Malaysian trans men subjectivities, in which they presently locate themselves on a 'spectrum called transmasculinity' which includes masculine-acting women and self-identified men who were assigned female (and woman) at birth, and that their subjectivities are 'still in the process of being worked out, [in which they may] remain in the spectrum, [or] later separate [them] selves' (Appendix 2: Interviewing Dorian Wilde, paras. 1–2). Moreover, many find that they have already been named, stereotyped, reviled and taxonomised in accordance with normative conventions in a disenabling environment, and their best efforts for self-actualisation trivialised.

I recognise my linguistic limitations in being mainly fluent in English and Malay, but I am certain that there are no autochthonous terms for Malaysian trans men in the Malay, Chinese, Indian or various indigenous languages in the country that manifest sociocultural approval or self-empowerment. It is also worthwhile to note that there is often no distinction between gender and sexual identities in Malaysia, or even discrete concepts of gender and sexual identities, as is the case in many parts of Southeast Asia (Jackson 2003; Peletz 2006). The Malay term *pak nyah* was used briefly by mostly Malay trans men as a masculine version of *mak nyah* but soon fell into obsolescence due to its inaccuracy and lack of popularity.[12] Many Malaysian trans men have never had a 'female history' (Hansbury 2005, 249) or lesbian history but are misgendered in the Malay language as *wanita keras* (literally 'hard' or 'rough' women) or '"masculine" or "butch" lesbian women' (J. N. Goh 2018, 170; also Lee 2011, 108; 2010, 150), *tomboy*, or *pengkid*, 'a localized synonym for a masculine-looking Malay-Muslim lesbian who is outlawed in Malaysia through Islamic discourses' (Y. Wong 2012, 436). In some rarer cases, trans men are addressed as, and referred to pejoratively as *pondan*.

Conceptually, the Malay term *pondan* 'works against the elaboration of distinctions ... between transvestism, transsexualism, hermaphroditism, homosexuality, and effeminate behavior' (Peletz 1996, 123) among men. *Pondan*, like other Malaysian terms, troubles the neat, discrete categories of gender and sexuality. It remains a subjective puzzle that does not resolve transgender and queer embodiments. Shanon Shah (2018) has uncovered its potency as a derogatory term for trans women, but I argue that its presence is felt most keenly at the grassroots as a scornful

[12]WhatsApp conversation with Wilde, 24th April 2018.

'catch-all to "feminise" every manner of non-heteronormative male subjectivity' (J. N. Goh 2018, 61) and as an accusation of abnormality levelled against masculine-acting individuals who were assigned female at birth. In my estimation, *pondan* is a particularly caustic appellation.

An anecdote may help elucidate my point: I clearly remember an incident more than a decade ago when a Malaysian father whom I knew relatively well and regarded as a friend condemned his masculine-presenting daughter as a disappointment and source of humiliation to the community because she was a *pondan*. When I visited, the entire family was present. The callous remark which fell from his lips was deliberately meant for the ears of this young adult who smiled at me in embarrassment. I believe that my attempts to defend her by reminding my friend that she was still his child were futile. Shame had eclipsed all logic and rationality. I lost touch with this family soon after the incident, and had neither the opportunity to speak to her about her father's reaction nor learn of her actual gender identity.

My research experiences inform me that *pondan* transgresses gender boundaries and insinuates 'an ingrained defectiveness and unworthiness that resides in the crevices of human embodiment' (J. N. Goh 2018, 61) when any person refuses and/or is unable to abide by gender norms. In this sense, despite its somewhat uncommon deployment, *pondan* is perhaps the most rancorous term used on Malaysian trans men. 'Trans man' remains the preferred identity for Malaysian individuals who were Assigned female at birth but live their adult lives as men. The jettisoning of *pondan*, *pak nyah*, *wanita keras*, *tomboy* and *pengkid* in favour of 'trans man' likely serves as a ratification of personal-communal empowerment and a repudiation of derision. It is even more likely that 'trans man' reflects a deep-seated desire to imitate and participate in 'collective identification' (Hines 2007, 58), notably that which is cultivated in North American (and European) contexts, 'in order to demand rights, equal citizenship, and welfare' (Chatterjee 2018, 312) among other goals in Malaysia. This is hardly surprising. Technological advances facilitate unprecedented accessibility to copious resources on transgender issues and imagine a global transgender community in borderless solidarity. Travis S. K. Kong points out however, that 'globalization is an uneven process that reproduces spatially uneven development, and the flow of capital, commodities, people, images, and ideas is never equal among locations' (2010, 11).

The Malaysian trans man thus experiences unequal and unstable access to the bounty of globalisation due to local limitations in education, economic means, social and cultural capital, class, ethnicity, religious affiliation, educational levels, infrastructure and health services. He continues to be experience 'disjunctive modernities' (Yu 2019) which exhibit 'irreducible plurality and local specificity' (Martin and Ho 2006, 186), thus dispelling the myth of trans(national) homogeneity in transgender identity. The trans men I interviewed interpret their life stories through the rubric of local contexts that dispel any suspicion of a mere mimicry of western-styled transgender identities.[13] Malaysian re/mouldings of 'trans man' speak to 'experiences of multiplicity in gender identification ... embedded within specific social, cultural, and interpersonal contexts [that] create altogether new, emergent forms of experience and identity' (Diamond and Butterworth 2008, 366).

These processes are replete with possibilities of self-realisation, but they can also prove to be occasions when trans men experience a 'diminishment of subjectivity [which] signals the insignificance and ludicrousness of their bodies among many in Malaysian society' (J. N. Goh 2012a, 221). While this reality needs to be acknowledged, as 'transmasculine discourse must leave room for localized, individuated identification of marginalization, discrimination and violence ... it must be careful to not obscure uncomfortable conversations and sweep dynamics that affect some, but not all transmen under a convenient banner of victimhood' (heinz 2016, 229). The dialectical dynamics of deep materiality towards self-realisation evince lived realities that bear the effects of repudiation, antagonism and persecution, but also resistance, liberation, empowerment and self-actualisation.

An Ethic of Unsilencing[14]

Despite his belief that 'Malaysians generally have a positive attitude towards transgender people' (quoted in Fong 2015b), Wilde has commented publicly on the various challenges that he and other trans men encounter in society, including parental objection and dismissal (cited in Cheh 2017; Fong 2015b; Uthaya 2013), gender incredulity when

[13] Dennis Altman's article 'On Global Queering' (1996) comes immediately to mind.

[14] The title of this section is inspired in part by Alwyn Lau's formulation of an 'ethic of astounding love' (2011, 30).

dealing with public services (cited in Irin News 2014), bullying at school (cited in Pragalath 2018), problems with gender-specific public toilets, hospital wards and access to healthcare (cited in Minderjeet 2017; Pragalath 2018), and defamatory depictions of LGBTIQ people in the media (cited in Qishin 2016).

Malaysia is not exempted from 'the medical and psychiatric discourses of the twentieth and twenty-first centuries [which] have tended to frame transgender people as sometimes ill, deviant, and even menacing' (Abelson 2019, 13). Moreover, the overwhelming and far-reaching effects of patriarchy, heteronormativity and cisnormativity[15] in Malaysia compel the vast majority of trans men (and many LGBTIQ individuals) to remain silent in the face of discrimination, persecution and violence. Trans men join other transgender and queer communities in being subjected to repeated pronouncements of their identities, expressions and behaviours as unnatural, perverted and iniquitous. Fully aware that such pronouncements are coupled with secular and/or religious penalties that serve as a 'disciplinary pedagogy marginalizing non-normative sexualities and genders' (Boellstorff 2004, 472), few trans men are inclined to speak up and talk back to their antagonists.

An immediate consequence of coerced silence that is imposed on transgressive bodies which have been accused of aberrant recalcitrance is the presumption of insignificance and ensuing devaluation. In the process, human lives can be relegated with great ease to sites of inconsequentiality and worthlessness. Wilde also observes that 'it's very hard to find people who are willing to step up and … join activism and … work on issues, because a lot of people are very comfortable' (Appendix 2: Interviewing Dorian Wilde, para. 7). What I can decipher here is that *invisibility correlates positively to inertia*—hiddenness supplies a much sought-after sense of security and relief, and that any form of activism could risk exposure to a female or lesbian history.

Wilde notes that an additional layer which adds to the silence and consequent invisibility of trans men is the prominence of trans women

[15]Patriarchy is 'a system of society or government in which men hold the power and women are largely excluded from it' (Brown 2016, 207). Heteronormativity 'refers … to the myriad ways in which heterosexuality is produced as a natural, unproblematic, taken-for-granted, ordinary phenomenon' (Kitzinger 2005, 478). In the same vein, cisnormativity 'highlights the privileging of a non-trans norm' (Pyne 2011, 129) as 'trans bodies are rendered unintelligible and unwelcome' (Pyne 2011, 133).

in the public sphere. He contends that 'when people think trans issues, they mostly think trans women … issues affecting trans men … are not taken into consideration' (Appendix 2: Interviewing Dorian Wilde, para. 7). That *mak nyah* are more frequently thrust into the limelight (cited in Fong 2015b) is hardly surprising as they are constantly caricaturised as failed men and invalid citizens in a heteropatriarchal country (J. N. Goh 2014b). As epithets of gender and sexual misdemeanour, many endure gross brutality (Free Malaysia Today 2017; Zachariah 2014). Muslim *mak nyah* bear the additional stigma of Islamic wrongdoing (Teh 2008a) which they share with trans men. Recent *mak nyah* matters that have caught the country's attention include a court case that challenged a *Syariah* (Islamic) legal ban on 'cross-dressing' (Reuters Staff 2015), the appointment of a *mak nyah* political secretary (Jalleh 2013), investigations over a local entrepreneur's 'real' identity (Qarami and Tang 2018) and the designation of a *mak nyah* as a committee member of the Country Coordinating Mechanism (CCM) Malaysia which aims to combat HIV/AIDS (The Star Online 2019).

I propose another consideration, which is that there are between 20,000 to 30,000 *mak nyah* in Malaysia (Khartini 2005; Yeow 2001) as compared to 172 trans men who have registered with ToM (Appendix 2: Interviewing Dorian Wilde, para. 46). Sheer numeric dominance will attract greater scrutiny. As a much smaller community than *mak nyah*, and possibly one of the smallest populations in the Malaysian LGBTIQ spectrum even though no official census of Malaysian trans men has ever been performed, trans men form a minority within a minority. Admittedly however, the prodigious public attention that is cast on *mak nyah* due to these reasons inevitably creates a hierarchy of trans-significance that intensifies the silence and invisibility of trans men.

In recognition of the silence, invisibility, persecution and indifference that Malaysian trans men experience in varying forms and intensities, I deploy an *ethic of unsilencing* throughout this volume to recuperate what Foucault refers to as 'subjugated knowledges' which 'have been disqualified as inadequate to their task or insufficiently elaborated: naïve knowledges, located low down on the hierarchy … low-ranking knowledges' (1980, 82). An ethic of silencing is aware that this type of knowledge regularly 'owes its force only to the harshness with which it is opposed by everything surrounding it' (Foucault 1980, 82).

In order to ensure its effectiveness as a strategy of deep listening for deep understanding and deep learning, an ethic of unsilencing foregrounds four complementary perspectives. First, it incorporates Jason Cromwell's notion of 'untying the tongues of transpeople', in which transgender communities 'have every right to use whatever terms they wish' and 'articulate their transsubjectivity differently [than] medico-psychological discourses have allowed' (1999, 24–25). Crucial to this idea is the conviction that transgender people are 'experts for the predicaments of their situation' (Lucius-Hoene 2000, para. 3) and indeed for all dimensions of their existence. Many LGBTIQ people who have often being spoken at and against, rather than spoken with, cherish avenues in which they can speak on their own terms about their lives. As a masculine presenting cis gay man and avowed trans ally, I consciously speak *with*, not *for* Malaysian trans men.[16]

Second, an ethic of unsilencing harkens to Sally Hines' *sociology of transgender*, in which 'practices of gender diversity are analysed in relation to wider social positionings and divisions, and should work to counter universal theorising' (2010, 12). This framework is concerned with the formation of gender identity as a relational act, rather than a presumption of privatised trans homogeneity, and which takes into serious consideration 'how structures of difference are mutually constructed and lived out in the "everyday"' (Hines 2010, 12). The intersectionality of age, class, ethnicity, relationship and medical accessibility does not accessorise (trans)gender identity, but rather, constitutes it. Through a methodology that investigates the interpenetrability of the discursive and the material in lived experiences, a sociology of transgender contextualises and situates transgender individuals in the world in which they live.

In augmenting a sociology of transgender with queer theoretical dimensions, Hines is convinced that '(trans)gender identities are cut through with difference' (2006, 64). In other words, the self-professed identities of transgender individuals do not only depart from the mainstream by transgressing gender and sexuality binaries (Hines 2007). Such self-realisations transpire in accordance with the particularities of both individual and collective contexts. As such, 'the concept of difference itself is contingent upon social, cultural, political, temporal and embodied considerations' (Hines 2006, 63). (Trans)gender identities are re/formed according to a host of interactive dynamics on macro and micro levels which involve interiorised self-comprehension, 'affective relations

[16] See 'Appendix 1: Designing the Research Project'.

and intimate networks' (Hines 2006, 64), and access to pertinent healthcare.

Third, an ethic of unsilencing looks to Fran Martin's and Josephine Ho's insistence on the *subjective authority of Asian transgender lives* in place of representational objectification that fulfils the fantasies of 'traditional, Eurocentric forms of exotic ethnography' (2006, 185). This authority stems from 'the *specificity of place*' (Martin and Ho 2006, 185; original emphasis) or the geopolitical and sociocultural peculiarities that allow transgender people to make sense of who they are. Hence, even if Malaysian trans men co-opt global terms such as 'transgender' or 'trans man', they cannot escape the inevitability of 'locally particular histories of transgender community and activism [that] shape the conditions of possibility for critical transgender cultures in the present' (Martin and Ho 2006, 185).

Finally, an ethic of unsilencing privileges research efforts involving Asian transgender communities by Asian scholars. It concurs with Marcus Greatheart that 'trans man identities are not white' (2013, 78) by default and conscripts the determination of Howard Chiang, Todd A. Henry and Helen Hok-Sze Leung to dismantle 'the "ghettoization" of trans-in-Asia as a small subfield about minority bodies in the quantitative sense of representing a small number of people ... in the overall scope of human experiences' (2018, 298). This ghettoisation provincialises Asian transgender academic scholarship and devalues Asian transgender lived experiences. It is precisely on account of this double-pronged discriminatory stance that Chiang, Henry and Leung champion an appreciation for 'empirical and theoretical insights ... on nonnormative bodies and their embodiments' which will galvanise greater cognisance of 'new issues and processes that should interest those who study and write about Asia' (2018, 298). An ethic of unsilencing underscores the synergy between Malaysian transgender studies and Malaysian transgender lived experiences, as well as the unsilencing of studies on Malaysian trans men in global transgender scholarship.

Therefore, an ethic of unsilencing operates as an unwavering principle to amplify life stories and magnify subjectivities that have generally been undisclosed and unheard, or permitted to emerge only in safe spaces that are often clandestine and intentionally exclusive. In disclosing how their 'gendered bodies can take up diverse subject positions that move back and forth across the ideologies that surround the boundaries of binary sex and gender' (Yue 2017, 11), trans men are thus afforded the freedom to tell of the transgression, dissension, malleability and accomplishment that constitute, signify and operationalise human embodiment. An ethic of unsilencing acts as a lens that permits the visibility of a highly variegated interweaving and confluence of 'crosscuts, intersections, overlaps, simultaneity, fragments, arbitrariness and continuing evolution' (Wickramasinghe 2010, 36). It labours to make sense of the multi-faceted subtleties, complexities and constraints that determine the direction and magnitude of gender, sexuality and sex. It foregrounds Asian academic endeavours on Asian issues.

Wilde's preparedness to appear in public forums, and canvass for gender and sexuality justice is clearly a departure from the norm of silence and invisibility among trans men, but it is not wholly unexpected due to his unerring commitment to human rights. Furthermore, his constant presence at the frontlines of activism with fellow LGBTIQ activists and allies may supply an unassailable source of strength and security through solidarity.

Expanding Malaysian Transgender Studies

Corresponding to the greater visibility of trans women in the public domain vis-à-vis trans men, the lion's share of Malaysian transgender studies focuses on contemporary Malaysian *mak nyah*. Teh Yik Koon is very likely its sympathetic frontrunner. Writing as a cis woman, her seminal text *The Mak Nyahs: Malaysian Male to Female Transsexuals* (2002) discusses a gamut of issues in relation to pre- and post-operative trans women, and includes sections that feature interviews with religious leaders, government officers, a medical professional, a psychologist and the police, as well as personal testimonies.

Other works on *mak nyah* focus on oppression and empowerment (Khartini 2005), gender identity formation (Guy 2003), dismissive and affirming religious perspectives (J. N. Goh 2012a, b, c; Nasrudin et al. 2013; Samsul et al. 2016), the use of a specific *mak nyah* 'secret' code known as *Bahasa Seteng* (DeAlwis and David 2010), and *mak nyah* sex workers and HIV (Gibson et al. 2016; Teh 2008b). Some scholars approach *mak nyah* issues unfavourably, including accusations of gender confusion and disorder (Ani Amelia and Zaleha 2017; Wan Azmi 1991), traumatic childhood experiences as responsible for transgender subjectivities (Amran and Suriati 2013) and simplistic conflations of *mak nyah* with transvestites (DeAlwis and David 2010). *Mak nyah* has been featured extensively in the Malaysian news media (Shahrin 2012; The Star Online 2016) and international human rights reports (Human Rights Watch 2014). A critical history of ***mak nyah*** activism in the 2000s which I co-wrote with Thaatchaayini Kananatu draws on many such resources (2018).

In contrast, there is a pronounced scarcity of academic literature on Malaysian trans men. I return again to examples from the United States—and include Canada—to briefly demonstrate how academic efforts that focus singularly on trans men have gained admirable momentum since the twentieth century, particularly by scholar-activists who identify as transmasculine or trans men. Patrick Califia, Jason Cromwell, Aaron Devor,[17] Jamison Green, C. Jacob Hale and Jay Prosser are often regarded as pioneers in this regard. More recent personages include Aren Z. Aizura, Michael Eric Brown, Paisley Currah, Jakob Hero, Griffin Hansbury, matthew heinz, Justin Edward Tanis, C. Riley Snorton, Dean Spade and Morgan M. H. Seamont. This list is anything but exhaustive. heinz's observation that 'transmasculinity research and scholarship coincides in time with the re-emergence of global, critical men's and masculinity studies' (2016, 222) hints at a growing acknowledgement and recuperation of trans men's identities as alternative forms of manness.

Scholarship on trans men straddles issues of anthropological, sociological, emotional, physical, discursive and linguistic developments of masculine and transgender identities (Brown 2016; Budge et al. 2015; Cromwell 1999; Devor 1987; Hansbury 2005; heinz 2016), embodiment and sexuality (Cromwell 1999; Devor 1993, 1994, 2002; Edelman and Zimman 2014; Seamont 2018; Schilt and Windsor 2014), healthcare and disease (Greatheart 2013; heinz 2016; Reisner et al. 2013; Rowniak et al. 2011; Rowniak and Chesla 2013), media representation (heinz 2016), love and relationships (Pfeffer 2017), law and citizenship (Adair 2019; Currah and Minter 2000), and Christian religiosity, theology and ethics (J. N. Goh 2019; Hero 2012; Kolakowski 1997; Tanis 2003).

In the country, there is a greater number of semi-academic and activism-inspired publications by human rights advocates which combine issues of LGBTIQ as opposed to dedicated scholarly work on trans men. For instance, Knowledge and Rights with Young People through Safer Spaces (KRYSS), a local advocacy platform for gender and sexuality rights published a multi-country report entitled *ON THE RECORD:*

[17] Throughout this volume, I refer to this scholar and his works solely by the name 'Aaron Devor'.

Violence against Lesbians, Bisexual Women and Transgender Persons in Malaysia (2014). In this report, trans men are discussed as part of a larger cohort of LGBTIQ Malaysians. Justice for Sisters (2016), a grass-roots campaign to champion transgender rights in Malaysia has produced a media guide in both Malay and Chinese languages on gender and transgender identities that includes trans men.

At the time of completing this monograph, I did not come across any published academic resources that are devoted exclusively to Malaysian trans men aside from Sharon A. Bong's chapter entitled 'The Power of *Trans*formation and *Trans*forming Power: A Malaysian Female-to-Male *Trans*gender Person's Narrative' in a forthcoming anthology, and my own article 'Untying Tongues: Negotiations and Innovations of Faith and Gender among Malaysian Christian Trans Men' (2019) in the Taylor & Francis journal *Culture & Religion*. Through an intentional focus on trans men, this book is an effort to expand transgender studies in Malaysia and beyond.

Overview

This section explains how the ensuing Chapters are structured. Narratives of trans men which are sampled here provide grounded contexts of the major issues at hand and act as a prelude to the upcoming thematically arranged Chapters based on gender identity, societal interaction, Gender Dysphoria, medical transitioning and belief systems—*constitutive elements that are crucial to the becomings of Malaysian trans men*. While themes of ethnicity, age, economic status, education and space were either absent, or did not feature prominently or explicitly in my conversations with trans men, it was clear from their narratives that issues of identity, society, culture, body, health and faith were deeply coloured by these themes.

Earlier, I had briefly mentioned the frustration that trans men experience due to the near impossibility of changing the names and gender identities assigned to them at birth that appear on their *MyKad* or Malaysian Identity Card. This situation, which is not unfamiliar to trans women either (Malaysiakini 2011), has frequently paved the way for harassment and humiliation (Malaysiakini 2011; Minderjeet 2017). As a case in point, Warp shares a traumatic experience at a Malaysian airport that stemmed from a disparity between how he looked in his *MyKad* and in person:

> The immigration officials they were, FUCKED UP (raises voice)! Like at that time I haven't changed my *MyKad*, so it was still the long hair ... they pulled me aside and they asked me like ... very personal questions. Like, er, so you're a man but actually you're a woman, so do you like women? How do you do with them? ... After a while they got bored, and so he just sent me on my way ... one of the officers actually pointed to me and told his colleague very loudly, '*nah yang* tu *yang perempuan* tu'! (there, that's *that* woman)[18]

By referring to the airport 'immigration offic[ers]' he encounters as 'fucked up', Warp is expressing his frustration over complete strangers who pose extremely inappropriate 'personal questions' to him due to the disparity between his *MyKad* and actual appearance. Their initial curiosity may have been justified due to their inability to match his official documents with the person they see before them, but their puzzlements quickly become inappropriate intrusions into Warp's personal life. These intrusions take the form of questions about his sexual attractions and practices. Warp is eventually permitted to proceed, but their fetishisation of his gender identity continues. Their continuing gossip about him is well within earshot, and may have even been intended to be so as a continuing indication of their disapproval. Warp's experience evinces the boorish savagery of cisnormativity and the sore lack of public conscientisation on transgender needs and concerns in Malaysia.

A matter of particular concern to Wilde, which is reflected in his experience, is the inability of Malaysian trans men to gain 'legal gender recognition' and 'proper documentation whether one is in university or when one goes to the police' (quoted in Pragalath 2018). Neither is there provision for a 'third gender' in the country. Trans men ordinarily find their needs and concerns belittled due to the disparity between their official documents and their outward appearances, thus impeding their quality of life (cited in Minderjeet 2017).

The *MyKad* perpetuates this problem as trans men are prohibited from officially changing their names and gender identities therein even though there is no actual legal prohibition in this regard. In fact, the National Registration Department Guidelines of 2007 allow for amendments to the *MyKad* if the sex—a category that is conflated with gender

[18] Warp's narrative here evinces a blend of English and Bahasa Malaysia, common among Malaysians.

identity—of an individual is incorrectly stated or 'legitimately' changed. Wilde recalls how 'in the 2000s, there [were] people who successfully went and changed their [*MyKad* details]' (Appendix 2: Interviewing Dorian Wilde, para. 10). The Department only requires 'a court declaration regarding her/his sex; a government doctor's confirmation that [Gender Affirmation Surgery] was completed; a verification from the hospital where the sex change was done; and a copy of the birth certificate' (KRYSS 2014, 30).

Today, such concessions are more accessible to intersex individuals than transgender people. The requests of the latter for any changes to their *MyKad* are ordinarily declined (KRYSS 2014). Wilde surmises that trans men who are 'denied their fundamental rights to liberty, equality before the law, freedom of movement and expression as contained in the Federal Constitution' (quoted in Fong 2015a) are invisibilised. In a certain sense, and similar to other official documents, the *MyKad* becomes an implement of violence, a license of citizenship and a regulatory marker of eligibility for movement in the public sphere (Adair 2019; see also Bishop and Myricks 2004; Taylor et al. 2015).

Hence, in Chapters 2 and 3 of this monograph, I discuss the complex negotiations of gender, sexuality and society. In Chapter 2, 'Engendering Identity', I investigate the construction of (trans)masculinity, manliness, man and manness by trans men through multitudinous and often conflicting strategies. Chapter 3, 'Engaging with Society', scrutinises trans men's interactions with family, friends and co-workers, struggles with disclosures of gender identity, and negotiations with social norms and systems that expect, favour and reward patriarchy, heteronormativity and cisnormativity.

The two ensuing Chapters deal with issues of physical ambivalence, medical transitioning and healthcare. Healthcare in Malaysian public hospitals and rural clinics has customarily been heavily subsidised by the state and funded by taxation. Since the 1980s, there has been an uptake in the privatisation of healthcare that caters to the needs of more financially stable urbanites. Although the availability of such services complements government-funded health facilities, scholars have highlighted their profit-driven agendas (Chee 2008; Rasiah et al. 2009). The procurement of medical and health insurance also correlates directly to financial means, and many Malaysians are subjected to out-of-pocket payments (Shafie and Hassali 2013; Zuriah and Norzaidi 2010).

Nonetheless, there are no official Malaysian state-sanctioned health programmes or insurance schemes that cater *specifically* to any form of medical transitioning. Public health concerns over *mak nyah* often centre on issues of HIV (Gibson et al. 2016; Teh 2008b) and are usually influenced by Islamic moralistic interpretations (Barmania and Syed Mohamed 2016). This situation is not unlike the manner in which religiously inflected stigma and shame often occlude access to health services for LGBTIQ people in the Asia-Pacific region (J. N. Goh 2016; Hendricks 2013). Malaysian medical professionals often discriminate against People Living with HIV and AIDS, a substantial percentage of whom are MSM (Earnshaw et al. 2014) and TG sex workers (Gibson et al. 2016). In the United States, academic studies on sexual and overall physical among trans men (Reisner et al. 2013; Rowniak et al. 2011) are complemented by transgender clinics that cater to needs of medical transitioning and overall physical health (Tom Waddell Health Center 2012). Such services are absent in Malaysia. Experts have noted that some healthcare providers express apprehension in treating transgender Malaysians due to a broad range of misconceptions and preconceived ideas (Vijay et al. 2017).

The plight of transgender Malaysians who suffer general healthcare discrimination has seized media attention. In sharing her experiences and that of other trans women in a local newspaper, trans activist Sulastri Ariffin reiterated that 'all [that trans women] want is to be able to walk into a clinic when [they] are sick, and not be turned away because of who [they] are' (quoted in Yeow 2001). Wilde has also publicly divulged the problems that trans men experience in healthcare, such as being located in female wards (cited in Minderjeet 2017) and listening to 'stupid questions (on gender and usage of facilities)' by medical personnel in hospitals (quoted in Pragalath 2018) who are uninitiated in transgender issues. Hence, transgender people frequently find themselves exposed to ridicule, misgendering, discrimination and denouncement in Malaysian healthcare systems.

Malaysian trans men whose journeys of medical transitioning involve 'modifying [their] physical body with hormones, surgery, or other techniques' (Aizura 2018, 32) often meet with medical neglect and indifference. For example, Schulz deplores the lack of state support in his medical transitioning:

> I'm very happy with the changes that hormone replacement therapy has done for me. But of course I am scared too, you know, of the lack of medical attention that we have available here. Even if it is, it's private sectors … It requires you to pay quite a hefty amount … I don't have that financial stability to support myself … to have a proper, full medical check-up and things like that … when I have the financial ability to someday, go for a full mastectomy, and phalloplasty, I would definitely want to go for it.

During the interview, Schulz was effusive about the positive responses he elicited from his friends due to the physical changes that they detected in him. Specifically, he was elated by 'the changes that hormone replacement therapy' had accorded him in the ongoing materialisation of his gender identity. This happiness is, however, tempered by a sense of fear that comes from 'the lack of medical attention' that is accorded to trans men. He is cognisant that endocrinal treatment requires consistent 'full medical checkup[s]', but he is unable to access such services on a regular basis due to the lack of 'financial stability' (see also Appendix 2: Interviewing Dorian Wilde, paras. 25, 50).

Yet his fear does not deter him from imagining a more enabling future, in which a robust 'financial ability' will permit him to 'go for a full mastectomy' or 'the surgical removal of part or all of a breast' (Fallon and Alic 2015, 3214)—or both breasts—and 'phalloplasty' or 'the surgical construction of a penis [to create] a functional and esthetic neophallus that provides tactile and erogenous sensation and the ability to void while standing' (Kim et al. 2018, 181). Schulz's subscription to HRT and hopes for more radical surgical procedures implies a sense of dissatisfaction with the current physical and physiological processes that he experiences, which is frequently referred to as Gender Dysphoria, or 'perceived inconsistencies between one's biological sex and gender identity [that] are often accompanied by significant distress' (Atkinson and Russell 2015, 792). His despondency is emblematic of the sense of forlorn faced by many trans men for whom a holistic route of medical transitioning proves to be beyond their reach due to monetary barriers.

Therefore, I explore issues of the trans man's body, Gender Dysphoria and coping strategies in Chapter 4, 'Dealing with Gender Dysphoria'. In Chapter 5, 'Embarking on Medical Transitioning', my attention is turned to the various complexities that surround Gender Affirmation Surgery, Gender-Affirming Hormone Therapy, peer support during gender-affirming transitioning and the financial difficulties that complicate these processes. Chapter 6 is devoted to the discussion of religiosities and spiritualities as factors that play an integral role in the becomings of many trans men of faith in Malaysia, but are typically overlooked or dismissed, or command little relevance in similar processes outside the country.

Ethnicity and religious affiliation continue to be crucial identity markers for many contemporary Malaysians, and trans men are no exception. Based on 2010 statistics, Malaysia comprises more than 28.3 million inhabitants. The majority of the population comprises the Malays (54.6%), followed by the Chinese (24.6), non-Malay *Bumiputeras*[19] (12.8%), Indians (7.3%) and other ethnic compositions (0.7%). Muslims form the largest percentage of the population (61.3%), with Buddhists (19.8%), Christians (9.2%), Hindus (3.4%), and the non-religious, other-religious, practitioners of unknown faiths and adherents to traditional religions trailing modestly behind (6.3%) (Department of Statistics, Malaysia 2010).[20] A Malay person is constitutionally one 'who professes the religion of Islam' (The Commissioner of Law Revision, Malaysia 1957, art. 160(2)), and any attempt to leave the religion is criminalised.

Both overt and covert forms of discrimination, oppression and violence in regard to LGBTIQ people need to be situated within the context of a wider policing of gender and sexuality in a mostly Muslim country that still adheres strongly to moral conservatism (see Lee 2011, 2018). Non-Muslims are generally subjected to the Federal Constitution and Penal Code. Muslims fall under the purview of these civil laws while being held accountable to *Syariah* or Islamic laws in what appears to be a double system of law in the country. Over the years, Malaysians have seen an increasing encroachment of Islamic legalities on its non-Muslim populace in custody battles (Malay Mail Online 2016), the right to burial rites (Aliran 2005), the banning of the use of the term 'Allah' among non-Muslims (R. B. H. Goh 2005) and obligatory conversions to Islam for non-Muslims who wed Muslims (Malay Mail Online 2013).

The escalating Islamisation of various levels of Malaysian life which became more pronounced in the 1980s under the administration of

[19] Literally, *Bumiputeras* means '"sons (or princes) of the soil"'. The contentious category is often used 'to justify preferential treatment in … politics and the economy' (Holst 2012, 35) for Malaysians of Malay and indigenous descent.

[20] Malaysia conducts its Census every ten years, and the next one is slated for 2020.

the country's longest serving Prime Minister Mahathir Mohamad has intensified the potency of *Syariah* legalities, including the relentless surveillance of gender and sexuality matters (Zainah 2005). For example, Muslims can be arrested under the Syariah Criminal Offences (Federal Territories) Act 1997 by Islamic authorities for '*khalwat* ("close proximity") between a man and woman, and *zina* ("fornication" or sex outside marriage)' (Vignato 2012, 242; see also The Commissioner of Law Revision, Malaysia 2006, secs 2(1), 27).

Such laws also criminalise *liwat*, 'or sexual relations between male persons', *musahaqah*, or 'sexual relations between female persons', and a 'male person ... in any public place [who] wears a woman's attire and poses as a woman for immoral purposes' (The Commissioner of Law Revision, Malaysia 2006, secs 2(1), 25, 26, 28). As indicated earlier in this Chapter, masculine-acting lesbian women, *tomboy* and *pengkid*—and by extension, trans men—are subjectivities which have been proscribed through a *fatwa* or Islamic opinion that can carry the force of law (Jabatan Mufti Kerajaan Negeri Sembilan 2008). Similarly, *Syariah* laws in the states of Perlis, Pahang and Sabah that fine and imprison women who appear as men (Legislature of the State of Perlis 1993; Legislature of the State of Pahang 2013; Legislature of the State of Sabah 1995).

Over the years, politicians and state agencies have shown injudicious discrimination towards LGBTIQ people, often using religious rhetoric. For instance, *Jabatan Kemajuan Islam Malaysia* (JAKIM) or the Department of Islamic Development Malaysia referred to the public outcry over human rights abuses as part of an LGBTIQ conspiracy to erode the authority of Malaysian Islam (cited in Syed Jamal 2013). Deputy Minister of Human Resources Mahfuz Omar remarked that affirming the rights of LGBTIQ Malaysians must parallel, if not supersede efforts to restore them to the gender assigned to them at birth. According to his rationale, 'if they were originally men, then they need to return to being men, and the opposite as well (if originally women, return to being women) ... Otherwise, there would be chaos in our society' (cited in Petah 2018). Despite using the term 'LGBT', it was evident that the politician had little knowledge of the distinction between contemporary conceptual distinctions between gender and sexuality, and ended up berating transgender communities. Additionally, Deputy Prime Minister Wan Azizah warned LGBTIQ Malaysians against 'glamourising' their lifestyles due to state legalities and Islamic sensibilities (quoted in Shazwan 2018).

Wilde has publicly spoken up about the role that organised religions, chiefly Malaysian Islam and Malaysian Christianity play in the unremitting discrimination of transgender people, including trans men. He realises that 'the growing Islamisation of Malaysia [is] making life difficult for [trans men] by worsening the stigma [about them]' (quoted in Fong 2015a). He laments how 'the persecution and clampdown against sexual minorities is viewed as a sort of testament of a person's religiosity within society' (quoted in Shazwan 2015), and transgender people become collateral damage in these pursuits of the moral high ground. During his brief foray into Christianity at a younger age, he found himself subjected to pulpit aggression against LGBTIQ people (cited in Uthaya 2013). Transgender Malaysians, he says, are manipulated in religio-political rat races as 'pawns' who can be 'sacrifice[d] for [a] larger agenda' (quoted in K. H. Wong 2018).

The succinct words of SR captures the climate of moral policing in the country. Despite being a staunch Muslim, he appears to be disconcerted by the arbitrary religio-legal arrests of Muslim Malaysians due to suspicions of sexually inappropriate behaviour:

> The *Syariah*, yes, Muslim, again, which is, I'm not satisfied actually. Because this is what I saw by my own eyes. You know they are like the Islamic erm, director, you know, JAWI, JAIS, JAKIM, they were like go and catch people this and that ... Yes, we are Islamic country, yet you were in karaoke? With the GRO sort of thing lah.[21]

SR is troubled by how sexual matters are (mis)handled by 'Islamic ... director[s]' comprising JAWI or *Jabatan Agama Islam Wilayah Persekutuan* (Department of Federal Territory Islamic Affairs) (2014), JAIS or *Jabatan Agama Islam Selangor* (Department of Selangor Islamic Affairs) (2018) and JAKIM (2015). These are state-sanctioned Islamic mechanisms that are often tasked to police issues of morality, conversion, apostasy and family life among Muslims.

SR seems dismayed by how these Islamic departments 'catch people like this and that' during occasions of suspected immorality. He cites an instance when 'people'—presumably Muslim men—are arrested for

[21] 'Lah' is a suffix that is added to casual conversations in multiple languages in Malaysia, Singapore and Brunei Darussalam as a '"solidarity/familiarity/emphasis" marker' (Ooi 2001, 113).

consorting with the 'GRO', an acronym for 'Guest Relations Officers' or women who accompany male patrons in bars, clubs and 'karaoke' lounges, and who periodically supply sexual favours in exchange for money and other forms of compensation. Almost mockingly, SR rehearses the condescending rhetoric used by the morality police to shame Muslim men who have the audacity to revel in the company of the GRO on morally reprehensible premises in what he calls an 'Islamic country'—a misnomer for a Muslim-majority rather than theocratic Malaysia.

Yet, SR's first hand experiences of witnessing such events '[through his] own eyes' informs him that some charges and arrests may have been haphazard, unfounded and unjust. I propose that his consternation does not stem solely from such incidents. His cognisance of erratic forms of moral surveillance and the seemingly 'unMuslim' thuggish behaviour with which these representatives of Malaysian Islam conduct their raids does affect him adversely as a pious Muslim who holds his faith in high regard. There is also a possibility that SR harbours fears of being similarly wantonly arrested for being a trans man, even though no trans man has been officially charged or incarcerated by *Syariah* laws on the basis of gender to the best of my knowledge.

In the final chapter, 'Epilogue', I revisit previous discussions on the major elements that constitute the becomings of Malaysian trans men, namely gender identities, engagements with society, Gender Dysphoria, medical transitioning and faith negotiations. The subjectivities of trans men are also reconsidered against instances of transgression and disruption in Malaysian history.

Bibliography

Abelson, Miriam J. 2019. *Men in Place: Trans Masculinity, Race, and Sexuality in America*. Minneapolis, MN: University of Minnesota Press.

Adair, Cassius. 2019. 'Licensing Citizenship: Anti-Blackness, Identification Documents, and Transgender Studies'. *American Quarterly* 71 (2): 569–94.

Aizura, Aren Z. 2018. *Mobile Subjects: Transnational Imaginaries of Gender Reassignment*. Durham, NC: Duke University Press.

Aliran. 2005. 'The Moorthy Maniam Case: Compassion and Justice Missing'. *Aliran Monthly* 25 (11). https://aliran.com/archives/monthly/2005b/11b.html.

Altman, Dennis. 1996. 'On Global Queering'. *Australian Humanities Review*, no. 2 (July). http://www.australianhumanitiesreview.org/archive/Issue-July-1996/altman.html.

Amran Hassan, and Suriati Ghazali. 2013. 'Sexual Abuse and Childhood Traumatic Experience: A Case Study on the Psychological Health of Transsexuals in Malaysia'. *International Journal of Environment, Society and Space* 1 (1): 33–42.

Ani Amelia Zainuddin, and Zaleha Abdullah Mahdy. 2017. 'The Islamic Perspectives of Gender-Related Issues in the Management of Patients With Disorders of Sex Development'. *Archives of Sexual Behavior* 46 (2): 353–60.

Atkinson, Sean R., and Darren Russell. 2015. 'Gender Dysphoria'. *Australian Family Physician* 44 (11): 792–96.

Barmania, Sima, and Syed Mohamed Aljunid. 2016. 'Navigating HIV Prevention Policy and Islam in Malaysia: Contention, Compatibility or Reconciliation? Findings from in-Depth Interviews Among Key Stakeholders'. *BMC Public Health* 16: 524.

Bishop, Elena P., and Noel Myricks. 2004. 'Sex Reassignment Surgery: When Is a "He" a "She" for the Purpose of Marriage in the United States?' *American Journal of Family Law* 18 (1): 30–35.

Boellstorff, Tom. 2004. 'The Emergence of Political Homophobia in Indonesia: Masculinity and National Belonging'. *Ethnos* 69 (4): 465–86.

———. 2005. *The Gay Archipelago: Sexuality and Nation in Indonesia*. Princeton, NJ: Princeton University Press.

Brown, Michael Eric. 2016. *A Herstory of Transmasculine Identities: An Annotated Anthology*. Miami, FL: Boundless Endeavors, Inc.

Budge, Stephanie L., Joe J. Orovecz, and Jayden L. Thai. 2015. 'Trans Men's Positive Emotions: The Interaction of Gender Identity and Emotion Labels'. *The Counseling Psychologist* 43 (3): 404–34.

Butler, Judith. 1993. *Bodies That Matter: On the Discursive Limits of 'Sex'*. New York: Routledge.

———. 1999. *Gender Trouble: Feminism and the Subversion of Identity*. New York: Routledge.

Chatterjee, Shraddha. 2018. 'Transgender Shifts: Notes on Resignification of Gender and Sexuality in India'. *TSQ: Transgender Studies Quarterly* 5 (3): 311–20.

Chee, Heng Leng. 2008. 'Ownership, Control, and Contention: Challenges for the Future of Healthcare in Malaysia'. *Social Science & Medicine*, Future Health Systems, 66 (10): 2145–56.

Cheh, Samantha. 2017. 'How Life Is Tough for Transgender People in Conservative Malaysia, Who Face Violence, Religious and Official Bias, and Abusive Media'. *South China Morning Post*, 15 November. http://www.scmp.com/lifestyle/article/2119847/how-life-tough-transgenders-conservative-malaysia-who-face-violence.

Cheng, Patrick S., and Joseph N. Goh. 2012. 'Queer Asian Spirit'. Queer Asian Spirit. http://www.queerasianspirit.org/.

Chiang, Howard, Todd A. Henry, and Helen Hok-Sze Leung. 2018. 'Trans-in-Asia, Asia-in-Trans: An Introduction'. *TSQ: Transgender Studies Quarterly* 5 (3): 298–310.

Chong, Joyce Ma Lai. 1990. 'Social Assessment of Transsexuals Who Apply for Sex Reassignment Therapy'. *Social Work in Health Care* 14 (3): 87–105.

Chua, Hang Kuen. 2014. 'Malay Muslim PLU Men in Peninsular Malaysia: Negotiating Non-Heteronormative Sexualities and Sexual Identities in Malay Muslim-Dominant Society'. PhD diss., Melbourne, Australia: La Trobe University.

Cromwell, Jason. 1999. *Transmen and FTMs: Identities, Bodies, Genders, and Sexualities.* Urbana, IL: University of Illinois Press.

Currah, Paisley, and Shannon Minter. 2000. 'Unprincipled Exclusions: The Struggle to Achieve Judicial and Legislative Equality for Transgender People Symposium: (De)Constructing Sex: Transgenderism, Intersexuality, Gender Identity and the Law'. *William & Mary Journal of Women and the Law* 7: 37–66.

DeAlwis, Caesar, and Maya Khemlani David. 2010. 'Language and Identity of Malay Teenage *Mak Nyah* (Transvestites) in Kuching'. *JATI—Journal of Southeast Asian Studies* 15: 39–52.

Department of Statistics, Malaysia. 2010. 'Population Distribution and Basic Demographic Characteristics 2010'. https://www.dosm.gov.my/v1/index.php?r=column/ctheme&menu_id=L0pheU43NWJwRWVSZklWdzQ4Tl-hUUT09&bul_id=MDMxdHZjWTk1SjFzTzNkRXYzcVZjdz09.

Devor, Aaron. 1987. 'Gender Blending Females: Women and Sometimes Men'. *American Behavioral Scientist* 31 (1): 12–40.

———. 1993. 'Sexual Orientation Identities, Attractions, and Practices of Female-to-Male Transsexuals'. *The Journal of Sex Research* 30 (4): 303–15.

———. 1994. 'Toward a Taxonomy of Gendered Sexuality'. *Journal of Psychology & Human Sexuality* 6 (1): 23–56.

———. 2002. 'Who Are "We"? Where Sexual Orientation Meets Gender Identity'. *Journal of Gay & Lesbian Psychotherapy* 6 (2): 5–21.

———. 2016. *FTM: Female-to-Male Transsexuals in Society.* Bloomington, IN: Indiana University Press.

Diamond, Lisa M., and Molly Butterworth. 2008. 'Questioning Gender and Sexual Identity: Dynamic Links Over Time'. *Sex Roles* 59 (5–6): 365–76.

Earnshaw, Valerie A., Harry Jin, Jeffrey Wickersham, Adeeba Kamarulzaman, Jacob John, and Frederick L. Altice. 2014. 'Exploring Intentions to Discriminate Against Patients Living with HIV/AIDS Among Future Healthcare Providers in Malaysia'. *Tropical Medicine & International Health* 19 (6): 672–79.

Edelman, Elijah Adiv, and Lal Zimman. 2014. 'Boycunts and Bonus Holes: Trans Men's Bodies, Neoliberalism, and the Sexual Productivity of Genitals'. *Journal of Homosexuality* 61 (5): 673–90.

Fallon, L. Fleming, and Margaret Alic. 2015. 'Mastectomy'. In *The Gale Encyclopedia of Medicine*, edited by Jacqueline L. Longe, 5th ed., 3214. Farmington Hills, MI: Gale, Cengage Learning.

Felix, Mark Stephan. 2014. 'Stigma as Part of Identity Development of Gay Men in Penang—A Qualitative Study'. *Pertanika Journal of Social Sciences & Humanities* 22 (1): 365–77.

Ferrarese, Marco, Joseph N. Goh, Julian C. H. Lee, and Caryn Lim. 2015. 'Identity Formations in Contemporary Malaysia: Traversing and Transcending Ethnicity'. In *Malaysia Post-Mahathir: A Decade of Change?* edited by James Chin and Joern Dosch, 41–69. Singapore: Marshall Cavendish.

Fong, Fernando. 2015a. 'Transgenders in Malaysia "vulnerable and Marginalised"—The Rakyat Post'. *The Rakyat Post*, 24 January. http://www.therakyatpost.com/news/2015/01/24/transgenders-malaysia-vulnerable-marginalised/.

———. 2015b. 'Born a Woman, but Always Been a Man'. *The Rakyat Post*, 26 January. http://www.therakyatpost.com/news/2015/01/26/born-woman-always-man/.

Foucault, Michel. 1980. *Power/Knowledge: Selected Interviews and Other Writings, 1972–1977*. Edited by Colin Gordon. New York: Pantheon Books.

Free Malaysia Today. 2017. 'Transgender Shot Three Times and Slashed'. *Free Malaysia Today*, 23 February. http://www.freemalaysiatoday.com/category/nation/2017/02/23/transgender-shot-three-times-and-slashed/.

Gibson, Britton A., Shan-Estelle Brown, Ronnye Rutledge, Jeffrey A. Wickersham, Adeeba Kamarulzaman, and Frederick L. Altice. 2016. 'Gender Identity, Healthcare Access, and Risk Reduction Among Malaysia's *Mak Nyah* Community'. *Global Public Health* 11 (7–8): 1010–25.

Giffney, Noreen. 2009. 'Introduction: The "q" Word'. In *The Ashgate Research Companion to Queer Theory*, edited by Noreen Giffney and Michael O'Rourke, 1–9. Surrey, UK: Ashgate Publishing Ltd.

Goh, Joseph N. 2012a. 'Mary and the *Mak Nyahs*: Queer Theological Imaginings of Malaysian Male-to-Female Transsexuals'. *Theology & Sexuality* 18 (3): 215–33.

———. 2012b. '*Mak Nyah* Bodies as Sacred Sites: Uncovering the Queer Body-Sacramentality of Malaysian Male-to-Female Transsexuals'. *CrossCurrents* 62 (4): 512–21.

———. 2012c. '*Nyah*-Islam: The Reconstruction of God and Institutional Islam by Malaysian Male-to-Female Transsexuals'. *in God's image* 31 (2): 33–44.

———. 2014a. 'Transgressive Empowerment: Queering the Spiritualities of the *Mak Nyahs* of PT Foundation'. In *Queering Migrations Towards, From, and*

Beyond Asia, edited by Hugo Córdova Quero, Joseph N. Goh, and Michael Sepidoza Campos, 123–37. New York: Palgrave Macmillan.
———. 2014b. 'Fracturing Interwoven Heteronormativities in Malaysian Malay-Muslim Masculinity: A Research Note'. *Sexualities* 17 (5–6): 600–617.
———. 2016. 'Christianity, Sexual Diversity and Access to Health Services'. APCOM. https://apcom.org/wp-content/uploads/2016/11/DiscussionPaper_Christianiy-2016.11.25.pdf.
———. 2018. *Living Out Sexuality and Faith: Body Admissions of Malaysian Gay and Bisexual Men*. London: Routledge.
———. 2019. 'Untying Tongues: Negotiations and Innovations of Faith and Gender Among Malaysian Christian Trans Men'. *Culture and Religion* 20 (1): 1–20.
Goh, Robbie B. H. 2005. *Christianity in Southeast Asia*. Singapore: Institute of Southeast Asian Studies.
Goh, Joseph N., and Thaatchaayini Kananatu. 2018. 'Mak Nyahs and the Dismantling of Dehumanisation: Framing Empowerment Strategies of Malaysian Male-to-Female Transsexuals in the 2000s'. *Sexualities* 22 (1–2): 114–130.
Greatheart, Marcus. 2013. *Transforming Practice: Life Stories of Transgender Men That Change How Health Providers Work*. Toronto, ON: Ethica Press.
Guy, Michelle Lee. 2003. 'Ungendering Gendered Identities? Transgenderism in Malaysia'. *Akademika* 63: 69–86.
Hansbury, Griffin. 2005. 'The Middle Men: An Introduction to the Transmasculine Identities'. *Studies in Gender and Sexuality* 6 (3): 241–64.
heinz, matthew. 2016. *Entering Transmasculinity: The Inevitability of Discourse*. Chicago, IL: Intellect Ltd.
Hendricks, Muhsin. 2013. 'Islam, Sexual Diversity and Access to Health Services'. APCOM. https://apcom.org/2013/05/22/islam-sexual-diversity-and-access-to-health-services/.
Hero, Jakob. 2012. 'Toward a Queer Theology of Flourishing: Transsexual Embodiment, Subjectivity, and Moral Agency'. In *Queer Religion*, edited by Donald L. Boisvert and Jay Emerson Johnson, 2:2: 143–165. Santa Barbara, CA: Praeger.
Hines, Sally. 2006. 'What's the Difference? Bringing Particularity to Queer Studies of Transgender'. *Journal of Gender Studies* 15 (1): 49–66.
———. 2007. *TransForming Gender: Transgender Practices of Identity, Intimacy and Care*. Bristol, UK: Policy Press.
———. 2010. 'Introduction'. In *Transgender Identities: Towards a Social Analysis of Gender Diversity*, edited by Sally Hines and Tam Sanger, 1–22. New York: Routledge.
Holst, Frederik. 2012. *Ethnicization and Identity Construction in Malaysia*. New York: Routledge.

Human Rights Watch. 2014. '"I'm Scared to Be a Woman": Human Rights Abuses Against Transgender People in Malaysia'. Human Rights Watch Report. Kuala Lumpur, Malaysia. http://www.hrw.org/node/129025.

I Am the T. 2014. *I Am the T: A Trans Documentary*. https://www.youtube.com/user/iamthetfilm/feed.

Irin News. 2014. 'Right to Dignity—Barriers to Healthcare for Transgenders'. *Irin News*, 14 August. https://www.irinnews.org/report/100488/right-dignity-barriers-healthcare-transgenders.

Ismail Baba. 2001. 'Gay and Lesbian Couples in Malaysia'. In *Gay and Lesbian Asia: Culture, Identity, Community*, edited by Gerard Sullivan and Peter A. Jackson, 143–63. New York: Harrington Park Press.

Jabatan Agama Islam Selangor. 2018. 'Jabatan Agama Islam Selangor'. 2018. http://www.jais.gov.my/.

Jabatan Agama Islam Wilayah Persekutuan. 2014. 'Jabatan Agama Islam Wilayah Persekutuan'. 2014. http://www.jawi.gov.my/.

Jabatan Kemajuan Islam Malaysia. 2015. 'Jabatan Kemajuan Islam Malaysia'. 2015. http://www.islam.gov.my/.

Jabatan Mufti Kerajaan Negeri Sembilan. 2008. 'Hukum Wanita Menyerupai Lelaki (Pengkid)'. Keputusan Mesyuarat Fatwa. 2008. http://www.muftins.gov.my/index.php/arkib2/himpunan-fatwa/171-keputusan-mesyuarat-fatwa/729-hukum-wanita-menyerupai-lelaki-pengkid.

Jackson, Peter A. 2003. 'Performative Genders, Perverse Desires: A Bio-History of Thailand's Same-Sex and Transgender Cultures'. *Intersections: Gender, History and Culture in the Asian Context*, no. 9. http://intersections.anu.edu.au/issue9/jackson.html.

Jalleh, Josephine. 2013. 'Transgender Political Sec of Tanjung Bungah Rep Hopes for Equal Treatment'. *The Star Online*, 12 July. http://www.thestar.com.my/News/Nation/2013/07/12/Transgender-Tajung-Bunga-rep/.

Jerome, Collin. 2011. 'Queer Melayu: Queer Sexualities and the Politics of Malay Identity and Nationalism in Contemporary Malaysian Literature and Culture'. PhD diss., Brighton, East Sussex, UK: University of Sussex.

Johnson, Katherine. 2016. 'Changing Sex, Changing Self: Theorizing Transitions in Embodied Subjectivity'. *Men and Masculinities* 10 (1): 54–70.

Justice for Sisters. 2014. *I Am You Campaign*. https://www.youtube.com/user/mytransally/videos.

———. 2016. 'Media Guides | Panduan Media BM & Chinese Language'. *Resources* (blog). 18 March. https://justiceforsisters.wordpress.com/2016/03/18/media-guides-panduan-media-bm-chinese/.

Khartini Slamah. 2005. 'The Struggle to Be Ourselves, Neither Men nor Women: *Mak Nyahs* in Malaysia'. In *Sexuality, Gender and Rights: Exploring Theory and Practice in South and Southeast Asia*, edited by Geetanjali Misra and Radhika Chandiramani, 98–111. London: Sage.

Khor, Samantha. 2014. '8 Influential Malaysian Transgenders You Didn't Know About'. *Says.Com*, 17 November. http://says.com/my/lifestyle/8-influential-malaysian-transgenders-you-didn-t-know-about.

Kim, Seunghwan, Margeaux Dennis, Jessica Holland, Mark Terrell, Marios Loukas, and Justine Schober. 2018. 'The Anatomy of Abdominal Flap Phalloplasty for Transgender Surgery'. *Clinical Anatomy* 31 (2): 181–86.

Kitzinger, Celia. 2005. 'Heteronormativity in Action: Reproducing the Heterosexual Nuclear Family in After-Hours Medical Calls'. *Social Problems* 52 (4): 477–98.

Kolakowski, Victoria S. 1997. 'Toward a Christian Ethical Response to Transsexual Persons'. *Theology & Sexuality* 3 (6): 10–31.

Kong, Travis S. K. 2010. *Chinese Male Homosexualities: Memba, Tongzhi and Golden Boy.* Hoboken, NJ: Routledge.

KRYSS. 2014. 'ON THE RECORD: Violence Against Lesbians, Bisexual Women and Transgender Persons In Malaysia'. New York: International Gay and Lesbian Human Rights Commission. https://www.outrightinternational.org/sites/default/files/MalaysiaCC_0.pdf.

Lau, Alwyn. 2011. 'Deconstruction and the Daring Church: A Brief Dis/(re)-assembling of Faith and Politics in Malaysia'. *Asia Journal of Theology* 25 (1): 24–41.

Lee, Julian C. H., ed. 2010. 'Against the Order of Nature'. In *The Malaysian Way of Life*, 149–55. Selangor, Malaysia: Marshall Cavendish.

———. 2011. *Policing Sexuality: Sex, Society and the State.* London: Zed Books.

———. 2018. *Women's Activism in Malaysia: Voices and Insights.* Cham, Switzerland: Palgrave Macmillan.

Legislature of the State of Pahang. 2013. *Enactment No. 11 of 2013—Syariah Criminal Offences Enactment 2013.* http://www2.esyariah.gov.my/esyariah/mal/portalv1/enakmen2011/Eng_enactment_Ori_lib.nsf/f831ccddd195843f48256fc600141e84/7a1794a47c1a932e48257d43000bf726?OpenDocument.

Legislature of the State of Perlis. 1993. *Enactment No. 4 of 1993—Criminal Offences in the Syarak Enactment 1991.* http://www2.esyariah.gov.my/esyariah/mal/portalv1/enakmen2011/Eng_enactment_Upd.nsf/f831ccddd195843f48256fc600141e84/3fedd97c89e2e8d3482576c500231b7e?OpenDocument.

Legislature of the State of Sabah. 1995. *Enactment No. 3 of 1995—Syariah Criminal Offences Enactment 1995.* http://www2.esyariah.gov.my/esyariah/mal/portalv1/enakmen2011/Eng_enactment_Ori_lib.nsf/f831ccddd195843f48256fc600141e84/a24f10def0a59d1e4825761f00281c44?OpenDocument.

Low, Wah-Yun, Ee-Ming Khoo, Hui-Meng Tan, Fen-Lee Hew, and Seng-Hin Teoh. 2006. 'Depression, Hormonal Status and Erectile Dysfunction in the

Aging Male: Results from a Community Study in Malaysia'. *The Journal of Men's Health & Gender* 3 (3): 263–70.

Lucius-Hoene, Gabriele. 2000. 'Constructing and Reconstructing Narrative Identity'. *Forum: Qualitative Social Research* 1 (2). http://www.qualitative-research.net/index.php/fqs/article/view/1087.

Malay Mail Online. 2013. 'Marriage Between Muslim and Non-Muslim Illegal, Says Jakim'. *Malay Mail Online*, 27 September. http://www.themalaymailonline.com/malaysia/article/marriage-between-muslim-and-non-muslim-illegal-says-jakim.

———. 2016. 'Shariah Laws Already Affect Non-Muslims, SIS Says'. *Malay Mail Online*, 26 November. https://www.malaymail.com/news/malaysia/2016/11/26/shariah-laws-already-affect-non-muslims-sis-says/1258895.

Malaysiakini. 2011. 'Transgender Aleesha Farhana Dies at 25'. *Malaysiakini*, 30 July. https://www.malaysiakini.com/news/171502.

Malaysian Digest. 2017. 'A Success For First Gay Iftar In Malaysia'. *Malaysian Digest*, 15 June. http://www.malaysiandigest.com/features/681176-a-success-for-first-gay-iftar-in-malaysia.html.

Martin, Fran, and Josephine Ho. 2006. 'Editorial Introduction: Trans/Asia, Trans/Gender'. *Inter-Asia Cultural Studies* 7 (2): 185–87.

Mellström, Ulf. 2003. *Masculinity, Power and Technology: A Malaysian Ethnography*. Burlington, VT: Ashgate Publishing Ltd.

Minderjeet Kaur. 2017. 'Transgender Wants NRD to Allow Change of Status in MyKad'. *Free Malaysia Today*, 23 September. http://www.freemalaysiatoday.com/category/nation/2017/09/23/transgender-wants-nrd-to-allow-change-of-status-in-mykad/.

Morrison, Jean. 1995. '"The Circulation of Men": Marriage Practices and Gender Relations among the Bajau of Sabah, East Malaysia'. *Indonesia Circle. School of Oriental & African Studies. Newsletter* 23 (67): 216–48.

Nasrudin Subhi, Mohd Suhaimi Mohamad, and Lokman Hamid. 2013. 'Potensi Konflik Di Antara Pegangan Islam Dan Identiti Seksual: Simptom Psikologikal Dalam Kalangan Mak Nyah'. *Journal of Psychology & Human Development* 1: 44–48.

Ng, Chirk Jenn, Hui Meng Tan, and Sarinah Wah Yun Low. 2008. 'What Do Asian Men Consider as Important Masculinity Attributes? Findings from the Asian Men's Attitudes to Life Events and Sexuality (MALES) Study'. *Journal of Men's Health* 5 (4): 350–55.

Nonini, Donald M. 1999. 'The Dialectics of "Disputatiousness" and "Rice-Eating Money": Class Confrontation and Gendered Imaginaries among Chinese Men in West Malaysia'. *American Ethnologist* 26 (1): 47–68.

Noritah Omar. 2006. 'Colonialism and Malay Masculinity: Malay Satire as Observed in the Novel *Kawin-Kawin*'. *SARI: Jurnal Alam Dan Tamadun Melayu* 24: 107–20.

Ooi, Vincent B. Y. 2001. 'Globalising Singaporean-Malaysian English in an Inclusive Learner's Dictionary'. In *Who's Centric Now?: The Present State of Post-Colonial Englishes*, edited by Bruce Moore, 95–121. Oxford, UK: Oxford University Press.

Peletz, Michael G. 1996. *Reason and Passion: Representations of Gender in a Malay Society*. Berkeley, CA: University of California Press.

———. 2006. 'Transgenderism and Gender Pluralism in Southeast Asia since Early Modern Times'. *Current Anthropology* 47 (2): 309–40.

Petah Wazzan Iskandar. 2018. '"Affirm LGBT Members" Rights, Original Identities"'. *New Straits Times*, 12 August. https://www.nst.com.my/news/nation/2018/08/400693/affirm-lgbt-members-rights-original-identities.

Peterson, V. Spike, and Jacqui True. 1998. '"New Times" and New Conversations'. In *The 'Man' Question in International Relations*, edited by Marysia Zalewski and Jane Parpart. Boulder, CO: Westview Press.

Pfeffer, Carla A. 2017. *Queering Families: The Postmodern Partnerships of Cisgender Women and Transgender Men*. New York: Oxford University Press.

Pragalath, K. 2018. 'Transgenders: Don't Discriminate Us'. *Berita Daily*, 7 February. https://www.beritadaily.com/transgenders-dont-discriminate-us/.

Pyne, Jake. 2011. 'Unsuitable Bodies: Trans People and Cisnormativity in Shelter Services'. *Canadian Social Work Review; Ottawa* 28 (1): 129–37.

Qarami Hashim, and Ashley Tang. 2018. 'Nur Sajat Says Meeting with Jakim Was "Positive"'. *The Star Online*, 17 January. https://www.thestar.com.my/news/nation/2018/01/17/nur-sajat-says-meeting-with-jakim-was-positive/.

Qishin Tariq. 2016. 'Media Guidebook on LGBT Issues'. *The Star Online*, 9 July. https://www.thestar.com.my/news/nation/2016/07/09/guidebook-on-lgbt-issues/.

Rasiah, Rajah, Abdillah Noh, and Makmor Tumin. 2009. 'Privatising Healthcare in Malaysia: Power, Policy and Profits'. *Journal of Contemporary Asia* 39 (1): 50–62.

Reisner, Sari L., Kristi E. Gamarel, Emilia Dunham, Ruben Hopwood, and Sel Hwahng. 2013. 'Female-to-Male Transmasculine Adult Health: A Mixed-Methods Community-Based Needs Assessment'. *Journal of the American Psychiatric Nurses Association* 19 (5): 293–303.

Reuters Staff. 2015. 'Malaysia Court Upholds Ban on Cross Dressing by Transgender Muslims'. *Reuters*, 8 October. https://www.reuters.com/article/us-malaysia-verdict-crossdressing/malaysia-court-upholds-ban-on-cross-dressing-by-transgender-muslims-idUSKCN0S21CE20151008.

Rowniak, Stefan, and Catherine Chesla. 2013. 'Coming Out for a Third Time: Transmen, Sexual Orientation, and Identity'. *Archives of Sexual Behavior* 42 (3): 449–61.

Rowniak, Stefan, Catherine Chesla, Carol Dawson Rose, and William L. Holzemer. 2011. 'Transmen: The HIV Risk of Gay Identity'. *AIDS Education and Prevention* 23 (6): 508–20.

Samsul Draman, Maliya Suofeiya, Liyana A., Farhani S., Jannah R., and Razman Mohd Rus. 2016. 'Psycho-Social and Spiritual Backgrounds, Experiences, and Needs as a Transsexual: A Qualitative Study Within Persatuan Insaf Pahang'. *International Medical Journal Malaysia* 15 (2): 27–36.

Schilt, Kristen, and Elroi Windsor. 2014. 'The Sexual Habitus of Transgender Men: Negotiating Sexuality Through Gender'. *Journal of Homosexuality* 61 (5): 732–48.

Seamont, Morgan M. H. 2018. 'Becoming "The Man I Want to Be": Transgender Masculinity, Embodiment, and Sexuality'. Boulder, CO: University of Colorado. https://scholar.colorado.edu/anth_gradetds/85.

Shafie, A. A., and M. A. Hassali. 2013. 'Willingness to Pay for Voluntary Community-Based Health Insurance: Findings from an Exploratory Study in the State of Penang, Malaysia'. *Social Science & Medicine* 96: 272–76.

Shah, Shanon. 2018. *The Making of a Gay Muslim: Religion, Sexuality and Identity in Malaysia and Britain*. Basingstoke, UK: Palgrave Macmillan.

Shahrin Yahya. 2012. 'Through Their Eyes: Sulastri Arrifin'. *FZ*, 1 November. http://www.fz.com/content/through-their-eyes-sulastri-arrifin.

Shamsul A. B., and Mohamad Fauzi Sukimi. 2006. 'Making Sense of Malay Sexuality: An Exploration'. *SARI: Jurnal Alam Dan Tamadun Melayu* 24: 59–72.

Shazwan Mustafa Kamal. 2015. 'Islam a "Wonderful Tool" for Political Mileage, Transgender Forum Told', 4 January. https://www.malaymail.com/s/826523/islam-a-wonderful-tool-for-political-mileage-transgender-forum-told.

———. 2018. 'Wan Azizah: LGBT Fine as Long as Kept in Private, Not "Glamourised"'. *Malay Mail*, 20 August. https://www.malaymail.com/s/1664056/wan-azizah-lgbt-fine-as-long-as-kept-in-private-not-glamourised.

Syed Jamal Zahiid. 2013. 'Human Rights a Facade to Destroy Islam, Says JAKIM in Friday Sermon'. *Malay Mail Online*, 18 October. http://www.themalaymailonline.com/malaysia/article/human-rights-a-facade-to-destroy-islam-says-jakim-in-friday-sermon.

Tanis, Justin Edward. 2003. *Trans-Gendered: Theology, Ministry, and Communities of Faith*. Cleveland, OH: Pilgrim Press.

Taylor, Jami K., Barry L. Tadlock, and Sarah J. Poggione. 2015. 'Birth Certificate Amendment Laws and Morality Politics'. In *Transgender Rights and Politics: Groups, Issue Framing, and Policy Adoption*, edited by Jami K. Taylor and Donald P. Haider-Markel, 252–72. Ann Arbor, MI: University of Michigan Press.

Teh, Yik Koon. 2002. *The Mak Nyahs: Malaysian Male to Female Transsexuals*. Singapore: Eastern Universities Press.

———. 2008a. 'Politics and Islam: Factors Determining Identity and the Status of Male-to-Female Transsexuals in Malaysia'. In *AsiaPacifiQueer: Rethinking Genders and Sexualities*, edited by Fran Martin, Peter A. Jackson, Mark McLelland, and Audrey Yue, 85–98. Urbana, IL: University of Illinois Press.

———. 2008b. 'HIV-Related Needs for Safety Among Male-to-Female Transsexuals (Mak Nyah) in Malaysia'. *SAHARA J: Journal of Social Aspects of HIV/AIDS* 5 (4): 178–85.

The Commissioner of Law Revision, Malaysia. 1957. *Federal Constitution*. http://www.agc.gov.my/agcportal/uploads/files/Publications/FC/FEDERAL%20CONSTITUTION%20ULANG%20CETAK%202016.pdf.

———. 2006. *Syariah Criminal Offences (Federal Territories) Act 1997*. http://www.agc.gov.my/agcportal/index.php?r=portal2/lom2&id=1431.

The Star Online. 2016. 'Nisha Dedicates Women of Courage Award to All Transwomen'. *The Star Online*, 30 March. http://www.thestar.com.my/news/nation/2016/03/30/transwoman-nisha-gets-women-of-courage-award-from-john-kerry/.

———. 2019. 'Controversy Over Transgender Appointment'. *The Star Online*, 11 July. https://www.thestar.com.my/news/nation/2019/07/11/controversyover-transgender-appointment.

Tom Waddell Health Center. 2012. 'The Transgender Clinic of the Tom Waddell Health Center'. 2012. http://www.twtransgenderclinic.org/.

Uthaya Sankar SB. 2013. 'Kisah Seorang "Pak Nyah"'. *The Malaysian Insider*, 9 December. http://www.theinsiderarchived.com/opinion/uthaya-sankar/article/kisah-seorang-pak-nyah/kisah-seorang-pak-nyah.

Vignato, Silvia. 2012. '"Men Come in, Men Go out": Single Muslim Women in Malaysia and Aceh'. *Social Identities* 18 (2): 239–57.

Vijay, Aishwarya, Valerie A. Earnshaw, Ying Chew Tee, Veena Pillai, Jaclyn M. White Hughto, Kirsty Clark, Adeeba Kamarulzaman, Frederick L. Altice, and Jeffrey A. Wickersham. 2017. 'Factors Associated with Medical Doctors' Intentions to Discriminate Against Transgender Patients in Kuala Lumpur, Malaysia'. *LGBT Health* 5 (1): 61–68.

Wan Azmi Ramli. 1991. *Dilema Mak Nyah: Suatu Ilusi*. Kuala Lumpur, Malaysia: Utusan Publications & Distributors Sdn Bhd.

Watts, Fraser. 2002. 'Transsexualism and the Church'. *Theology & Sexuality* 9 (1): 63–85.

Wickramasinghe, Maithree. 2010. *Feminist Research Methodology: Making Meanings of Meaning-Making*. London: Routledge.

Wilde, Dorian. 2010. *Dorian's Transition Weblog*. https://www.youtube.com/channel/UCk8EJRJyV_k7_KMJVICR7sg.

———. 2012a. 'Why Label?' *Queer Asian Spirit E-Magazine (QAS E-Zine)*, 2012. http://www.queerasianspirit.org/16.html.

———. 2012b. 'Labels'. *Potato Popstar: Resource for Transsexual Information in Malaysia* (blog). 22 May. https://potatopopstar.wordpress.com/2012/05/22/labels/.

Winter, Sam. 2006. 'What Made Me This Way? Contrasting Reflections by Thai and Filipina Transwomen'. *Intersections: Gender, History and Culture in the Asian Context*, no. 14. http://intersections.anu.edu.au/issue14/winter.htm.

Wong, Kai Hui. 2018. 'We Are Nothing but Scapegoats: LGBT Community'. *Malaysiakini*, 8 February. https://www.malaysiakini.com/news/411519.

Wong, Yuenmei. 2012. 'Islam, Sexuality, and the Marginal Positioning of *Pengkids* and Their Girlfriends in Malaysia'. *Journal of Lesbian Studies* 16 (4): 1–14.

Yeow, Julia. 2001. '"Women in Men's Bodies" Struggle for Basic Rights'. *Malaysiakini*, 9 September. http://www.malaysiakini.com/news/4611.

Yu, Ting-Fai. 2019. 'Reconfiguring Queer Asia as Disjunctive Modernities: Notes on the Subjective Production of Working-Class Gay Men in Hong Kong'. *Journal of Homosexuality* 0 (0): 1–22.

Yue, Audrey. 2017. 'Trans-Singapore: Some Notes Towards Queer Asia as Method'. *Inter-Asia Cultural Studies* 18 (1): 10–24.

Zachariah, Elizabeth. 2014. 'Spurned and Abused, Two Transwomen Now Push for Equal Rights'. *The Malaysian Insider*, 26 September. http://www.themalaysianinsider.com/malaysia/article/spurned-and-abused-two-transwomen-now-push-for-equal-rights.

Zainah Anwar. 2005. 'Law-Making in the Name of Islam: Implications for Democratic Governance'. In *Islam in Southeast Asia: Political, Social and Strategic Challenges for the 21st Century*, edited by K. S. Nathan and Mohammad Hashim Kamali, 121–34. Singapore: Institute of Southeast Asian Studies.

Zuriah Abdul Rahman, and Norzaidi Mohd Daud. 2010. 'Adverse Selection and Its Consequences on Medical and Health Insurance and *Takaful* in Malaysia'. *Humanomics* 26 (4): 264–83.

CHAPTER 2

Engendering Identity

I have often been asked how I differentiate between a straight or lesbian or masculine-acting woman and a trans man, to which I respond that I do not make such distinctions and definitions myself. I concur with Michael Eric Brown that 'it is up to each individual to define their own identity and their own version of what masculinity means to them [and that t] here are no absolutes when it comes to transmasculinity' (2016, 24). Malaysian trans men articulate and construct their subjectivities as life projects based on a simultaneous bid to resist and 'conform to codes of masculine behavior that are socially enforced' (Cromwell 1999, 12). In each instance of such projects, these individuals both reject and adhere to specific socially condoned attributes of manness, manliness and masculinity as anchor points, foregrounding the notion that 'one is not born a man but rather becomes one again and again as they encounter the gender, racial, and sexual knowledges and related expectations of different social contexts' (Abelson 2019, 61).

Queer theories have long been the favoured methodology to frame transgender identities (Currah et al. 2006; Stryker and Whittle 2006), and have done much to demystify, challenge and even undermine both nonnormative and normative gender and sexual identities (Bunch 2013; Butler 1999; Jagose 1996; Warner 1993). Identities are, and will always prove to be 'fragmented, unstable, discontinuous and contradictory' (Ridge et al. 1999, 45–46). Yet, queer theories have not contributed

J. N. Goh, *Becoming a Malaysian Trans Man*,
Gender, Sexualities and Culture in Asia,
https://doi.org/10.1007/978-981-15-4534-4_2

definitively to the demise of identities, as in the instance of men who deliberately retain 'gay' as personalised selfhood (Adam 2000).

Sally Hines posits that theorising transgender subjectivities via queer theories is 'limited by a lack of attention to lived experience, which often leaves non-performance-related transgender identities unaccounted for' (2007, 27). Hence, as Griffin Hansbury says, 'to dispel [identities] completely by forever citing the exceptions and many permutations, is to render them – and the people who stand behind them – invisible' (2005, 242). The elimination of identities can lead to the diminishment of lived embodiments of self-understanding and self-expression. Therefore, I understand identity in the sense of *identification*, 'where the suffix *–ation* marks a process' (Machart and Lim 2013, 37; original italics). Identity is thus a 'signifying practice' (Butler 1999, 184), an ongoing but permanently unstable negotiation of subjectivity that gestures towards potential agency, empowerment and realisation in lived experiences.

Therefore, my use of 'identity' in relation to the personal self-descriptions of gender among trans men builds on notions of becoming, subjectivity and personhood which I had discussed in 'Prologue'. The construction of gender identity, as evident in the testimonies of my research participants, is not a stagnant, ontological trait but a project that is vulnerable to uncertainty, open-endedness, and pliability. Powerfully conditioned by, and perpetually impacting spatial and temporal circumstances and contexts, identity is a project of reflexive self-conception and somewhat resembles Aaron Devor's idea of 'a person's acceptance of a sex, gender or sexual categorization as descriptive of themselves' (1994, 33), or Jason Cromwell's reference to a 'person's self-concept and how individuals perceive themselves, that is, self-image and the subjective sense of self' (1999, 8). As such, identity constructions are multifaceted, fluid, interlocking, contingent, unstable and impermanent on many other counts while also being *profoundly experienced embodied processes*.[1]

'Man' is a highly volatile and contested embodiment, and it proves crucial to examine how trans men comprehend themselves and where they situate themselves *purposefully* and *meaningfully* within the evolving nodes of Malaysian life, which in itself is also a highly variegated reality.

[1] It is worth noting that not all transgender people deploy 'transgender' as an identity, as some 'describe their transgender experience as a status or medical history' (Galupo et al. 2014, note 1, 461).

For instance, do trans men see themselves as transgender people who are embarking on a gender journey, or occupying a liminal social identity, or have accomplished the intertwined project of man and manliness? The diverse elements of everyday life with which they engage in these processes are, I propose, equally significant. This Chapter examines three major assemblages of man among Malaysian trans men, notably how man is named, performed and communicated. Each of these assemblages yields nuanced details of identity crafting within specific Malaysian contexts which nonetheless also actively 'tap onto the global circulation of discourse' (Tang 2012, 84) on collective, politically charged transgender identity (Currah et al. 2006; Taylor and Haider-Markel 2015).

Naming 'Man'

The scholarship on identity formulations of manness, manliness and masculinity among trans men is copious (Abelson 2019; Brown 2016; Cromwell 1999; Devor 2016; heinz 2016). While the majority of Malaysian trans men self-identify as 'trans men', others refer to themselves as 'Female-To-Male' (FTM), 'transgender', 'transmasculine', 'male' or simply 'man'. The understanding of these terms in the act of self-naming is vital for trans men as they journey towards self-understanding and self-communication, often amidst conflict, convolution and contradiction.

'Girls That Look Like Guys That Like Girls': Female-to-Male (FTM)

Michael shares how the 'discovery' of an FTM subjectivity paves the way for him to self-identify as 'male'.

Goh: How do you describe yourself in terms of your gender?

Michael: Well, I would describe myself as male, because that's what I wanna be ... identified as. Erm, I want people to respect me as what I identify myself.

Goh: Not a transgender man?

Michael: Ah, I wouldn't say transgender, because to be honest I hate describing myself as transgender, because, I don't know if it's like a bad thing ... I just want people to know me as a male. That's it ... So I went and looked for ... a specific term, saying 'girls that look like guys that like girls' ... last time like internet was in Malay, so I saw a few, like terms like '*pengkid*' ... then one, just one word hit me, and it

> was FTM. And then I went and clicked on FTM and I started searching about FTM and I saw FTM, what FTM stands for is actually 'Female-To-Male', and I was like … this is what I am, FTM, and … so the proper term for FTM is actually transgender … all this while I was thinking transgender is only meant for male-to-female, but I didn't know you can actually be from Female-To-Male as well, and I was like … so this is what I am.

Michael speaks of a period of exploration in which he is unable to articulate his subjectivity. Browsing on the 'internet', he chances upon the Malay word *pengkid* for masculine-acting and/or lesbian women who are seen as an affront to Malaysian Islam (Jabatan Mufti Kerajaan Negeri Sembilan 2008; Wong 2012). As is the case in other parts of the world, the media becomes a crucial tool that assists in the search for gender self-recognition (heinz 2016).

Marcus Greatheart notes the prevalence of 'a dominant sexuality discourse that problematically lumps trans people together with gay, lesbian and bisexual people[, whereby] gender identity and sexual identity are commonly confused' (2013, 144), a situation which resonates with the Malaysian context. In contrast to this view, Michael expresses how becoming a trans man requires the confluence of both gender identity (girls that look like guys …) and sexual attraction (… that like girls). Nevertheless, Michael is keenly aware that his own embodiment does not quite cohere with '*pengkid*'. His search for an apt description for himself that is free from a sense of ill-fittingness leads him to self-cognisance as 'FTM' rather than '*pengkid*'.

The FTM label 'is not claimed by all transmasculine individuals due to its binary connotations. Also, many do not believe they were ever "female", so there is no "transition" in the respect of female to male' (Brown 2016, 205). Consequently, 'the preferred [term is] "transman", which [is] appreciated as the most affirming of the [individual]'s identity[,] de-emphasize[s] the pathology model, and reflect[s] an active appreciation of the diversity model' (Elizondo et al. 2012, 16). Michael's zeal to uncover the meaning of FTM, which denotes a simultaneous acknowledgement and abandonment of his 'female socialization and history' (Cromwell 1999, 28), enables the evolution of an identity which 'is what [he is]'. His quip that '[he] never told anyone that [he] was transgender' despite the fact that '[he] knew that [he] was' because '[he] just didn't know' hints at an interior struggle towards comprehending and embodying a self-affirmed gender identity.

In other words, Michael wrestles with attempting to comprehend how he embodies both a departure from socially sanctioned gender representations and sexual attraction, an inner conflict reflected in his initial musings on whether transitioning was 'a bad thing'. Michael's self-enlightenment and twice-repeated affirmation that he is indeed FTM suggests that trans men experience relief in bringing a category of identity to a recognisable, comforting gender logic as advised by sexual desire. That he is 'okay' and 'fine' with this 'discovered' category is a case in which self-definition becomes an exercise of authenticity and confident 'being-himself-ness' (Goh 2016, 135) as a trans man. Michael shows that there is a certain experiential profundity that exceeds societal expectations and is 'basic to beingness' (Cromwell 1999, 42).

Akin to several other research participants, Michael both disavows and accepts the identity of transgender. Michael conceptualises the terms 'Female-To-Male' and 'transgender' as strategic interim phases in order to understand and map the journey towards being male, which is his ultimate goal. It this final recognisability as male, which I argue is a metonym for man, that he desires for himself and for society to 'respect [him] as what [he identifies himself]'.

'Closer to the Male Side': Transmasculine

Ray favours the term 'transmasculine' over 'trans man' or 'man'. As the following narrative reveals, his choice of self-identification interplays intimately with sociocultural presuppositions of man:

> *Ray*: I would consider myself as transmasculine person … as far as my understanding of it goes, is a person who is on a gender spectrum … closer to the male side of the gender spectrum than the female side. So for me is like I am more personally comfortable being addressed as male, treated as male …
>
> *Goh*: What is difference between transmasculine and trans man?
>
> *Ray*: I guess … this is just my personal feelings lah. The thing is, a lot of people when they say trans man they expect trans men to be super masculine, macho and all that. For me … I'm not necessarily that way, because sometimes … I do prefer like, what you call feminine-identifying thing if that makes sense … not that I say I call these activities like make up or clothes making as feminine per se, but some people view it as feminine, so I say I'm more comfortable being a transmasculine person.

Ray presents his understanding of 'transmasculine' as fundamentally constitutive of 'being addressed [and] treated as male'. Sari L. Reisner and colleagues 'use the term *transmasculine* as an inclusive umbrella term that refers to transgender people assigned a female sex at birth and who identify on the masculine spectrum, including as a man of transgender experience, transgender man, transman, female-to-male (FTM), genderqueer, or "other" masculine identity' (2013, 293; original emphasis; see also Peitzmeier et al. 2017).

Despite the fact that 'there are no absolutes when it comes to transmasculinity' (Brown 2016, 24) and 'transmasculine' is thus a catch-all term, Ray uses it to *replace* 'trans man' and 'man'. Upon my probing, he offers two insights that unpack this personalised category that leans towards gender nonconformity. First, becoming 'transmasculine' requires the cognisance that one 'is closer to the male side of the gender spectrum', a description which exemplifies the popular understanding of transmasculine individuals as those 'assigned female at birth, but identify with masculinity to a greater extent than with femininity' (Brown 2016, 209). Ray recognises that while he was assigned female at birth, his embodiment resonates more closely with sociocultural designations of male identity, behaviour and traits. Logically therefore, the ways in which 'transmasculine persons' talk about the body reveal how discourse can indeed disrupt some of the most common-sense "facts" (i.e., ideologies) about, sex, sexuality, and desire' (Edelman and Zimman 2014, 674). By deconstructing the female-feminine imperative, Ray reveals the significance of reconstructing an ongoing discursive identity of embodied transmasculinity that ruptures the seeming unassailability of gender ideologies.

Second, his self-affirmed gender identity builds on his 'personal feelings' that he does not match up to sociocultural expectations of being 'super masculine [and] macho'. Both perceptions indicate that the construction of transmasculinity negotiates intimately with stereotypical expectations of hyperbolised hegemonic (trans)masculinity to become man. Here, Ray discloses his penchant for 'make up or clothes' that are popularly interpreted as 'feminine-identifying'. Owing to his proclivity for activities that are associated with women, he feels somewhat disentitled to be a trans man and settles on 'transmasculine' as an identity with which he feels more 'personally comfortable'. Although transmasculinity acknowledges a male dimension in its doings, and transmasculine men may be 'more fluid in their identifications with the signs or props of masculinity and maleness' (Cromwell 1999, 109), transmasculinity can also be attenuated by 'feminine-identifying' activities.

Yet for Ray, becoming transmasculine is the negotiation of polarised tensions in living primarily as man without relinquishing favoured acts that are 'feminine-identifying'. The nexus between 'discourse and the body [is] inextricably linked such that discourse does not override the truth of the body but rather brings it into social existence' (Edelman and Zimman 2014, 64). In Ray's case, the intersection of discourse and embodiment that makes him socially intelligible conscripts 'feminine-identifying' activities that defy stereotypical scripts of hypermasculinity. Ray thus instantiates a 'a self-identification that relates in some way to masculinity, but that relation is [as] diverse as gender and sexuality' (Brown 2016, 24) itself.

'Very Much Male': Trans/Man

Many Malaysian trans men understand themselves as trans men, while others see themselves as simultaneously trans men and men. The perceived eligibility of becoming a trans man or simply man is, however, laced with richly diverse nuances. For instance, Alco speaks about managing his identity as a trans man with 'the anatomy of a woman':

> *Goh*: How do you describe yourself in terms of your gender?
>
> *Alco*: In terms of gender, well, how I describe myself ... for me I'm a trans man.
>
> *Goh*: And what does that mean to you?
>
> *Alco*: A man going through transitioning (laughs). I mean ... if you talk about male or female, it's very specific right? You know, they got all the (air quotes) 'necessities' of being, you know, biologically male, biologically female, right? But I'm a mixture of both.
>
> *Goh*: (chuckles) What do you mean by that?
>
> *Alco*: Meaning that ... I have the anatomy of a woman, but overall, erm, the other different aspect of me is very much male ... some people say that, you know, you don't have to have a penis to be a man. I totally agree with that. But for me, it's my, my own perception of myself ... I'm more comfortable with being identified as a trans man.

By describing himself as 'a man going through transitioning', Alco establishes his identity as a trans man in a two-fold manner as man and an individual who is undergoing Gender-Affirming Hormone Therapy

(GAHT).[2] Alco's assertion that 'the other different aspect of [him which] is very much male' is very likely an allusion to a partially accomplished mental feat of self-identity as man.

Nevertheless, Alco holds a belief, shared by many Malaysian trans men, in what he perceives as the biological dimensions of maleness that constitute the obligatory 'necessities' of achieving a full status of man in the Malaysian context. A simultaneous acknowledgement of being 'biologically female' and the unattainability of being 'biologically male' due to the absence of a penis reinforces 'the binary sex system [in which] the material body must align with its prescribed gender' (Yue 2017, 11). That manness for Alco is a matter of 'specific' physical representation as much as it one of mental certitude in order to align with dominant gender scripts or that which 'some people say' embraces the idea that 'conceptualizing essentialist and constructionist positions as divided and separate appears an oversimplification of the unavoidable parallelisms in human thought and bodily perception' (heinz 2016, 227).

I argue that Alco experiences a liminal subjectivity that generates gender dis/placement due to the lack of a penis, an irreconcilable melange of confidence and non-confidence. Despite agreeing with popular perception that the penis is a non-essential element 'to be a man', the lack of this appendage precludes the 'full' status of manhood for him. In order to address this dysphoric tension with some measure of manageability, Alco seems to subscribe to a coalesced subjectivity in which the trans man subjectivity occupies 'a mixture of both' elements of biological maleness and femaleness.

Griffin Hansbury asserts that American trans men of the twenty-first century identify as men but 'also embraced their transness, which lent them a blended quality that made them more gender fluid than the Woodworkers and the "just men"' (2005, 253).[3] In contrast, Alco's testimony suggests that there are trans men for whom this 'transness' almost assumes a state of temporary setback, a transitionary stage before establishing what they believe to be a 'complete' status of manliness. It is

[2] For a richer discussion of GAHT, see 'Embarking on Medical Transitioning'.

[3] According to Hansbury, Woodworkers 'are your run-of-the-mill, Joe-six-pack, female-to-male transsexuals. They would most likely identify themselves as men, minus any transspecific prefixes, and are sometimes called Woodworkers by other transpeople because of their tendency to blend into the woodwork' (2005, 246).

within this framework of 'perception' and reasoning that Alco feels that his self-naming as a female-to-male transgender person becomes justified.

Axman differs from Alco in that he holds a preference to identify as 'male' rather than as a trans man. Not unlike Michael, Axman's idea of 'male' is also a referent to the doing of man:

> *Goh*: How would you describe yourself in terms of your gender?
> *Axman*: Male.
> *Goh*: Just male?
> *Axman*: Yeah.
> *Goh*: Not trans man?
> *Axman*: Why would I want to … I think we're over that, you know? Once you assimilate into society … just want to be … binary, okay? So to the general population I mean, you go and explain to people what's a trans man about. I think, it's not that I don't want to educate people, but generally, society around us they, not to say they're narrow-minded or what but I think we just keep all the, what do you call that, the explanation lah. Because I already pass, there's no point I want to explain some more. Unless … for research purposes I will explain, but to general people that I meet day to day I don't see the need to explain, unless you know, you start asking me, what is that on my IC (Identity Card) like that, okay, I'm forced to explain, I will explain, yes.

Axman's active rejection of the label 'trans man' as a bid to 'assimilate into society' is an attempt to be successfully invisible in a mainstream society that taxonomises human persons into normative categories of man/male and woman/female. He expresses a desire to move beyond a trans identity and settle unproblematically into the gender binary due to his ability to 'pass', or to be socioculturally recognised, perceived and treated as male and man.[4] Axman expresses a preference to eschew being what Brown calls 'transgressively gendered' or residing in the amorphous interstices of gender, and settle instead into an embodiment that is 'more "binary" – more male or more female' (2016, 80).

The fact that Axman deliberately resists 'trans man' implies a dissonance with how he truly feels as 'male'. This reactionary expression seems to imply that 'trans' points to an ersatz man, as 'to be discovered or revealed as FTMs/transmen is often to be treated as less than real or

[4]The notion of passing is highly complex and contentious, as I will discuss further in the section 'Passing'.

artificial' (Cromwell 1999, 12). Thus, while he may be socioculturally categorised as a trans man, he feels male and needs to slip 'legitimately' into invisibility in order to become man. Axman's resolution in gender identity resonates with Cromwell's idea that 'in spite of transpeople's female bodies, which society insists means that they are women, they become men and in many ways behave like other men in their respective communities[, and] often become invisible as transgendered people and only visible as men' (1999, 11–12).

Furthermore, Axman does not seem to have any desire to dismantle the fixities of the gender binary. What I find noteworthy in this regard is that transitioning to man effectively corroborates, rather than challenges hegemonic gender categorisations in the pursuit of gender recognisability and acceptance. The keen pursuit to be male is at once the heartfelt desire to be 'non-male' or female, which entrenches the gender binary and underscores the fact that 'each gender status claim is a simplification of the complexity inherent in the immense diversity of human nature' (Devor 1994, 38–39).

The exception he makes in this regard 'for research purposes', an obvious reference to his willingness to meet with me for an interview, and as a 'forced' explanation of the incongruity between his gender appearance and details on his Malaysian Identity Card or *MyKad* is particularly significant.[5] I propose that Axman's unwillingness to 'explain' is concomitantly his unwillingness to qualify and justify his gender identity to meddlesome onlookers 'that [he meets] day to day'—perhaps akin to Warp's experience as discussed in Chapter 1. His desire to steer away from those who may have no other interest than to callously objectivise, fetishise and pathologise him as a gendered aberration or who may find his gender complexities incomprehensible constitutes what I call a trans-technique of averting the anomalizing and abnormalizing gaze that harbours the risk of reducing the trans man to a man who is 'less than real or artificial' (Cromwell 1999, 12).

On the other hand, Axman interprets 'research' projects and official procedures that require him to divulge his gender identity in detail as because such requests emerge from genuine interest or out of manifest necessity. The act of delineating casual questions from more substantial enquiries on his gender identity becomes a means for him

[5] I address the interlocking significance between gender identity and the *MyKad* in Warp's experience in 'Prologue'.

to avoid publicising what he sees as the privacy of gendered existence as male. The trans man subjectivity, as such, is a concomitantly private and public negotiation of embodied identity that actively resists cultural reductionism.

Axman's aversion towards having to explain himself as a trans man and zeal in assimilating into the gender binary is reflected and elaborated in Schulz's co-optation of 'man' due to 'a slight stigma' of being transgender:

Goh: Why do you not like being referred to as a trans man or referring to yourself as a trans man?

Schulz: Erm, maybe there's still a slight stigma. Er, that when you're seen as a trans man, people immediately start questioning, like, does this guy have a dick or a penis, or how does he have sex or things like that. And for me, it's something very private. You shouldn't be asking people like that (laughs). Things like this is very personal and private. What people do in their bed, dude it's none of your business. But that, maybe that's one of the reasons why I still, when people ask me, I still prefer to just be seen as a man, to avoid those kind of questions. Yes. So, but, when you tell them you're a trans man and things like that, and they start questioning you, into details which I believe is not necessary at all (laughs).

What Schulz refers to as 'stigma' is actually the objectification and fetishisation of transgender people in terms of their genitalia, which is not uncommon in Malaysia (see Goh 2014; Khartini 2005).[6] While Axman's uneasiness is not as explicitly mentioned, I suggest that he is also wary of, and abhors the awkward and insensitive questions that will be levelled against him if he were to publically divulge his gender identity as a trans man. Schulz seemingly enfleshes Axman's detestation of having to 'explain' himself by naming absurd enquiries that he has encountered, including questions of whether he possesses 'a dick or a penis' and how he engages in sexual activity.

Despite arguments that the penis as a signifier of manness and masculinity is always determined by sociocultural particularities (for instance, Cornwall 1994), the penis—particularly the erect penis—ordinarily

[6] Refer to Warp's experience in 'Prologue'.

remains indexed as, borrowing from Tony Ayre's words, 'the most aggressive symbol of masculinity' (1999, 94) or in this context, manness. Malaysia is no exception. Hence, I argue that the inappropriate questions directed towards Schulz are in reality inordinate interrogations that challenge and potentially disintegrate the cohesiveness which a trans man belabours to accomplish man. In other words, his self-construction as a man who was assigned female at birth is vulnerable to a society that expects men to be exclusively biologically male.

Schulz uses a two-fold strategy to cope with these destructive elements of 'stigma' that are akin to Axman's. First, he insists that as both his gender identity and gender expression are 'personal and private', he is not obliged to provide any explanation of who he is. Here, I suggest that both privacy and the construction of society as an inquisitive agent act as important deployments to secure the trans man subjectivity. Second, by 'just be[ing] seen as a man' rather than a trans man, he is able 'to avoid [inappropriate] questions' that erode his gender identity. In other words, what Schulz does on one hand is to label society as an inimical force that seeks to invade the privacy of his personal space as a transgender person. On the other hand, Schulz seemingly befriends society by aligning himself to sociocultural expectations of the gender binary, thus identifying as man. Hence, the dialectics of criticising and befriending socioculturally sanctioned gender norms maintains a space that preserves a self-affirmed gender identity.

While Axman self-declares as male and Schulz as man, Warp expresses the lack of certitude in his gender identity:

> *Goh*: And what does it mean for you to be a man?
>
> *Warp*: That is a good question. That is something I've asked myself forever. But I feel like the only thing that determines a man is your self-identity. Your self-determination. If you say you're a man, then you are a man.
>
> *Goh*: And for you as Warp, how do you identify as a man?
>
> *Warp*: I don't know. It's just a, it's just a preference maybe like, I would prefer erm, like I feel more connected to the body and the physicality of a man than I would with a woman. And more with the identity of a man, than of a woman. Or anything in between, really. Or maybe I'm still in the process of self-discovery, who knows. So, erm, in that sense for now in this time and place, I am, I identify as a trans man who, whose gender expression is very fluid.

Despite identifying as a trans man, Warp candidly remarks that his gender identity 'is something [he's] asked [him]self forever' or that he continues to unravel the complexities of his subjectivity. In the midst of this bewilderment, Warp employs the terms 'self-identity', 'self-determination' or 'preference' as constitutive of a self-affirmed gender identity. This dependence on a resolute process of self-actualisation, which is an awareness of the self that facilitates an ongoing endeavour of self-determination, self-creation or self-definition as a recognisable subject in the world is indicative of the fact that 'the process of recognizing and realizing one's transmasculine identity is fundamentally understood as a search for self' (heinz 2016, 154).

Rather than deferring to secondary sex characteristics or specific genitalia like Alco, or focusing on non-engagement with a largely uninformed public in order to maintain a gender identity like Axman or Schulz, Warp relies on a personally developed deep-seated conviction. Although he was assigned female at birth, he has a stronger connection with 'the body and the physicality' as well as 'the identity of a man'. Comparable to Michael's experience, Warp heeds the '*somatic wisdom*' (Goh 2018, 65; original emphasis) that wells from within himself and lives his life as man. The identity of a trans man arises from an acute awareness of, and ability to follow through with the methods in which he desires to appear and live in a gendered world in accordance with experiential profundity.

Warp's self-determination is not without its precariousness. What I find to be of particular significance is that Warp identifies 'as a trans man … whose gender expression is very fluid'. By naming himself as 'anything in between', Warp demonstrates that a trans man is not always one who uncritically and unequivocally corresponds to stereotypical appearances and roles of men, or who feels the need to conform to the gender binary. His self-understanding resonates with Devor's contention that 'gender roles are not uniquely defined but rather have multiple interpretations possible within different contexts[, and that a]ctions which would seem masculine in one context may seem quite feminine in another by contrast to the still more masculine conduct of other actors' (1994, 38). I argue that Warp sees himself as a situated trans man, or one who is comfortable with particular gender expressions according to specific times and spaces.

His gender interstices are captured in the term 'trans', which acts as 'a modifier … [a] prefix perpetually in the act of changing, forever crossing from one side to the other, it means "across," "beyond," and "through"' (Hansbury 2005, 252). In this context, becoming a trans man can thus be understood as a continuous 'process of self-discovery' that 'has nothing to do with arrival, or departure [but is] forever about the journey' (Hansbury 2005, 252).

'I Feel Like a Man': Non/Woman, Non/Feminine

Although a number of trans men discover a need to engage in a strategic distancing from sociocultural perceptions of womanliness and femininity in order to draw up a contrast with their own identities as man, some like Ray believe that it is possible to be man without relinquishing woman. Conversely, Adam speaks from the depths of this embodied experience in terms of a sense of discomfort as woman:

Goh: How, how do you live your life as a man?

Adam: I've always felt ... not female (laughs). I think it's easier to, to explain this by saying that when I was living in a woman's body, and I did not feel comfortable as a woman. I did not feel comfortable being viewed as a woman, being in a woman's body, as well as a, kind of a gender expectations of what a woman should be. Erm, so opposite of that is a man. And I always feel like I'm a man, from, things like my, my mannerisms, to I think ... we've been taking their space in this world. There's a different way of how a man takes space in this world and, women taking their space ... when I was in a woman's body, I would have, comments when I was younger. Like why do I sit like this, can you not close your leg ... I think I'm doing that because naturally I feel like a man, taking that space.

Adam introduces the notion of having 'always felt ... not female' which is similarly shared by many Malaysian trans men whom I interviewed. The fact that he 'did not feel comfortable as a woman ... in a woman's body', or even 'being viewed' as one reflects a sense of body discomfort in which he finds himself unable to perfectly conform to a phantasmic construction of woman and the 'gender expectations of what a woman should be'. It is interesting that the capacity to discern *who he is not* is accompanied by the capacity to know *who he is.*

Adam speaks of a sense of ease with the 'opposite' of woman from two particular perspectives. That '[he] always feel[s] like [he's] a man' describes a sense of clarity in his self-affirmed gender identity which he has experienced over a period of time. Becoming a trans man is a protracted and sustained feeling of congruence with the identity of man, rather than mere capricious mimicry. Adam's declaration that he is a man is premised on two elements of human practice.

First, he is guided by '[his] mannerisms' which match socioculturally lauded comportments of 'male normalcy' that are 'constructed through learning what behaviors, mannerisms, and speech patterns are marked for the culturally gendered category "men"' (Cromwell 1999, 43). Second, Adam's way of sitting without 'clos[ing] his leg[s]' defies and exposes him as being 'unladylike' and thus 'manlike'. Malaysian women of all ethnicities are expected to sit with their legs pressed together or one leg crossed modestly over the other in order to appear 'ladylike' as a marked distinction from men. As 'access and use of space is inexorably tied to issues of gender, class and power' (Hall 2005, 143), the spatial liberties he co-opts are concomitantly the act of accumulating the male privilege and power of 'manspreading', 'a neologism used to refer to men who sit with their legs in a wide v-shape [and] a blatant example of the sorts of "everyday" sexism suffered by women as a result of men's inflated sense of entitlement' (Jane 2017, 459–460).

Ironically, it is this experience of being subconsciously mannish rather than womanish that advises him of his self-affirmed gender identity as 'naturally … feel[ing] like a man'. In this respect, 'naturally [acting] like a man' could reflect how 'people do feel that aspects of their being are essential (natural)' (Cromwell 1999, 43)[7] as well as 'signify an individual who orients himself along a binary gender system as much as it could signify an individual who does not [as] such rhetorical flexibility increases the significance of *contextualized* understanding' (heinz 2016, 8; added emphasis) of being a man in Malaysia.

Jon does not harbour the same conviction with which Adam speaks on constructing gender identity through the rejection of any form of womanliness:

> I feel, now I feel comfortable with my body, I am a woman. So I accept people respect me as a woman, I also accept people respect, accept me as a man. So I don't, I don't er, so put the quite hard time or feel hard feelings when people respect me as a woman. Because it's nothing wrong, this is their, their view, okay? But some of my friend, they are hundred percent

[7] See my discussion on this issue in 'Epilogue'.

> trans men even though they don't go to hormone pills, they don't go to operation, but they will feel offend when they stay with me. Because I feel comfortable. For me … I don't feel … cleaning the house, I'm doing the housework, I'm doing the kitchen's work, I cooking, I do the lady works, well, cut down my manhood …

Despite initially intimating his identity to me as a trans man and a person who has 'the soul of a man',[8] Jon eventually also identifies as 'a woman' in the course of our conversation. The multiple identities which he holds—although man is his primary category of identification—stems from a shrewd observation that he is now 'comfortable' with being man who was assigned female at birth, a multifarious identity which he conflates with woman. It is within this gendered landscape that Jon is receptive to interpellations of man and woman, insofar as they are executed with 'respect'. In order to substantiate his sense of versatility in gender identity, he subscribes to the popular feminisation of reproductive labour (Chang et al. 2011; Gutiérrez Rodríguez and Brites 2014) and the added identity of 'woman' by referring to 'cleaning the house', 'housework', '[kitchen] work', 'cooking' and 'lad[ies'] work'.

Similar to Ray, Jon incorporates seemingly 'feminine tasks' into his gender identity rather than reject them as solely and validly constructive of womanliness. These perspective lies in polarity with 'some of [his] … hundred percent trans men' friends who 'feel offend[ed]' by his willingness to undertake activities that are stereotypically ascribed to women, thus corroborating the notion that 'men's identity is structured by their participation or nonparticipation in domestic work and child care' (Hoang and Yeoh 2011, 720). For Jon's friends, his passion for reproductive labour is unbecoming for a man. My use of 'unbecoming' here is deliberate as I wish to highlight the double entendre that this word evokes. His participation in such 'lady works' is unbecoming as in unbefitting or inappropriate for a man. At the same time, lady-like activities contribute to his unbecoming as man, or the undoing or unravelling of his subjectivity.

The fact that Jon qualifies his critics as 'hundred percent trans men even though they don't go [on] hormone pills' is significant.[9] He is

[8] Jon's description mirrors the conviction of Malaysian trans woman or *mak nyah* Nuk that she possessed '*jiwa wanita*' ("the soul of a woman"). See Goh (2014, 132).

[9] GAHT is discussed in greater detail in 'Grappling with Gender Dysphoria'.

offering the irony that these individuals who appeal to patriarchal concepts are not completely male despite claiming to be so because they are not on GAHT. Despite not being thoroughly men as perceived by Jon, they shun home-based labour as womanly and have the audacity to be 'offend[ed]' by his zeal for 'doing the housework'. Jon typifies 'transmasculine individuals [who] orient themselves and are oriented by a multiplicity of representations, including those that challenge transnormativity' (heinz 2016, 223). Transnormativity supports the idea that individuals who have abandoned a gender identity ought not to associate themselves in any way to it.

Thus, he is confident that his identity as a trans man who 'feel[s] comfortable' with 'lady works' does not 'cut down [his] manhood'. In other words, it is possible to simultaneously inhabit the sociocultural imaginaries of man and woman without being robbed of a predominant man identity as 'gender roles are not uniquely defined but rather have multiple interpretations possible within different contexts' (Devor 1994, 38).

'Actually a Man': Non-lesbian

As seen in Jon's narrative, adamant identifications of 'trans man' often rely on strict adherences to stereotypes of man, although some men who were assigned female at birth provide an insight into their abilities to live as men without renouncing life practices that they perceive as womanliness. While some trans men may admit to compromises for resemblances with woman, such compromises are absent in comparisons with a lesbian identity, regardless of whether they have gone through a 'lesbian phase'. 'Superman' expresses how a former relationship with a woman shed light on his gender identity:

Goh: Did you go through a phase where you lived your life as a lesbian woman?

Superman: I had lived a lesbian woman's life for about eight years. I came out first as a lesbian ... when I was 19 ... and I came out as a transgender properly last year.

Goh: And what was the difference, what caused the shift?

Superman: Erm, in one of my more recent relationships, I was with a woman who identified me as a man. She said 'you don't behave like a, lesbian'. Right? And when she called it out ... because intimacy as well ... none of my female lovers have ever expressed that I conduct myself

> as a woman in bed. And all of my female lovers have been bisexual, pansexual. I've never had a lesbian female lover. So, I guess secretly carried this, urge to present myself as male for a long time. And so one of my lovers who became my then partner, called me out on that one day. She said to me that 'performance in bed, you are actually a man, you just don't know it'.

Superman acknowledges his 'emergence into this world as [a] designated [female] who lived in the social construction of that gender for a number of years' (Brown 2016, 12) and who 'lived a lesbian woman's life' before '[coming] out as … transgender'. This personal disclosure is akin to an act of paying homage to a female past (Cromwell 1999; Hansbury 2005). It demonstrates a distinct shift from lesbian woman to trans man, which is also a shift in emphasis from sexual identity to gender identity.

As Superman had lived as a woman 'for about eight years' and appropriated a self-affirmed gender identity as a trans man a year before our interview, he had lived as a lesbian woman longer than he has 'properly'—or with resolute conviction and self-legitimacy—as a trans man. His experience resonates with many trans men who lived as women, specifically masculine-acting women, until an unbearable sense of discomfort propelled them to explore and redefine their masculine identities (Brown 2016). As Malaysian trans activist Dorian Wilde posits, some Malaysian trans men 'start off as butch lesbians, or lesbians in general, and then like slowly, feels weird, and … finally find out that there's such thing as trans man [which is] a light bulb moment' (Appendix 2: Interviewing Dorian Wilde, para. 5).

Superman speaks of a former lover who 'identified [him] as a man' by comparing him with, and being cognisant that his 'behav[iour]' departs from her familiarity with the (stereo)typical traits of a lesbian woman. It is the act of sexual 'intimacy' that corroborates her intuition that he is a man. His 'performance in bed' that leads to her conviction is reminiscent of Devor's findings in the 1990s among trans men that 'although their anatomy said that they were lesbian women, they were different from other lesbian women' (1993, 312).

Taken aback by her claims, Superman engages in a process of reflexive discernment that validates his former lover's conclusion of his gender identity and enables him to finally recognise it. He becomes cognisant that 'none of [his] female lovers' have perceived him 'as a woman in bed', which alludes to his sexual dynamics as man. His awareness that his 'female lovers have been bisexual [and] pansexual' rather than homosexual further contributes to his inner conviction that these non-monosexual lovers have skilfully and accurately named his sexuality as heterosexual, rather than homosexual. Hence, erotic encounters and relationships are gender light bulb moments, or instances of clarity for trans men in recognising their gender identity and situating their sexual attractions within that recognition. As 'all sexuality is gendered and such that all gender has sexualized elements' (Devor 1994, 35), the sexualisation of gender and the gendering of sexuality in Superman's self-discernment leads to the verification of gender identity.

Contrary to Superman, Hadi has never lived as a lesbian:

Goh: What is your gender identity?
Hadi: For now, I think I'm trans man …
Goh: Did you ever go through a stage where you felt like you were lesbian?
Hadi: Erm, no.
Goh: Why do you choose to describe yourself as trans man?
Hadi: Because, because I am different (laughs). No because, I think I'm a man … I feel I am man. Because you know lesbian and tomboy, who couple with other girl? I feel they're wrong. Why? Lesbian is wrong. But I'm right because I'm, even people looking at me they say, oh you're woman, partner with another woman. But I feel I'm right because I'm man. I don't know why. Even, erm, there's a girl come to me and say, don't couple with tomboy anymore, go … find a real man.
Goh: Can you say something about your relationship with your wife, your partner?
Hadi: Oh we live together. For almost five years we live together.

Hadi's tentative identity as a person who 'think[s]' and 'feel[s]' like a man without a lesbian history is evocative of Brown's contention that '*all transmen are not and may never have been lesbians*' (2016, 9; original emphasis). What piques my interest in this narrative is Hadi's formulation of ethics in his relationship with a woman,[10] which he constructs based on his opinions of 'lesbian[s] and tomboy[s]'. His firm opinion that 'lesbian[s] and tomboy[s] who couple with other girl[s]' are 'wrong', which corresponds to Malaysian *Syariah* law (The

[10] I further discuss ethics for trans men in 'Performing Faith'.

Commissioner of Law Revision, Malaysia 2006, sec. 26) and *fatwa* or Islamic opinion (Jabatan Mufti Kerajaan Negeri Sembilan 2008),[11] is based on the idea that they are involved in romantic and sexual relationships *with women as women*.

Despite complexities that often render it difficult 'to make tidy distinctions between FTMs/ transmen and butch lesbians [due to] much overlap and many similarities between the types' (Cromwell 1999, 63), Hadi's self-perception is that of a man who is involved in a heterosexual relationship with women, which coheres with the idea that 'when an individual self-identifies as a man ... and chooses women as sexual partners, then his erotic choice is heterosexual' (Cromwell 1999, 111). Thus, the appropriation of both cisgender and heterosexual identities by trans men ratifies what would otherwise be 'wrong' same-sex relationships.

Hadi is well aware that his romantic pursuits are easily misconstrued as 'lesbian' or 'tomboy' liaisons, as 'where there is transgendered behavior there is a presumption of homosexuality' (Cromwell 1999, 44). Based on his experience with 'a girl' who exhorted him not to 'couple with [a] tomboy' and 'find a real man', Hadi is aware that society still perceives him disapprovingly as a woman who is in a same-sex relationship. The act of delineating himself from a lesbian and a tomboy acts as an indispensable strategy to authentically affirm Hadi's identity as a man, a non-lesbian, and a non-tomboy, as well as to embrace a 'valid' relationship with a woman with whom he has lived 'for almost five years'.

Passing

My decision to discuss the notion of passing in this particular Chapter stems from my focus here on the fervent desire of Malaysian trans men to become men and establish masculinity through a 'convincing' projection of gender interiority to the exterior demands and expectations of society as the ultimate yardstick of gender approval. Gender, as Judith Butler (1993, 1999) famously postulates, is a reiterative performativity of socioculturally accepted corporeal props, scripts, patterns and motions that produce the illusion of a gender 'naturalness', a 'naturalness' towards which many of my research participants aspire.

[11] For an explanation of *fatwa*, see (Sirry 2013).

These doings of man in order to be acknowledged as man are often referred to as 'passing', or 'the degree to which a person is regarded as a member of the gender with which they physically present' (Greatheart 2013, 44, note 3). As a method of 'blending in and becoming unnoticeable and unremarkable as either a man or a woman' (Cromwell 1999, 39), passing for many transgender individuals 'constitutes a positive goal in the process of actualizing and affirming their gender identity' (Bockting et al. 2013, 949).

Scholars in transgender studies highlight the risk of allowing passing to be the sole umpire of pronouncing gender validity and invalidity (heinz 2016; Ho 2006; Pfeffer 2017). Greatheart offers the caveat that 'some trans men may choose to not pass for personal or political reasons while others simply are not able to pass due to genetic factors and biological responses to [GAHT]' (2013, 140). In Judith Halberstam's opinion, 'passing as a narrative assumes that there is a self that *masquerades* as another kind of self and does so successfully' (1998, 21; added emphasis). I am inclined to agree with Halberstam, as well with Carla A. Pfeffer who sees 'passing' as problematic because it implies that

> only some people hold a legitimate claim to maleness or femaleness, manhood or womanhood, heterosexuality, or queerness [and that] only certain individuals legitimately "belong" to various groups of gender and sexual identity, while others may only hope to "pass" into relatively inauthentic membership as (often tragic) "wannabes". (2017, 38)

Aside from harbouring connotations of deceit, inauthenticity, artificiality, secrecy and shame (Ho 2006), passing can become a destructive device that qualifies or disqualifies gender identity as predicated on societal acceptance and approval. Passing can create power-ridden hierarchies of gender legitimacy and illegitimacy by bestowing the labels of success and failure to transgender people. By a similar token, I find that 'presenting' sometimes insinuates at a gender portrayal that may not necessarily accompany a deeply experienced identity.

Hence, this section uses the term 'passing' with a certain degree of tentativeness and without any pretext of being absolute or exhaustive. It frames the discussion with the idea that passing is an enterprise on which trans men embark to prioritise an embodied conviction and recognition that they are men before and/or when they educate themselves on which 'learning behaviors, mannerisms, and speech patterns are marked for the culturally gendered category "men"' (Cromwell 1999, 43), and project these patterns to society thereafter. This section foregrounds the notion of passing as the active and multifaceted endogenous and/or exogenous architecturings of gender identity that trans men experience in pursuing the deepest core of meaningful embodied existence in which they speak truth to self.

'A Man Outside': Physical Appearance

In the following narrative, Pokerface speaks of the significance of a 'male outlook'[12] or 'the physical appearance of a man' for himself:

> *Goh*: What's the male outlook for you?
> *Pokerface*: Male have a more solid structure, and they will have like more facial hair ... but for female will be more chubby, softer, then for me I have half is because, because from different angles, sometimes I will look more male, masculine, and from another angle I will look feminine.
> *Goh*: So when you say outlook, you mean physical appearance.
> *Pokerface*: Yes.
> *Goh*: Okay, is it important for you to have the physical appearance of a man?
> *Pokerface*: Yes.
> *Goh*: Why? Is it not enough for you to feel like a man inside? Why do you have to feel like a man outside?
> *Pokerface*: Well, for me it's like being comfortable if I'm a man outside. And I don't have to fear that how people look at me, or raise an eyebrow, think that whether I'm a male or female. That's why I prefer my outlook to be similar to my inner.

Pokerface appeals to socioculturally sanctioned sexual differences between 'male[s]' and 'female[s]' as a method to continuously measure his maleness as a man who was assigned female at birth. He is cognisant of the fact that his maleness is unstable because he '[has] half' and 'look[s] more ... masculine [or] feminine' according to the 'different angles' in which he finds himself. These angles can either portray him as a man with 'a more solid structure [and with] facial hair', or as a woman who is 'more

[12] Several Malaysian Chinese trans men whom I interviewed used the term 'outlook' to mean 'physical appearance' rather than thought processes or worldviews.

chubby [and] softer'. Physical characteristics are thus predictably and conveniently recruited to achieve an aspired gender identity. Unlike Jon, this 'half' situation is not a desirable feature for Pokerface. He strives to attain a congruence between his 'outlook' and his 'inner' gender. A 'complete' representation of man would prevent 'people look[ing] at [him] or rais[ing] an eyebrow' in doubt of his self-affirmed gender identity.

Masculinity, as Brown envisions, 'is a social construct, and those who were born female-bodied experience this masculinity differently according to the time and setting ... depending on the perceptions of the individuals around him or her' (2016, 24). Pokerface's desire for a parallel between the 'man outside' and the 'man inside' in order to achieve manly invisibility indicates a dependence on the combination of a personal standpoint, physical appearance and societal approval that does not simply cohere with the *abstract* elements of social construction as Brown seems to imply.

Miriam J. Abelson's assertion that 'the social experience of being a man is a becoming that happens through *recognition* rather than a static or fixed trait, or individual identity' (2019, 61; added emphasis) veers closer towards what I am trying to say, which is that Pokerface exemplifies trans men who strive for male masculinity as indubitably and thoroughly grounded in material recognisability, both to themselves and to society. A trans man's subjectivity is therefore an interminable pursuit of personal and sociocultural recognition of the outward appearance of man towards 'the normative desire to look "like other men"' (heinz 2016, 105) via the physical body. In other words, for some trans men, a 'flawless' gender representation is the goal towards which they aspire in order to become 'truly' men to themselves and the society in which they are embedded.

Adam shares Pokerface's apprehension in not being sufficiently 'manly':

> In my case after the transition ... I became actually more and more invisible. Because I became just another bloke. Which is good ... and the voice thing is a very strong indicator in gender. Er, before that I was, even though I looked like a guy, but the moment I opened my mouth, thinness of the voice, the female voice, and then everybody would just take a second look, and that's a giveaway. But now after transitioning, hormone therapy, now I speak with a lower voice, thicker voice. Erm, that's one of the indicators of being man in this society. The voice definitely, the look, the facial hair, these are physical indicators.

The 'physical indicators' which Pokerface yearns for are already attained by Adam who 'became just another bloke' or rendered invisible as man in society. He refers to the process of acquiring 'the look', or 'a lower [and] thicker voice' as well as 'the facial hair' as stereotypical male traits in '[becoming] more and more invisible' in his journey of transitioning. Not unlike Axman, Adam holds invisibility as a gender ideal. The trans man subjectivity achieves 'success' once it merges seamlessly into social anonymity and the process of passing acts as the erasure of transgender subjectivity (Cromwell 1999).

Manliness is invisible, not only because it is normative, but also because it is considered a permanent and stable fixture of 'man in … society'. By becoming 'just another bloke', Adam achieves a persuasive 'gender realness'. The attainment of such a state suggests that 'an individual is no longer a member of the stigmatized group of transsexuals … he has completed "transition" and is now "just a man" [for] to do otherwise is to fail' (Cromwell 1999, 39).

Nonetheless, the confidence with which Adam 'carr[ies him]self' after he begins transition is somewhat compromised due to his 'female voice'. He recalls how his appearance 'like a guy' was somehow incomplete as a man due to 'the thinness of [his] voice' that became evident 'the moment [he] opened [his] mouth'. Adam is aware that 'a second look' is the exercise of casting doubt in relation to his manness. Pokerface's feminine 'angles' parallel 'the female voice' for Adam and acts as the 'giveaway' to his gender identity. For some Malaysian trans men, the physicality of man is the cogent performance of both bodily appearance and sonic projection, a necessary step to achieve manness.

'Treating Me Like a Man': Interactions with Women

Trans men also engage in additional forms of gender communication beyond appearance and gender-discernible audibility. One such element comprises interactions that trans men have with women. Aarone socialises with other men and performs 'manly' activities in order to '[be] who [he] really [is]' by 'being a man'. The reciprocity which he experiences constitutes defining moments of 'manliness':

> Being a man is being who I really am, that is the most important thing … I don't understand when the, my female cousin talk among themselves. When they talk about shopping, or boyfriends … I really don't understand

> ... Even now, I don't really hang out with my female cousin ... You know? The female language, which I find it ... very ... mushy? Or probably erm, something that it's all about shopping? And, clothes ... I just like move away and go and find my uncles, or my cousin brother and like we just hang out there, outside. And talk about guns ... catapults, what kind of trees, so those kind of things ... I like to hang out with my brother, like to hang out with my dad. We talk about trees, we talk about cars, I like cars. I like to just like open up a car and, or a motorbike and take a look at what's going on inside.

Aarone experiences a certain sense of ignorance in relation to the topics of conversation that thrill his 'female cousin[s]', namely 'shopping, or boyfriends ... and ... clothes'. By claiming that he 'really [does not] understand what they talk about among themselves', Aarone locates himself in polarity with stereotypical depictions of womanly interests that are 'mushy'. His use of the term 'female language' to describe such topics of interest indicate a sort of talking away from women in order to disengage from woman and approximate man, perhaps expressing a subconscious knowledge that 'masculinity does not exist except *in contrast* with "femininity"' (Connell 2005, 68; added emphasis).

Aarone further expands on this contrast by asserting that he 'move[s] away' or disengages from socialising with women in order to socialise with male relatives such as his father, male sibling, 'uncles', or male cousins whom he refers to as 'cousin brother'. In other words, he moves away from an uncomfortable gendered space to one of greater comfortable belonging like other men who 'live "normal, average" lives as their own fathers and brothers did' (Hansbury 2005, 247). Bonding with men who were assigned male at birth in a reciprocal manner forms 'the social relationships that are the basis of men in groups' (Tiger 2007, vii) and constitutes a method of passing as man. It is within this space that he can freely discuss topics such as 'guns', 'catapults', 'trees' and 'cars', which are popularly touted as—and which he designates as—'manly' matters. As 'homosociality is heterosexual and masculine' (Flood 2008, 345), and 'masculinity and homosociality are crucial components of male storytelling practices' (Vaynman et al. 2019, 3), Aarone purposefully immerses himself within masculine homosocial discourses as a strategy of effective passing.

Aarone further expresses a participatory interest in such matters, in which he 'likes to ... open up a car ... or a motorbike' in order to learn of their mechanisms. Womanliness is thus constructed as passive, dull and unimaginative, while 'being a man' is active, exhilarating, exploratory and intelligent. A simultaneous bonding with men and distancing from women allows him to pass as man. Through this strategy, Aarone both becomes acutely cognisant that 'being a man is being who [he] really [is]', echoing that which matthew heinz deduces as a trans man's 'desire to live openly in [his] felt gender, to not deceive others by pretending to be something [he] is not' (2016, 146). Aarone thus strives towards an interminable performativity of manliness in order to blend in as a form of 'gender normalcy'. 'Blending in as normal', as Cromwell holds, 'means that one has succeeded and become a "real" man' (1999, 39).

Just as Aarone talks away from women, SR *talks towards* women as a way to 'do as a man':

> *Goh*: Is there anything that you do that you say to yourself, ah, this is what I do as a man now?
>
> *SR*: You know … going out with guys, and I'm talking about girls, you know chit-chatting about, you know I'm more into that. I'm more comfortable with the guys. So when I'm going out with them, I feel … it was really good … because some of them, because my close friends, they were treating me like a man. So I feel like I'm a man … Like, for example, if I hanging out with my with my guy, which is a straight guy, they were like, SR (coughs) look at that girls … you're gonna like it. So they were treating me, they were talking about sex … I can BE a part of it. And they were talking about a lot of things, because that is how they treated me. So I did ask them, guys, did you ever think that … I am a girl? No, man. You are my bro.

SR, like Aarone, draws on bonding with men as part of his self-affirmed gender identity in possible recognition of the reality that 'friendship as a form of relatedness is … crucial for learning about masculinity' (Mellström 2010, 261). Nevertheless, while Aarone bonds with men as a way of disengaging from women, SR's fraternal interactions are focused on women. When he is 'out with guys', they find themselves 'chit-chatting' and 'talking about girls'. In addition to conversations about women, SR's 'straight guy' friends prompt him to 'look at … girls [whom he is] gonna like'. SR interprets the talking about and looking at women as 'talking about sex', which Abelson refers to 'backstage talk [which] most frequently consist[s] of open discussions of sex and … misogynist talk about women' (2019, 79).

I propose that while SR does not appear to speak 'about sex' in terms of graphic retellings of sexual exploits, the practice of active admiration of women is a method of objectivising women that anchors and stabilises his gender identity. His discursive account manifests the reality that 'the use of degrading and objectifying language, profanity, bragging and boasting may help men bond as men, while separating them from what is perceived as "feminine"' (Vaynman et al. 2019, 3; see also Abelson 2019; Nguyen 2008).

The objectification of women through a collective and herd-like 'male gaze' (Mulvey 1975)—imagined and/or recounted—evokes a thrilling process that '[he] can be part of' through which he feels like he is being 'treat[ed] … like a man'. Communicating man can also be a microcosmically communal gendering process in which an interiorised gender identity is validated by one's male peers through fraternal camaraderie that acknowledges one's manness. An obsessive but appreciative fascination with women that is shared by cisgender men and SR becomes a constitutive factor for him to 'feel like' [he's] a man' and a 'bro'. For both Aarone and SR at this stage of life, such 'gender props' or physical gender markers 'are not the most important aspect of communicating gender to others; rather, styles of relating to others are among the strongest markers of gender' (Devor 1993, 303).

The experiences of Bottle, adding to those of Aarone and SR, demonstrate that a rigid adherence to stereotypical gender, sociocultural and ethnic performativities also plays an important role in the becomings of trans men:

> *Goh*: When you say that you are a man, what are some of the things that, how do you live up your life as a man concretely? In everyday life.
>
> *Bottle*: Oh, right, so for day to day life, I make it simple. To me, I'm a very typical Chinese man, okay it's like er, okay there's definitely no makeups and all … those small stuff like, you know, the laundries in the house, I have the time but I won't do. To me, that is like a lady's job … And then let's say when you're out … let's say they want to go for *makan* (meals) and all, man will pay … When people look at me, I just want them to know me as a simple man, okay, fair and square, so I always positive and happy-go-lucky …

Bottle's refusal to apply cosmetics and do 'laundr[y] in the house' is predicated on his belief that such tasks which are both 'small' and 'like a lady's job' constitute womanliness, a belief that is a distinct departure from Jon' vistas. The establishment of manliness thus assimilates notions of feminising and belittling household tasks. Conversely, Bottles upholds credence for certain practices and attitudes that are frequently masculinised—and subsequently valorised—in Malaysian societies. Bottle's insistence on paying for the meals of others in public eating places as a definition of manliness coheres with Ulf Mellström's study on Malaysian Chinese cisgender masculinities in the state of Penang where 'to pay for drinks and to be generous is another important element in proving worthiness as a man' (2010, 267). This practice, alongside what Bottle perceives to be manly traits, such as being 'a simple man … fair and square … always positive and happy-go lucky', 'is tied to consumption practices, commodity culture and identity politics specific not just to transmasculinity but also to masculinity at large' (heinz 2016, 213) in achieving manliness.

Sally Hines' notion that 'transgender identities are cut through with multiple variables such as gender, sexuality, "race" and ethnicity, class, age, transitional time span and geographical location' (2007, 49) is particularly helpful in parsing this situation. In speaking from his own experiences as 'a very typical Chinese man' in what I had asked in relation to his 'everyday life' in a Malaysian society, Bottle manifests clear adherences to certain forms of sociocultural performances while rejecting others to fortify his gender identity.

The conscription of the qualities of financial stability, generosity, simplicity and fairness, a favourable and carefree disposition, and the avoidance of womanly activities as part of 'Malaysian Chineseness' is an important facet of becoming a trans man, and captures the reality of many trans men who 'conform to codes of masculine behavior that are socially enforced' (Cromwell 1999, 12; see also Ng et al. 2008) in order to be accepted as man. Bottle exemplifies how becoming man is not solely a matter of gender identity, but is informed by 'a coexistence of traditional and hybridised versions of masculinity within the process of globalization, with strong emphasis on urbanism, cosmopolitanism and middle-class sensibilities' (Kong 2012, 302).

Conclusion

Malaysian trans men co-opt transdiscursive self-descriptors such as 'Female-to-Male (FTM)', 'transmasculine', 'trans man', 'man' and 'male', while concomitantly rejecting identities and expressions of 'woman', 'lesbian' and 'feminine'. The complex negotiations of passing by trans men straddle strategies of physical appearance and interactions with women. Hence, their diverse forms of naming and living out of masculinity and manness within Malaysian context illuminates the intricate techniques that are taken up by trans men to identify, negotiate, produce and occupy their subjectivities.

Although some admit to a female and/or lesbian history, others experience a total alienation from such experiences. Some trans men interpret their gender identities and expressions as shifting and multifaceted. There are others, however, who are adamant that being a 'full', 'complete' and 'authentic' man is the ultimate accomplishment and point of arrival which often culminates in their desired corporeality.

Moreover, in personal negotiations of gender at the intersection of biology and social expectation, 'transpeople can, and do, recognize that gender is an essential part of their beings [yet] acknowledge that it is constructed' (Cromwell 1999, 43). There are trans men who are comfortable with becoming men without any surgical or hormonal intervention just as there are those who crave for radical bodily alterations and changes. In regard to the latter, Cromwell's somewhat generic claim that 'transpeople not only shake the foundations of the biological foundationalist and essentialist theories but also undermine them *completely*' (1999, 43; emphasis added) needs to be revisited and rethought according to Malaysian contexts.[13]

Most of the Malaysian trans men I interviewed are zealous to become 'unremarkably, men' (Cromwell 1999, 247), thus displaying a dichotomous mentality of gender which nuances the position of Jami K. Taylor, Daniel C. Lewis, and Donald P. Haider-Markel that gender identity is 'a continuum rather than a dichotomy' (2018, 13). In this regard, 'continuum' can be better understood as the interminable process of achieving an identity that is securely positioned at the desired side of the gender dichotomy. Endeavours to become invisible as men are not solely abstract constructions or cerebral enterprises, but often indefatigably centred on the physical body and its operations towards the achievement of subjective 'success'. Engendering identity is thus always and everywhere a conscious process of embodiment.

[13] A lengthier discussion is found in 'Grappling with Gender Dysphoria' and 'Embarking on Medical Transitioning'.

The heterogeneous navigations of self-comprehension among trans men are intrinsically linked to strivings for self-determination and meaningful existence in a country that continues to exhibit disdain and discrimination towards nonnormative genders and sexualities. These signifying practices may not be unique to Malaysia contexts, but they constitute the conditions of possibility and modes of production for the becomings of Malaysian trans men.

Bibliography

Abelson, Miriam J. 2019. *Men in Place: Trans Masculinity, Race, and Sexuality in America*. Minneapolis, MN: University of Minnesota Press.

Adam, Barry D. 2000. 'Love and Sex in Constructing Identity Among Men Who Have Sex with Men'. *International Journal of Sexuality and Gender Studies* 5 (4): 325–39.

Ayres, Tony. 1999. 'China Doll-The Experience of Being a Gay Chinese Australian'. *Journal of Homosexuality* 36 (3–4): 87–97.

Bockting, Walter O., Michael H. Miner, Rebecca E. Swinburne Romine, Autumn Hamilton, and Eli Coleman. 2013. 'Stigma, Mental Health, and Resilience in an Online Sample of the US Transgender Population'. *American Journal of Public Health; Washington* 103 (5): 943–51.

Brown, Michael Eric. 2016. *A Herstory of Transmasculine Identities: An Annotated Anthology*. Miami, FL: Boundless Endeavors, Inc.

Bunch, Mary. 2013. 'The Unbecoming Subject of Sex: Performativity, Interpellation, and the Politics of Queer Theory'. *Feminist Theory* 14 (1): 39–55.

Butler, Judith. 1993. *Bodies That Matter: On the Discursive Limits of 'Sex'*. New York: Routledge.

———. 1999. *Gender Trouble: Feminism and the Subversion of Identity*. New York: Routledge.

Chang, Hongqin, Fiona MacPhail, and Xiao-yuan Dong. 2011. 'The Feminization of Labor and the Time-Use Gender Gap in Rural China'. *Feminist Economics* 17 (4): 93–124.

Connell, Raewyn. 2005. *Masculinities*. 2nd ed. Cambridge, UK: Polity Press.

Cornwall, Andrea. 1994. 'Gendered Identities and Gender Ambiguity Among *Travestis* in Salvador, Brazil'. In *Dislocating Masculinity: Comparative Ethnographies*, edited by Andrea Cornwall and Nancy Lindisfarne, 111–32. London: Routledge.

Cromwell, Jason. 1999. *Transmen and FTMs: Identities, Bodies, Genders, and Sexualities*. Urbana, IL: University of Illinois Press.

Currah, Paisley, Richard M. Juang, and Shannon Price Minter, eds. 2006. *Transgender Rights*. Minneapolis, MN: University of Minnesota Press.

Devor, Aaron. 1993. 'Sexual Orientation Identities, Attractions, and Practices of Female-to-Male Transsexuals'. *The Journal of Sex Research* 30 (4): 303–15.

———. 1994. 'Toward a Taxonomy of Gendered Sexuality'. *Journal of Psychology & Human Sexuality* 6 (1): 23–56.

———. 2016. *FTM: Female-to-Male Transsexuals in Society*. Bloomington, IN: Indiana University Press.

Edelman, Elijah Adiv, and Lal Zimman. 2014. 'Boycunts and Bonus Holes: Trans Men's Bodies, Neoliberalism, and the Sexual Productivity of Genitals'. *Journal of Homosexuality* 61 (5): 673–90.

Elizondo, Paul M., Willy Wilkinson, and Christopher Daley. 2012. 'Working With Transgender Persons'. *Psychiatric Times* 29 (9): 16–18.

Flood, Michael. 2008. 'Men, Sex, and Homosociality: How Bonds Between Men Shape Their Sexual Relations with Women'. *Men and Masculinities* 10 (3): 339–59.

Galupo, M. Paz, Shane B. Henise, and Kyle S. Davis. 2014. 'Transgender Microaggressions in the Context of Friendship: Patterns of Experience Across Friends' Sexual Orientation and Gender Identity'. *Psychology of Sexual Orientation and Gender Diversity* 1 (4): 461–70.

Goh, Joseph N. 2014. 'Transgressive Empowerment: Queering the Spiritualities of the *Mak Nyahs* of PT Foundation'. In *Queering Migrations Towards, From, and Beyond Asia*, edited by Hugo Córdova Quero, Joseph N. Goh, and Michael Sepidoza Campos, 123–37. New York: Palgrave Macmillan.

———. 2016. 'Imaginative Assemblages of Transcendent/Desire: Non-Heteronormative Malaysian Men Speak Up and Talk Back'. *Critical Research on Religion* 4 (2): 125–40.

———. 2018. *Living Out Sexuality and Faith: Body Admissions of Malaysian Gay and Bisexual Men*. London: Routledge.

Greatheart, Marcus. 2013. *Transforming Practice: Life Stories of Transgender Men That Change How Health Providers Work*. Toronto, Canada: Ethica Press.

Gutiérrez Rodríguez, Encarnación, and Jurema Brites. 2014. 'Feminization of Labor: Domestic Work Between Regulation and Intimacy'. *Women's Studies International Forum* 46: 1–4.

Halberstam, Judith. 1998. *Female Masculinity*. Durham, NC: Duke University Press.

Hall, C. Michael. 2005. 'Shifting Spaces of Masculinity: From Carisbrook to the MCG'. In *Spaces of Masculinities*, edited by Kathrin Hörschelmann and Bettina van Hoven, 143–51. New York: Routledge.

Hansbury, Griffin. 2005. 'The Middle Men: An Introduction to the Transmasculine Identities'. *Studies in Gender and Sexuality* 6 (3): 241–64.

heinz, matthew. 2016. *Entering Transmasculinity: The Inevitability of Discourse*. Chicago, IL: Intellect Ltd.

Hines, Sally. 2007. *TransForming Gender: Transgender Practices of Identity, Intimacy and Care*. Bristol, UK: Policy Press.

Ho, Josephine. 2006. 'Embodying Gender: Transgender Body/Subject Formations in Taiwan'. *Inter-Asia Cultural Studies* 7 (2): 228–42.

Hoang, Lan Anh, and Brenda S. A. Yeoh. 2011. 'Breadwinning Wives and "Left-Behind" Husbands'. *Gender & Society* 25 (6): 717–39.

Jabatan Mufti Kerajaan Negeri Sembilan. 2008. 'Hukum Wanita Menyerupai Lelaki (Pengkid)'. Keputusan Mesyuarat Fatwa. http://www.muftins.gov.my/index.php/arkib2/himpunan-fatwa/171-keputusan-mesyuarat-fatwa/729-hukum-wanita-menyerupai-lelaki-pengkid.

Jagose, Annamarie. 1996. *Queer Theory: An Introduction*. New York: New York University Press.

Jane, Emma A. 2017. '"Dude … Stop the Spread": Antagonism, Agonism, and #manspreading on Social Media'. *International Journal of Cultural Studies* 20 (5): 459–75.

Khartini Slamah. 2005. 'The Struggle to Be Ourselves, Neither Men Nor Women: *Mak Nyahs* in Malaysia'. In *Sexuality, Gender and Rights: Exploring Theory and Practice in South and Southeast Asia*, edited by Geetanjali Misra and Radhika Chandiramani, 98–111. London: Sage.

Kong, Travis S. K. 2012. 'Chinese Male Bodies: A Transnational Study of Masculinity and Sexuality'. In *Routledge Handbook of Body Studies*, edited by Bryan S. Turner, 289–306. New York: Routledge.

Machart, Régis, and Sep Neo Lim. 2013. 'Identity *and* Language vs. Identification *Through* Language: A Historical Perspective'. In *Intersecting Identities and Interculturality: Discourse and Practice*, edited by Régis Machart, Choon Bee Lim, Sep Neo Lim, and Eriko Yamato, 22–44. Newcastle upon Tyne, UK: Cambridge Scholars Publishing.

Mellström, Ulf. 2010. 'The Cultural Construction of Masculinity Among Working-Class Malaysian Chinese in the Intersection of Race, Class and Gender'. In *Gendered Inequalities in Asia: Configuring, Contesting and Recognizing Women and Men*, edited by Helle Rydstrøm, 252–85. Gendering Asia. Copenhagen, Denmark: NIAS Press.

Mulvey, Laura. 1975. 'Visual Pleasure and Narrative Cinema'. *Screen* 16 (3): 6–18.

Ng, Chirk Jenn, Hui Meng Tan, and Sarinah Wah Yun Low. 2008. 'What Do Asian Men Consider as Important Masculinity Attributes? Findings from the Asian Men's Attitudes to Life Events and Sexuality (MALES) Study'. *Journal of Men's Health* 5 (4): 350–55.

Nguyen, Athena. 2008. 'Patriarchy, Power, and Female Masculinity'. *Journal of Homosexuality* 55 (4): 665–83.

Peitzmeier, Sarah, Ivy Gardner, Jamie Weinand, Alexandra Corbet, and Kimberlynn Acevedo. 2017. 'Health Impact of Chest Binding Among Transgender Adults: A Community-Engaged, Cross-Sectional Study'. *Culture, Health & Sexuality* 19 (1): 64–75.

Pfeffer, Carla A. 2017. *Queering Families: The Postmodern Partnerships of Cisgender Women and Transgender Men*. New York: Oxford University Press.

Reisner, Sari L., Kristi E. Gamarel, Emilia Dunham, Ruben Hopwood, and Sel Hwahng. 2013. 'Female-to-Male Transmasculine Adult Health: A Mixed-Methods Community-Based Needs Assessment'. *Journal of the American Psychiatric Nurses Association* 19 (5): 293–303.

Ridge, Damien, Amos Hee, and Victor Minichiello. 1999. '"Asian" Men on the Scene'. *Journal of Homosexuality* 36 (3–4): 43–68.

Sirry, Mun'im. 2013. 'Fatwas and Their Controversy: The Case of the Council of Indonesian Ulama (MUI)'. *Journal of Southeast Asian Studies* 44 (1): 100–117.

Stryker, Susan, and Stephen Whittle, eds. 2006. *The Transgender Studies Reader*. New York: Taylor & Francis.

Tang, Shawna. 2012. 'Transnational Lesbian Identities: Lessons from Singapore?' In *Queer Singapore—Illiberal Citizenship and Mediated Cultures*, edited by Audrey Yue and Jun Zubillaga-Pow, 83–96. Hong Kong: Hong Kong University Press.

Taylor, Jami K., and Donald P. Haider-Markel, eds. 2015. *Transgender Rights and Politics: Groups, Issue Framing, and Policy Adoption*. Ann Arbor, MI: University of Michigan Press.

Taylor, Jami K., Daniel C. Lewis, and Donald P. Haider-Markel. 2018. *The Remarkable Rise of Transgender Rights*. Ann Arbor, MI: University of Michigan Press.

The Commissioner of Law Revision, Malaysia. 2006. *Syariah Criminal Offences (Federal Territories) Act 1997*. http://www.agc.gov.my/agcportal/index.php?r=portal2/lom2&id=1431.

Tiger, Lionel. 2007. *Men in Groups*. New Brunswick, NJ: Transaction Publishers.

Vaynman, Margaret J., Sveinung Sandberg, and Willy Pedersen. 2019. '"Locker Room Talk": Male Bonding and Sexual Degradation in Drinking Stories'. *Culture, Health & Sexuality*, 1–18.

Warner, Michael. 1993. 'Introduction'. In *Fear of a Queer Planet: Queer Politics and Social Theory*, edited by Michael Warner, vii–xxxi. Minneapolis, MN: University of Minnesota Press.

Wong, Yuenmei. 2012. 'Islam, Sexuality, and the Marginal Positioning of *Pengkids* and Their Girlfriends in Malaysia'. *Journal of Lesbian Studies* 16 (4): 1–14.

Yue, Audrey. 2017. 'Trans-Singapore: Some Notes Towards Queer Asia as Method'. *Inter-Asia Cultural Studies* 18 (1): 10–24.

CHAPTER 3

Engaging with Society

The subjectivities of Malaysian trans men, according to my findings, appear to corroborate Raewyn Connell's[1] claim that 'gender is not fixed in advance of social interaction, but is constructed in interaction' (2005, 35). Becoming a man, as such, neither depends exclusively on biological assemblage or a definitive act of volition as a personal project of the mind, 'but is rather a process tied to social assessment and interaction' (Abelson 2019, 61) with the various units of society. This chapter, which plans to pursue the dynamics in which trans men subjectivities are conditioned and produced by social engagements in specific spaces, is three-pronged in its presentation.

First, it reveals how the manifold ways in which trans men's lives 'segue seamlessly in between overlapping, sequential, fragmented and disparate images and portrayals' (heinz 2016, 11) during interactions with immediate family members,[2] cisgender and transgender friends and colleagues frequently play a critical role in the negotiations of their self-affirmed gender identities. It concurs with Aaron Devor that 'styles of relating to others are among the strongest markers of gender' (1993, 303). Such interactions necessarily implicate 'the execution of external, stereotyped gender roles[,] the rhetorical weight of becoming or being a man [and] the difference between having been someone's wife,

[1]Throughout this volume, I refer to this scholar and her works solely by the name 'Raewyn Connell'.

[2]I use this term to refer to parents, siblings and more immediate relatives.

J. N. Goh, *Becoming a Malaysian Trans Man*,
Gender, Sexualities and Culture in Asia,
https://doi.org/10.1007/978-981-15-4534-4_3

daughter, mother, aunt, grandmother and becoming someone's husband, son, father, uncle or grandfather (heinz 2016, 154).

Second, this chapter problematises the dynamics of gender self-disclosure among Malaysian trans men, specifically being in the closet, coming out and stealth. My use of 'disclosure' is not restricted to the idea of 'sharing one's transgender history after transition' (Zimman 2009, 60), but any form of self-revelation in terms of a self-affirmed gender identity. Not unexpectedly, the self-disclosures of trans men's gender identities often lead to a mélange of dilemmas and conflicts. As such, the self-awareness, self-realisation and self-determination of trans men as processes of 'mastering a set of conventional signifying practices through which the identity "man" is established and upheld *in interaction*' (Schrock and Schwalbe 2009, 279, added emphasis) are never purely detached and individually customised labours of identity building.

Third, this chapter participates in, and supplements Judith Halberstam's critical explorations of the bathroom 'as an arena for the enforcement of gender conformity [and] a sanctuary of enhanced femininity' (1998, 24). Without a doubt, a great majority of trans men experience unsettling dilemmas and even terrifying encounters associated with fulfilling basic bodily needs in public toilets delineated for women and men. Trans activist Dorian Wilde reflects on how 'trans men are very loathed to use public toilets[and b]ecause [they]'re so scared, [they] *tahan … sampai balik* (withhold from urinating until they reach home)' (Appendix 2: Interviewing Dorian Wilde, para. 26). As I will show in due course, these '"sites of interaction" may not only serve as sites of oppression, but also as "sites of resistance" and "sites of liberation"' (Yee 2009, 54) that affirm the subjectivities of trans men.

Encountering Family, Friends and Colleagues

My exclusion of the girlfriends, partners and wives[3] of trans men in this section is purposeful. My focus on immediate families, cisgender and transgender peers, and co-workers is guided by the fact that *each* trans man I interviewed placed emphasis on all three groups in his social

[3] As same-sex marriage is not legally recognised in Malaysia, the term 'wives' here is reproduced from the narratives of some trans men who refer to their female partners as their wives.

interactions. This in turn galvanises my keenness to explore the diverse yet peculiar dynamics of both the acceptance and rejection of trans men's gender identities in these three particular social engagements.[4]

'People You're Supposed to Be Able to Count On': Fashioned by Family

In the following narrative, Pokerface speaks of the 'difficulties' of gender socialisation that occurred during the years of 'growing up' and growing into his own as a trans man:

> *Goh*: Did you have difficulties with your family as you were growing up, and even now being a transgender man?
>
> *Pokerface*: My parents passed away when I was ... twenty-one, erm when I was growing up, when I was small, I don't think that's a problem. I just can go swim in a trunk in the beach, until puberty hit, that's the worst experience. Because when puberty hits, women will develop breasts, and that's the time when my mum said, 'You can no longer go shirtless outside'. 'What'? Then she said 'Yes, girl, girls cannot go shirtless', so ever since I've been trying to find a way to hide chest, breast, feel uncomfortable, having a chest, whereby I'm just like, 'screw it, why, why, why me'?

Pokerface recalls a period in his life prior to the demise of his parents when he 'was small' and dressed only in swimming 'trunk[s]' at the 'beach'. He muses over a time when it was possible for him to appear topless in public and perform as 'man' without 'a problem'. The androgyny with which he is able to pass as man in his pre-pubescence, or 'regarded as a member of the gender with which [he] physically present[s]' (Greatheart 2013, 44, note 3) prior to adolescence, shudders to a halt at the moment when puberty descends as 'a subjective turning point in relation to an increased awareness of gender discomfort' (Hines 2007, 53).

It is at this moment that the socially defining hallmarks of femininity, notably gender-specific attire and the 'develop[ment of] breasts' disqualifies him from public performances of 'man' by 'go[ing] shirtless outside'. Akin to many other Asian societies, the social tolerance and acceptance

[4]My research participants hardly mention their interactions with lesbian, gay, bisexual or queer Malaysians. Scholars highlight the importance of such friendships among many trans men (Galupo et al. 2014b).

of Malaysian transmasculine individuals as simply displaying 'tomboy ish behaviour' during puberty is 'discouraged and frowned upon[, even] punished and forbidden' (Kuru-Utumpala 2013, S158) when they enter young adulthood.

In Pokerface's situation, a parent acts as the adjudicator of gender identity and the beach becomes a site of gendered im/permissibility in social interaction. In such spaces, breasts are swiftly interpreted and moderated as the unequivocal manifestation of womanhood, hence necessitating the relinquishment of manhood. As Devor postulates, 'it is breast development which most publicly marks the waning of childhood and the beginning of the march into womanhood' (2016, 182). Pokerface's mother's emphatic claim that 'girls cannot go shirtless' is a reiteration of gender predicated on biology which is at once a non-negotiable insistence on a biological feature that must not be interrupted as it fulfils its destiny.

Miriam J. Abelson holds that 'men typically have greater social permission to expose their chests than women, especially in public, largely because women's chests are viewed as sexual objects' (2019, 71). I do feel however, that the proscription of publicly revealing breasts cannot be restricted to a matter of sexual objectification, or even of 'sexual provocation' (Arneil 2000, 348). The general hiddenness of these body parts safeguards a metanarrative that has far-reaching consequences in the preservation of a socially comprehensible and ordered gender binary. The curtailment of exposing breasts is read as feminine (Arneil 2000) while its exposure is read as masculine. Any transgression of this gender script courts shame in a deeply conservative country where conversations on gender and sexuality issues are regarded as taboo (tan 2007).

In popular Malaysian discourse among all ethnic groups, and with the exception of breastfeeding as a manifestation of maternity in some spaces, the exposure of breasts is considered 'shameful' for women. Conversely, when men refuse to expose their chests, they risk becoming targets of emasculation and vitriolic feminisation. While the politics of nudity are far too complex to discuss here (for instance, Lunceford 2012), it is possible to conclude that this gender dichotomy becomes vital in retaining the specificities in which 'gender is a way in which social practice is ordered' (Connell 2005, 71).

Pokerface, who had to learn to associate breasts with femininity from adolescence but now identifies as man, continues 'to find a way to hide [his] breast[s]' and constantly 'feel[s] uncomfortable [in] having a chest'. In this regard, gender reiteration has achieved its goal of predicating—and therefore anchoring and solidifying—gender on corporeality. In order to remain true to his self-affirmed gender identity, Pokerface finds himself negotiating socially approved markers of his physicality in frustration, as attested to by the expletive 'screw it' and the repeated questioning of 'why' his body seems inflexibly gendered as woman. 'The incongruities of a mismatched *sex* and *gender* [which] are often felt by [trans] individuals prior to school age' (Brown 2016, 16, original emphasis) is a continuous experience for him although he currently exercises greater flexibility in determining the course of action in regard to this mismatch.

SR is also subjected to the life lessons of gender identity in familial interaction through the in/validation of 'appropriate' attire. Unlike Pokerface, he experiences greater acceptance from his parents in contrast with 'relatives':

> *Goh*: Were there objections from mother, from your relatives, from your brothers and sisters?
>
> *SR*: From my parents, no ... But from my aunt, yes. From my relatives, yes. They were like, 'oh, what are you gonna be? Ah? God already gave you the body like that ... you should this and that, be a girl this and that' ... it's quite sad because my mum had to dealt with it throughout my growth ... but the thing is, my mum understands me. That is the best part. And my dad always like, and he is kind of really cool with that ... I don't really care what people say. And at the time, we was really struggle because, relatives, anywhere I need to go ... *kenduri* (feast) ... they were forcing me to wear *baju kurung* (traditional Malay attire for women) ... So I was like when I was 7 years old ... I refuse to wear those kind of you know *baju kurung* whatsoever. And I really interested in *baju melayu* (traditional Malay attire for men), I really interested in boys' things.

Instead of having to resist gender prescriptions from his parents, SR finds that his insistence on a particular performativity of gender results in a kind of overall familial 'struggle'. On the one hand, he has a 'mum [who] understands [him]', and a 'dad [who is] really cool' and '[doesn't] really care what people say' in relation SR's projection as a man. On the other hand, he finds himself besieged by 'relatives' who express their unmitigated disapproval of his gender identity. That he is inundated by questions that cast doubt over 'what [he is] gonna be', or interrogations of what he sees as meaningful existence, demonstrates how 'masculinity ... is enacted through a number of different locally grounded social categories in daily life, such as brother, father, son, uncle, friends and husband' (Mellström 2010, 253).

Their interrogations are religiously inflected, as SR is seen to be someone who defies the immutable reality that 'God already gave [him a] body [in order for him to] be a girl'. The construction of a stable gender identity with its norms and stereotypes involves the notion of a divinely ordained imperative. This is significant, as the dis/approval of a divine creator lies at the heart of a Muslim trans man's attitudes towards his own existence because 'to be transgender is a sinful choice that merits penalties' (Goh 2019, 437).[5] Nevertheless, despite claiming parental support as 'the best part' of his journey, the series of 'this and that' or transnegative accusations that SR experiences do affect his parents in an adverse manner. By acknowledging that his decision to present as man incites a period of 'struggle' both for himself and his parents, SR demonstrates that 'shifts in gender identity mark shifts in family identifications, roles, and processes that may be quite challenging' (Pfeffer 2017, 22).

The *kenduri* is a particular potent site of gender contestation. As a communal feast among the Malay-Muslims to mark and celebrate specific life events, it also sets expectations on attendees to don traditional attire which fall along definitive and unwavering gender faultlines. As a person who was assigned female at birth, SR is expected to wear the loose-fitting *baju kurung* designated for women despite his keenness to wear the *baju melayu* as man. In this respect, the *kenduri* as an emblem of celebration is transmuted to a dreaded site of sociocultural surveillance and judgement.

His 'refus[al] to wear' a traditional dress and his propensity for 'boys' things' are not just an affront to the gender binary: they are also a transgression of his ethnic, religious and nationalistic identities' (consult Siti Nor Amalina and Noraini 2019). His perceived recalcitrance creates a personal conflict as well as a source of struggle for his parents, such as his mother who 'had to [deal] with [his transgender subjectivity] throughout [his growing up]'. As such, just as a transgender subjectivity is a privately experienced challenge, it can also spur familial tribulations because

[5] I examine the relationship between gender identity and faith in 'Performing Faith'.

'the family as an institution [makes] for a complex site of recognition' (Abelson 2019, 66) within the wider ethos of ethnicity, religiosity and nationalism.

Speaking from the experiences of an Indian Malaysian for whom the nuclear family 'is a huge factor' that holds gravitas for the formation of his self-affirmed gender identity, Warp shares a personal reflection in the following narrative:

> Family is a huge factor, because it like basically changes everything. Er if you have an accepting family, your chances of suicide and your ability to deal with society, no matter how *teruk* (atrocious) the society could be, is immediately so much better, you know. Whereas family is seen as the first bastion of ... that's supposed to be your place ... these are people who are supposed to have your back, no matter what. And if you lose that, if you lose people that you're supposed to be able to count on for anything, then everything else automatically becomes even worse. Then it'll be, it's my own fault ... So yeah, your first layer of protection is gone.

Warp's insight is representative of many other trans men I interviewed who regard the family as 'the first bastion' against the intolerance, discrimination and violence that are levelled against them. He is cognisant that society can be *teruk* in their approach to transgender individuals. Echoing SR's experiences, Warp suggests that familial affirmation and support are indispensable constituents of the performativity of man, as they form the 'first layer of protection' that ensures a life-giving gender-emergence. It is within the family that Warp feels compelled to 'place' himself, as it is in such a location that he can relish the active presence of trustworthy allies who '[have] his back, not matter what'. As is the case in many parts of Asia, many Malaysians elect to reside in their childhood homes out of a sense of loyalty and/or due to the lack of financial independence. For transgender individuals like Warp, however, 'home is, ironically, where they feel least at home' (Ho 2006, 233). Such experiences are not uncommon among transgender Malaysians.

Unconditional familial acceptance and support that he can 'count on for anything', Warp muses, is vital for his well-being. While the burden of confronting gender norms, expectations and stereotypes can be shared with members of 'an accepting family', a family that refuses its support will inevitably relocate the disapproval of non-acquiescence to cultural dictates of gender solely on the trans man as '[his] own fault'.

I am certain that akin to Malaysian gay men who are judged and treated accordingly as traitors to their families for their inability and/or refusal to conform to sexual norms (Bong 2011b; Ismail 2001; Peletz 2002), transgender people are ostracised for betraying '"traditional" heterosexual family values' (Lee 2011, 103) and for bringing shame upon the family.

Without this 'layer of protection', Warp is rendered vulnerable to the transnegative ravages of society. The 'chances of suicide' escalate, and the 'ability to deal with society' as a trans man undergoes a significant attenuation.[6] 'Everything', meaning a transgender subjectivity and its attendant challenges, 'becomes even worse'. Rather than playing an ancillary role, familial dynamics are indisputably formative of trans men's subjectivities on multiple levels.

'Their Level of Acceptance': Un/Forging Friendships

My findings suggest that engagements with friends hold as much significance for trans men as familial relationships. Some trans men experience affirming and supportive friendships. Others realise that any disclosure and sharing of their gender identity can be fraught with difficulty, hence necessitating strategic forms of revelation and purposeful selections of friendship, even with fellow trans men. As such, they experience *both* circulations *and* interruptions in their gender identities through the doings of friendship. Michael recounts his encounters with 'supportive' friends:

> To be honest I have a really small circle of friends. And I'm perfectly fine with that. It's like, all my friends are very supportive … all my friends have like told their parents about it, and their parents are really supportive … they wanna know … what I'm going through, like they wanna see the changes that I'm going through, and they are all like very proud of me, because it's like a big step that I've taken in my life … they also said like, 'We kinda knew that you were gonna come out soon, because we know how you've lived, and er, how you have feelings for girls and stuff like that, so it's okay and you know, we're still going to be around you no matter what'.

[6] Refer to 'Grappling with Gender Dysphoria' for an analysis of suicidal ideation in relation to Gender Dysphoria.

Albeit comprising 'a really small circle', Michael's friends prove to be 'very supportive' towards him in his gender-affirming transitioning. The endorsement of his friends is further fortified by the approval of their parents. This supportive stance takes on two main forms. The first is an interest in 'see[ing] the changes that [he's] going through', which I suggest can well be an unresolved vacillation between genuine, caring interest and raw curiosity in witnessing physical transformations due to the process of transitioning. It is impossible to determine if they in fact 'read [Michael's] success at blending in and becoming unnoticeable and unremarkable [man] as disguise, masquerade, and pretense' (Cromwell 1999, 39). Perhaps they were merely trans-exoticising him (Nadal et al. 2014). Despite the ambiguity of intent, the fact remains that he is acclaimed for taking 'a big step … in [his] life', which in turn elicits a sense of pride in him from his friends and their parents. Being lauded rather than decried for their gender identity becomes for trans men a source of encouragement, possibly due to the fact that 'validation [is] more powerful from someone with [a] normative identity' (Galupo et al. 2014a, 200).

The second manifestation of support is directly related to the inklings of Michael's friends—and presumably their parents—of his self-affirmed gender identity. These individuals were cognisant of his way of life and 'feelings for girls', which they interpreted as the outward manifestations of transgressive gender and sexuality identities as 'where there is transgendered behavior there is a presumption of homosexuality' (Cromwell 1999, 44). The fact that they have prescience of this intimate part of his life, see it unfold, proclaim that 'it's okay' and pledge their support 'no matter what' is crucial for Michael's becoming. Their demeanour reveals both an unspoken and a spoken posture of non-judgement, affection, respect and unwavering support that exists even before he 'comes[s] out'—a performance of friendship that contributes positively to an 'individual's process of self-acceptance as a member of a marginalized community' (Galupo et al. 2014c, 26).

Some trans men exercise careful circumspection in revealing themselves to friends. For instance, Aarone develops specific methods of being 'out as a trans man':

Goh: Are you out as a trans man?
Aarone: Erm, to my friends, bit by bit … But in a subtle manner. Bit by bit.
Goh: When you meet people for the first time … How do you introduce yourself? … Are you comfortable with them knowing who you are?

Aarone: For new friends, yes. It's 'Aarone'. I introduce myself as 'Aarone' and ... for old friends, I will er, test them for a while. And see their level of acceptance. Then I will let you know, come out. If not, then I'll just let them think er, I'm that tomboyish friend that they had.

Aarone distinguishes between self-disclosure to 'old friends' and to 'new friends'. While these are friends, there is a risk that 'old friends' will reject who he is at the present moment. It becomes necessary to 'test them for a while' in order to gauge 'their level of acceptance'. While the nature of their rejection is unknown, studies show that transgender individuals often face macroaggressions from their friends and families due to their gender identities and expressions (Nadal et al. 2014). Aarone's experience suggests that trans men are more inclined to reveal that they were assigned female at birth only when they have elicited a satisfactory level of acceptance from their friends.

His approach to this group of people is through 'a subtle manner' or indirect, implicit and gentle strategies of divulging himself. He also believes in coming out 'bit by bit', or a steady, manageable portions of information about himself that is more likely to be accessible to his friends and family as these are individuals who have been acquainted with his female history and perhaps have become familiar with him as an individual with a female history. As such, while the process of revealing himself is executed among those who have previously known him as a woman, it must be done in a lighter manner in order to ease them into his current self-affirmed gender identity.

Conversely, Aarone is able to retreat and allow himself to be simply seen as a 'tomboyish friend'—a performance of gender that is ordinarily acceptable only during pre-pubescence (Halberstam 1998; Kuru-Utumpala 2013). In deploying the blurry boundaries between a masculine-acting woman and a man who was assigned female at birth to his advantage, Aarone seems to suggest that a masculine woman—or tomboy and *pengkid* (Wong 2012)—is often more socioculturally accepted or at least tolerated than a transgender individual. This strategy is, however, not repeated in relation to 'new friends'. With these individuals, there is no prior history of womanhood. He starts, as it were, on a clean slate as 'man' and enters stealth mode.[7] He is able to confidently

[7]Consider my discussion on stealth later in the sub-section '"Simply Seen as a Man": Stealth'.

and unproblematically 'introduce [him]self as Aarone'. A trans man's name, devoid of any allusions to femaleness, represents and assures the acceptance of an undisputed gender identity.

The complexity of interactions with friends also extends to other trans men. Although camaraderie among transgender people has been shown to be crucial for their well-being (Bockting et al. 2013; Emerton 2006; Hines 2007; Teh 2001), and while many of my research participants index positive experiences with fellow trans men, Bottle expresses ambivalence in engaging with those who share similar gender identities:

> *Goh*: Erm … do you have trans men friends?
>
> *Bottle*: I do, but I seldom mix with them … initially I actually eagerly wanted to know more and more, because I believe, it's not to say self-praise, I am a positive sign, and … most of them, they look down on themselves. Not to say their parents did them or whatever it is, but they themselves look down at themselves. So I would eagerly like to meet them up, you know, give them some positive words, feelings, and tell them how good the world is, but then most of the people I meet, they tend to … hide themselves from the society, don't want people to know. Just like they're cheating themselves. So why am I supposed to help people who are cheating themselves? So, it's a waste of time … and on and off, just meet up some … good friends among them.

Bottle expresses a form of swithering in regard to his relationship with other trans men, as he 'seldom mix[es] with them'. Evidently, he does not see them as on a par with him on 'an implied hierarchy of trans* experience' (Galupo et al. 2014b, 466). Bottle describes himself as 'a positive sign', which he qualifies as someone who confers 'positive words [and] feelings' in a bid to uplift other trans men and assist them in appreciating 'how good the world is'. His keenness to impart inspirational ideas underscores 'the value of transgender individuals connecting with similar others, possibly providing the opportunity to question stigma from the majority culture and reappraise their experiences in a self-affirmative way' (Bockting et al. 2013, 949). This desire, however, is met with defeatist attitudes from fellow trans men. His personal experience is that he is engaging with men who 'look down on themselves' or possess low self-esteem, who 'hide themselves from … society' or those whose interactions with the world are kept at a bare minimum, and who 'don't want people to know', meaning that they prefer to live without disclosing their gender complexities.

Although the need to anonymise and detach themselves from a society that neither understands nor approves of them may be an important strategy of self-preservation for trans men, Bottle feels that they are 'cheating themselves'. He may be alluding to the decision of many trans men to refrain from divulging themselves as individuals who were assigned female at birth, but I am more inclined to believe that 'cheating' for Bottle is a reference to the defeatist attitudes that many trans men adopt due to sociocultural disapprobation. His embodiment of 'a specific masculinity is constituted in relation to other masculinities and to the structure of gender relations as a whole' (Connell 2005, 154).

For him, such attitudes not only render futile any form of assistance to these trans men. To 'help people' with such attitudes constitutes 'a waste of time' or a fruitless endeavour, as they are already deeply entrenched in the moroseness that surrounds their gender identities, rather than publicly revel in them. Bottle's decision to maintain a distance from such individuals and solely to 'meet up' with trans men who are his 'good friends' is significant. Disassociation is a crucial strategy to avoid being overwhelmed by what a trans man sees as the exudence of negativity, which may potentially be disempowering. Strategic negotiations of friendship with fellow trans men are formulative of one's own gender identity. There is neither a homogeneous trans man experience (Galupo et al. 2014b) nor a guaranteed camaraderie or solidarity among trans men based solely on gender identity (Boyer and Galupo 2018).

'Who Is This Person?': Contemplating Collegiality

Similarly, the workplace is often experienced as a site of gender confrontations and negotiations, often culminating in discriminatory practices and policies (Minter and Daley 2003). Aside from engagements with family and friends, the becoming of the trans man is also greatly conditioned by unpredictable interactions with colleagues. The workplace often takes on the role of an inquisitor of gender identity and expression, and trans men risk being publicly exposed (Hines 2007). Bottle recalls a situation in which he needed to present himself in a more aggressive manner when his gender identity was questioned:

Bottle: I experience this with my recent colleague, he actually came up to me er, he's saying ... in like a teasing way, 'I heard from someone that you are a female'. Okay, the first sentence I ask him, I look at his face ... 'Who told you that'? He keep quiet. The second sentence I told him, 'Follow me to the toilet now', and then from that day onward, he keep quiet and still becomes my friend until today ... Because he tend to throw me a challenge, so I throw him back. You want to know, you follow me to the toilet ... He don't ask any more questions.

Goh: Okay, I don't understand 'follow me to the toilet'. What ... does that mean?

Bottle: Because he tend to throw me a challenge, so I throw him back. You want to know, you follow me to the toilet.

Goh: Did he?

Bottle: No.

Goh: So what did he do after that? Did he treat you like a man?

Bottle: Yes.

Goh: Did he ask you any more questions?

Bottle He don't ask any more questions.

That a 'recent colleague' or someone who has just recently become a co-worker would actually confront Bottle with a claim from hearsay undermines Bottle's ability to pass 'successfully' as man at the workplace. Although Bottle refers to this colleague as speaking in a 'teasing way', I suggest that it is not so much a tone of chaffing as it is 'thro[wing a provocative] challenge' to Bottle to prove his gender identity.

Seemingly unfazed, Bottle responds to his colleague's challenge by 'throw[ing] him back with' another challenge. He does so by interrogating his antagonist on the source of the latter's information, and orders his colleague to 'follow [him] to the toilet' immediately. This two-fold response reflects a demeanour that is often associated with machismo – 'a pervasive and persuasive male-centered discursive paradigm' (Horton and Rydstrom 2011, 547) which personifies 'exploration, risk, adventure [and] danger [as] stereotypically masculine attributes' (Devor 1993, 311). Bottle's demand to know how his colleague came to his conclusion is a way to destabilise and debunk the seeming arrogant certitude that accompanies this colleague's accusation.

The insistence that this colleague follows Bottle to the toilet is not a measure taken to prove his gender identity as established on genitalia, as he would evidently not be able to enact biological 'proof' of gender. What Bottle strives to do is 'throw … a challenge' or pose a dare that would throw his opponent off guard by instilling doubt in him through the display of a '"rugged", nonfeminine veneer' (Swain 2003, 376). It is unsurprising that the toilet acts as an arena in which a battle over gender certitude plays out, even though Bottle is not subjected to misgendering or scorn due to (mis)perceptions of presentation.[8] The intended consequence is for this colleague to suffer the embarrassment of poor judgement when he is finally able to witness Bottle's male genitalia directly, which obviously holds great risk for Bottle himself.

Although the dare is not taken up, its intended purpose achieves fruition. Bottle's colleague ceases 'ask[ing him] any more questions', 'keep[s] quiet' and has '[become his] friend' who now 'treat[s him] like a man'. Through a strategic move, Bottle befriends an adversary and his gender identity remains intact. He has 'take[n] his place (indeed … carve[d] out a place for himself) alongside other men' (Buchbinder 2013, 79).

Not all trans men suffer direct confrontations at work. Pokerface experiences awkwardness from his 'big boss' who is confused about his gender identity:

> *Goh*: And, have you ever experienced er, difficulties, challenges [at work]?
> *Pokerface*: A few times. Because … when I first joined, my manager told me that every time my big boss saw me, she will ask 'who is this person? Is he a male or female'? Because when we're wearing our lab coats, we cannot see whether you are male or female. You only can see the head. So she had problem explaining that to the big boss. But now the big boss seems okay, because she talk to me for a few times, and I think that should be better, but there's one time where we have to do a demo for client, my [Head of Department] eventually call me 'miss'. That is the moment I feel like very awkward, because I don't really like people calling me 'miss', but I don't know how to tell him.

Rather than assimilating into an indistinguishable crowd of gender-neutral 'lab coats', Pokerface finds that the ability for people to 'see [his] head' makes him obtrusive. Specifically, he piques the curiosity and elicits the

[8] More of the significance of the toilet is given prominence in the section 'Revisiting the Bathroom Problem: Possibilities at Public Toilets'.

confusion of his 'big boss' or 'Head of Department' in relation to his gender identity. Pokerface's 'manager' is at a loss to explain him to the 'big boss' in a manner that best presents his self-affirmed gender identity. Evidently, both the manager and the Head of Department are struggling to position Pokerface in familiar and readable categories of gender.

I propose that this struggle highlights the workplace as a site where it is often considered necessary for gender taxonomies to be indisputably defined. Pokerface's office somewhat becomes, borrowing from Abelson's words, one of many 'amplified sites [or] spaces structured such that processes of categorization for gender, sexuality, and race, as well as the norms and social actions that reinforce them, play out in heightened ways when people interact in them' (2019, 156). Nevertheless, it is gender, rather than sexuality or ethnicity that acts as a contributory factor to the amplification of what appears as ambiguous subjectivity to his 'big boss'. This demand for clear demarcations of 'male or female' exemplifies the gendered dynamics of bureaucracy in many workplaces, where a clear recognition, delineation and even segregation of individual demographics ensures efficient interaction, order and hierarchy. It arguably proves more difficult to define and control ambivalent subjects than it is well-defined ones.

The Head of Department eventually converses with Pokerface who feels that such a personal connection 'should be better' as he expects the former to accept his gender identity as a consequence of this interaction, even if a definitive line of questioning about his gender identity is absent. Instead, Pokerface becomes aware that constant interactions with his superior have led to the latter's conclusion that he is 'miss', possibly due to the latter's unfamiliarity with, and/or inability to interact with transgender people. He becomes increasingly aware that 'ambiguous gender, when and where it does appear, is inevitably transformed into deviance, thirdness, or a blurred version of either male or female' (Halberstam 1998, 20). His hope for an intuitive understanding of who he is transmutes into a quandary whereby he has been misgendered but lacks a clear strategy of how to enlighten the Head of Department. Colleagues are not just co-workers or work superiors, but agents of gender policing who mould workplace spatialities according to the rules of the gender binary. The confusion over who he really is, he realises, persists, and he is ultimately taxonomised as 'miss'.

Hadi realises that the way he presents himself,[9] either as woman or man, has a direct bearing on the way his capabilities are viewed at work:

> I go interview I wear *tudung* (veil or headscarf) then on my first day I didn't wear my *tudung* because they didn't want. Maybe they see, 'oh *boleh buat kerja ke tak boleh buat kerja?* (can this person do the job or not?)'. Sometimes they feel that way. '*Oh ini, tak boleh* (oh, this is impossible)' … last time I worked as a technician. I worked with another technician. They don't like because me, er, I don't want to work with *abang-abang* (elder brothers), he say, say like that. Then because I'm, that time it's a, *ekonomi gawat* (economic downturn) … Then I don't have a job. So … I really need the job, then I changed myself, so I wear *tudung* for that time so I can work with him … I just er, have my *tudung* in my car, then I go, when I'm going to my office then I wear *tudung*. Just outside the gate I take out (laughs).

I find Hadi's experiences fascinating because he faces challenges irrespective of whether he presents as woman or man at work. Both identities attract different sets of discriminatory attitudes. He speaks of difficulties in securing employment as a woman with 'short hair' who dons a *tudung*, also known as a *hijab*. There is a popular perception in Malaysian Muslim societies that is based on Qur'ān ic interpretation—and which then leads to popular practice—that Muslim women are forbidden to expose their hair in public as they are meant to hide their *'awrah*[10] (modesty) from public view. While Muslim women are not legally bound to wear the *tudung* and numerous interpretations abound as to their exact enactment and significance, many do so out of peer pressure, and as displays of Muslim respectability and differentiation. An unveiled head is frequently interpreted as defying Malaysian Malay-Muslim ideals of femininity and religiosity (Izharuddin 2018).

This demand of Islamic social respectability appears to be so prevalent that Hadi puts on a *tudung* in hopes of a better chance to secure a job. 'For women who do not wear the hijab in the context of Islamization, their nonveiled status is shaped by daily social pressures and tensions as they very visibly deviate from the normative identification of Muslim

[9] In 'Engendering Identity', I briefly discuss the problematics of using the terms 'presenting' and 'passing', due to connotations of deceit and superficiality associated with transgender subjectivities. As such, I use such terms in this chapter with some tentativeness.

[10] This term is commonly spelled and pronounced as '*aurat*' in Malaysia.

femininity' (Izharuddin 2018, 156), and may consequently be disentitled from gainful employment. Ironically, upon donning the *tudung*, he realises that his employers 'didn't want' him to do so because they were sceptical of whether a woman could 'do the job'. The eventual removal of the *tudung* becomes necessary due to a form of gender-based discrimination that a (veiled) woman would find this particular job an 'impossible' task.

Soon, Hadi discovers resistance in working as a woman 'technician' with an exposed head. Working in close quarters with male technicians proves to be an uncomfortable experience. There is no way by which these technicians could know of Hadi's self-affirmed gender identity, as he is not out to them.[11] Yet their unwillingness 'to work with *abang-abang*' is an insinuation that they are reluctant to work with women who appear in a masculine fashion, be they masculine-acting lesbians or trans men. Although he did not explicitly mention it, Hadi's experience suggests an attenuation in career satisfaction due to his gender identity, consistent with many studies on transgender people in the workplace (Brewster et al. 2012).

Owing to sheer necessity for 'a job' during a period of '*ekonomi gawat*', Hadi decides to feminise himself by wearing the *tudung* in order to ease the tension and awkwardness. Not unlike SR and his dilemma between donning a *baju kurung* or a *baju Melayu*, the *tudung* therefore becomes both a potent semiotic of ethnicity, religiosity and nationalism as well as gender identity that can potentially command credibility and respectability as a 'proper' Malay-Muslim woman in Malaysia. The act of having 'changed [him]self' is a strategic one, as he keeps the veil in his car, wears it during work and removes it once he is 'outside the gate' of his workplace. While he identifies as man, Hadi displays an interesting deployment of situational, context-fluid gender identity which embodies a particular gender identity that provides optimal benefits in accordance with particular socio-economic circumstances.

Conformity to the gender binary appears to be a *sine qua non* for employment in many instances in Malaysia, and many transgender people—particularly *mak nyah*—face great difficulty in securing stable jobs (Goh 2014a; Khartini 2005) due to the unpredictability of gender norms and expectations.

[11] See the following section, 'Problematising Disclosures'.

Problematising Disclosures

The copious amount of academic documentation on disclosures of sexuality or 'coming out' for lesbian, gay and bisexual people demonstrate that these issues are pivotal to their life journeys and identity politics (LaSala 2000; Lewis 2012; Li and Orleans 2001; Seidman et al. 1999). Family involvement is also crucial in this respect (Bong 2011a; LaSala 2000; Wang et al. 2009), and practices of coming out in Asian countries have occasionally taken the form of bringing life partners home to meet parents (Tan 2011; Wong 2007). Studies suggest that transgender people who come out register greater overall life happiness (Teh 2001). In contradistinction with lesbian, gay and bisexual people however, the pressing concern for transgender people is often the predicament of revealing a (trans)gender history rather than sexual or gender identity (Zimman 2009).

The workings of man as undertaken by trans men stretch beyond the imaginings of self-naming and passing. In order to become men, many find themselves negotiating with issues of coming out, or disclosing and/or undisclosing their gender history or gender journey. The journeys of living as trans men are also paved with issues of choosing the 'correct' public toilet.

'Just Feel Inside': Un/Disclosing

Hadi's lived sociocultural realities pose as elements that hamper the possibilities of coming out as a trans man. In this sense, he lives as a closeted trans man:

Goh: So what do you mean when you say, you're not out as a trans man?

Hadi: Because I never out to anybody except my wife. Except my group, trans men group. I'm not ready for my family. I think they cannot except it. Because I'm from a … very, very religious family.

Goh: So if you're not out means, in your everyday life, how do you tell people, what is your gender identity that you tell people?

Hadi: Oh I don't. I don't. I just feel inside … I never came out to my family. Erm, they just, because my family … very religious family, then they keep asking me to wear the *tudung* (veil) lah, as a Muslim. Everywhere you go you have to wear the veil, don't take off your veil …

For Hadi, 'not [being] out as a trans man' means that he neither discloses his self-affirmed gender identity or presents as man in public. As Jason Cromwell says, 'becoming invisible as transmen/FTMs and only visible as men is precarious and dependent upon how "out" someone is [because t]here is always some risk of being found out and marginalized as a result' (1999, 12). During our interview, I noticed how his physicality adhered rather closely to popular expectations of womanly appearance and comportment. As such, I find little difficulty in understanding Hadi's definition of 'never [being] out to anybody' with the exception of his wife and other trans men. By 'not [being] out as a trans man', he chooses to pass as woman in order to disclose his gender identity to a select few. Non-disclosure, or being in the closet as popularly phrased, is irreducible to stealth whereby 'stealth [is used] *instead of* in the closet' (Zimman 2009, 61, added emphasis). Through a dynamic of double invisibility, a trans man is able to invisibilise himself as woman in public in order to invisibilise himself as man in private.

While the closet is a regulating device that preserves 'the relations of the known and the unknown, the explicit and the inexplicit around homo/heterosexual definition' (Sedgwick 2008, 3) for gay and lesbian people, being closeted for trans men is the act of publicly presenting the gender identity that was assigned to them at birth. Becoming 'man' for Hadi is something that he 'just feel[s] inside'. In other words, gender identity is primarily an interior conviction and sense of ease. The socio-religious ethos in which he finds himself proves to be a pervasive factor that exacerbates his disinclination towards divulging his gender identity. Hadi is 'not ready [to disclose his gender identity to] his family' due to their religious fervour that could possibly favour transnegativity. He is repeatedly admonished for not 'wear[ing] the veil' in a consistent manner, as is the custom that is observed by many pious Malay-Muslim women. As mentioned variously earlier, for many Malaysian-Muslim trans men, religion, cultural assumptions, familial life and gender presuppositions often interlace in a debilitating capacity. Malaysian-Islam operates along unflinchingly cisnormative tracks that insist on the unnegotiable performance of rigid gender markers (Chua 2019; Goh 2014b, 2015; Goh and Kananatu 2019).

'Simply Seen as a Man': Stealth

A transgender person in stealth is one 'who is read as their affirmed gender at all times and may live apart from those who knew their gender history' (Greatheart 2013, 44, note 4), or who 'pass[es] as cisgender and mak[es] no effort to inform people otherwise[,] similar to remaining closeted as a gay or lesbian [person]' (Seamont 2018, 56). While Hadi finds it necessary to shield his identity by living as a woman, Schulz organises his disclosures in strategic ways that he refers to as 'stealth' by distinguishing it from 'coming out':

> *Goh*: [What about] being in the closet?
> *Schulz*: Okay. That's different because when you come out, erm, let's talk about the circle of your family first, yeah? You come out of the closet to your family, they are the ones that grew up with you, saw you growing up and things like that. So they are going to understand you coming out as a man, because you're telling them 'I don't see myself as a woman, I see myself as a man'. So, that's what I did. I didn't introduce myself as a trans man to my family.

Schulz provides an interesting contrast between stealth, which I will discuss in his next narrative, and the act of coming out by using his 'circle of … family' as a case study. He speaks of a reiterative disavowal of woman that is in tandem with 'see[ing him]self as a man'. This performativity of a self-affirmed gender identity occurs within a community with members that 'grew up with [Schulz and] saw [him] growing up'. His narrative of gender disclosure indicates that coming out of the closet for a trans man is a gradual concomitant process of information for, and adaptation by those who are most familiar to him. Hence, coming out is both a personal and familial process.

Coming out for Schulz is thus constituted of the revelation of a former gender identity assigned to him at birth that is accompanied by the profession of a current gender identity that is currently embraced. In this regard, 'coming out does not mean revealing a gender *identity*, but rather a particular kind of gender *history* characterized by the movement from one gender category to another' (Zimman 2009, 54; original emphasis). Coming out is concurrently a present embrace of man and the disclosure of a history of woman which he differentiates from stealth:

> Basically being stealth is like you acknowledge that you're a trans man, you acknowledge and you know that, it's just that you don't want other people from your past, your present and the people who are going to be in your future to know that you're trans. So you just simply want to be seen as a man ... I go out, and I meet people who are in my present, or my future, I tell them that I'm a man. Unless ... they get really intimately close to me, like, I feel that there's a trust between me and them, then yes, I do tell them that I am trans.

Schulz explains that 'stealth' is a twofold, simultaneous process in which trans men 'choos[e] to be known only as their current gender presentation' (Brewster et al. 2012, 61–62). It is first the '[self-] acknowledge[ment] that [one is] a trans man', a coming out to oneself. In other words, it is a veracious self-recognition that one was assigned female at birth but now identifies and lives as man. Second, stealth is the decision to not let 'other people from [the] past ... present and ... future ... know that [one is] trans', and conversely 'simply ... to be seen as a man'. Stealth is therefore the strategic aesthetics of cogent appearance through which one passes convincingly and unproblematically in society, whereby one foregrounds one's present gender identity and harbours in secrecy a former gender identity. When we met for the first time, I was admittedly doubtful that Schulz was assigned female at birth, due to his manly appearance and comportment.

Similar to Schulz's own gradualness of coming out as a transgender person, stealth professes a politics of partial revelation 'when a person chooses to be secretive about their gender history, either after transitioning or while successful passing' (Brown 2016, 208). The difference between coming out and stealth is that the latter conceals the fact that one was assigned female at birth. Lal Zimman posits that 'while *in the closet* or *closeted* may be used to talk about pre-transition transgender people who hide their gender identities, *stealth* refers specifically and exclusively to post-transition transgender people who opt not to disclose their transgender status' (2009, 62, original emphasis). Like almost all my other research participants, Schulz has not undergone any surgical procedure and does not see surgery as imperative for his subjectivity as a man.[12] His purposeful self-description as being stealth democratises and augments the concept beyond the perimeters envisioned by Zimman.

[12] Navigate to 'Embarking on Medical Transitioning' for a fuller discussion.

Although stealth is a refusal to reveal one's (trans)gender identity to the general populace, it ceases to be the purview of the private when the trans man establishes 'trust between [him] and them'. Those who 'get really intimately close' to the trans man dismantle stealth and become privy to his coming out, which becomes unmerited in mutually trustworthy relationships. I argue that stealth acts as a protective barrier from potentially injurious interactions in which a female history is deployed as an abusive arsenal to attack an appropriated identity of man. Stealth prepares the groundwork for selective and safer disclosures.

Living in stealth does not, however, preclude the continuous operations of the closet, a matter I had discussed earlier and which I further unpack below. For Schulz, the secrecy associated with stealth extends beyond his present and future acquaintances to 'people from [his] past'. Although he does not specifically mention it, there is a likelihood that being stealth towards 'people from [the] present and future' is accomplished through the sole presentation of man, but stealth towards 'people [from] the past' translates to presenting as both woman and man according to circumstances:

> *Goh*: What was it like to be in the closet? What did you, how were you in the closet?
>
> *Schulz*: Maybe it's safe to say that I'm still in the closet as being as a trans man. To put it into context, so I was living in the closet previously as a woman ... and now I'm still living in the closet (chuckles). Maybe that's what stealth means. Being in the closet as a trans man.

Schulz's assertion that he 'was living in the closet previously as a woman' suggests that he is aware of a phase in life where he had lived contradictorily as a woman despite being cognisant of his self-affirmed gender identity. For him, the closet was a state of life in self-concealment, 'linked, perhaps inseparable from, the notion of "coming out" [which] gives expression to the dramatic quality of privately and publicly coming to terms with a contested social identity' as Steven Seidman et al. (1999, 9) comment in relation to sexually diverse individuals. Being in the closet means that Schulz, like Hadi, had yet to 'come out', or publically divulge his gender identity as man.

That Schulz continues to uphold a multi-layered understanding of the closet suggests that being stealth does not contribute to an utter resolution of the closet. The partial, strategic disclosures which are commanded by stealth are still shared with the dynamics of the closet. To exist in stealth is ironically to hide and unhide. Schulz conceals and reveals the fact that he was assigned female at birth to 'people from [his] past … present and … future' by strategically closetting and unclosetting himself as a man.

Therefore, by admitting that he is 'still in the closet as … a trans man', the double element of un/disclosure persists in his living in stealth. I argue that stealth is a reworking of the closet and coming out. Stealth is neither the state of being completely out or being completely in. Although stealth simultaneous dismantles and reassembles the closet for the benefit of the trans man's preservation of privacy and security, the closet remains. Stealth, closet and disclosure are neither fait accompli projects nor collapse in definition into each other. They travel interminably in intersectional tracks that may not necessarily demonstrate absolute linearity either.

SR engages in similar strategies of stealth, and utilises the level of intimacy in his interactions as the yardstick for disclosure:

> Like with friends, I'm gonna be very open. They know, because they know me since I was like, erm, who I am before, female (clears throat). I'm gonna be very open to them, okay, I'm a trans man. Like for the outsider, I'm gonna be very closed. Like, I'm gonna be like so, private. I keep it in private, because they don't even know me before … So I don't owe anyone an explanation, so whatever you look at me … if you wanna judge me that way, go ahead, I'm okay. But for me, because I don't owe people any explanation. Accept me for who I am, man. That's it. And for like, the outsider, the outsider yes of course, if you have a beard, if you have a moustache, you're not gonna think you're a girl.

Like Schulz, SR's understanding of stealth involves 'be[ing] very closed' to 'outsider[s]' but 'be[ing] very open' to friends in terms of his transition to 'man'. A lack of intimacy means that 'outsiders' who 'don't even know [him from] before' cannot be privy to his 'private' life. SR's tactics of stealth do not include people from his past as he abides by the decision to 'be very open' as a 'trans man' to them, rather than 'choos[ing] not to share certain aspects of [his] life history or embodiment with others' (Zimman 2009, 62) who are friends.

In affirming that friends are those who have 'known [him when he was] female', SR conflates female and woman, which echoes Judith

Butler's (1999, also 1993) now classic postulation that sex is already gendered rather than being a purely prediscursive, ontological state. As the denouncement of femaleness is also the denouncement of womanness, there is a high probability that the appropriation of manness is also the taking on of maleness. As evident from my interview with him, SR presents as a smooth-faced man. Yet it is perhaps his gender vision that prompts him to consider 'a beard [and] moustache' in order to solidify his self-affirmed gender identity. The ability to be male, insofar as he is able to, is concomitantly the ability to be a man. Passing is not only a venture undertaken in society. In spotting facial hair, '[he is] not gonna think [he's] a girl'. Through such means, he is able to pass to himself before he passes to 'outsider[s]'.

Like Schulz, the access to SR's female history is permitted only in cases of established familiarity. In this sense, outsiders become insiders who share the knowledge of his lived reality. SR is aware that acting in stealth does not guarantee that he completely passes in society. Outsiders continue to hold him in suspicion. In a nonchalant manner, he speaks of the judgemental gaze of those who 'look at [him]'. Although such actions that are directed towards him elicit responses that do not appear to unnerve him, I suggest that he is still adversely affected. He still asks to be accepted 'for who [he is]'. In reality, the outsider/insider dynamics continue to determine the direction of stealth for him.

Revisiting the Bathroom Problem: Possibilities at Public Toilets[13]

There are no Malaysian laws that accommodate transgender people's choice of public toilets. Some gender-sensitised establishments in Malaysia provide 'single occupancy-style gender-inclusive' (Abelson 2019, 202) toilets, but such instances are rare, transient and often arbitrary. The bathroom, as Halberstam points out, continues to preserve and police gender binaries through strict segregations of sex and gender visibility. For instance, Malaysian trans men who encounter 'the accusation "you're in the wrong bathroom"' are actually encountering the accusation that their 'apparent masculinity ... is at odds with [their]

[13]While the term 'bathroom' is commonly used in the U.S., most Malaysians are inclined to refer to 'toilet', 'washroom', 'loo', 'gents' or 'ladies'. 'Lavatory' and 'WC' (water cooler) are hardly ever used.

supposed femaleness' (Halberstam 1998, 23–24) and thus disqualified from this space. In visiting public toilets, they experience a coerced yet implicit declaration of their anatomies in these sites of 'urinary segregation' (Abelson 2019, 169).

This section features the narratives of trans me who enter men's toilets. Here, I discuss the processes through which trans men negotiate unyielding societal demands for self-taxonomy in terms of genitalia—and by extension, gender identity—in response to bodily needs. For instance, Jon is cognisant that his presence in a public toilet designated for men is a source of tension for other users:

> Every moment I need to struggle. Can you imagine, every time you go to toilet, go to the washroom, I will stand in front the washroom and struggle almost one hour. I don't know where I want to go into the gentleman toilet or I go to the ladies washroom … I try my best because I dress, I wear ties, I dress like men, I go into the men washroom, but I don't like the thing I watch, I observe surrounding me. Because why, deep inside my body I feel I uncomfortable… because … some of the guy, their acting in the toilet, er, the washroom, so I feel uncomfortable and some, I can feel offendable. I think, even though the guy also feel offendable … I am a woman, they also feel offendable. So, I feel uncomfortable.

For Jon, to 'stand' in uncertainty is to undergo an unresolved dilemma in choosing between entering the toilet for men or women. This dilemma is one that emerges from an acute realisation that he is a man who was assigned female at birth, and who will be pressured by society to conform to normative gender expectations. The liminality that thus arises disqualifies him from a facile cisnormative assemblage of sex and gender, and the toilet stands as the spatial adjudicator of a 'legitimate' correlation between biology and outward appearance, at which point he stands at the verge of being disqualified.

The conflation of male and man that I discussed earlier in relation to SR is pertinent here. The toilet bears a simultaneous potential to in/validate Jon's gender identity. The mention of his efforts to 'dress like men' indicates a desire to validly enter the men's toilet through the use of cogent props and patterns, yet his perception of how some men '[act towards him] in the toilet' reveals his efforts to pass as lacking, unconvincing and subsequently unsuccessful. Jon interprets such actions as provoking the ire of men who were assigned male at birth. Their reactions to his presence foreground the reality that both cissexism and heterosexism are 'likely below the level of consciousness for most men, [but] peppered throughout [trans] men's days as they enter these spaces' (Abelson 2019, 189).

Such an interpretation may either indicate physical expressions of resentment that were levelled against him, or personal perceptions of rejection, or both. Whichever the case may be, Jon's thrice-mention of 'offendable' indicates that what he 'watch[es and] observes surrounding [him]'—that other uses take offence at his presence—is real for him. 'Deep inside [his] body', he is cognisant that the toilet remains as a site in which the struggles and discomfort that encircle his self-affirmed gender identity are accentuated, interrogated and undermined.

While toilet quandaries remain unresolved for Jon, Aarone devises strategies to address negative responses at work:

Goh: When you work with your colleagues, yeah, when you were working and you had colleagues, erm, did you ever experience discrimination?

Aarone: Erm, yes. Yeah. Partly. Some of it. But I always er, try to minimise the impact on me, so that's why I said, er, I'm lucky, I was lucky because my work at that time took me about fifty percent of the time outside. Er, outstation. So I don't really meet with people at the office so often (clears throat).

Goh: Can you explain what form of discrimination?

Aarone: Oh. For example like going to the loo. You know, sometimes they, sometimes we bump into each other and they saw me coming out from the male toilet and they say like, 'eh why you, you know, like you go to this toilet'? I said like, 'well, so what, that toilet is full. I can just go into any other toilet, it's just the same'. But then I had to come up with that kind of excuse anyway … So, here are times when, after a few times, I had to remove myself, in a way where I just go to a different floor, where no one knows me.

Aarone's self-affirmed gender identity as a trans man is not without experiences of 'discrimination', including 'with [his] colleagues' when he was employed. He focuses on 'going to the loo' as emblematic of this discrimination. That his fellow employees question him on his use of the 'male toilet' suggests that he presents as woman at work, and/or puzzlement on their part in relation to his gender identity. There is no outright enquiry: the choice of a toilet itself mediates questions that seek to enlighten suspicions and confusions in connection with gender identity.

That Aarone is subjected to such misgivings likely indicates that he has not 'succeeded' in the execution of a 'perfect' passing. 'Being left alone in the men's room for most of the men is a form of social honor' (Abelson 2019, 170) that is denied him. Like for Jon, the toilet is potentially a 'dangerous' space that can compromise his self-presentation. Just as 'social recognition as a man can further legitimize the internal sense of being a man' (Abelson 2019, 62), the reverse is also true. It can be extremely unnerving and subsequently lead to an attenuation of gender identity.

Upon confronting such circumstances, Aarone subscribes to several plans of action. The first is serendipitous, in that his previous occupation required him to be 'outside', or away from the office 'about fifty per cent of the time'. The infrequency of 'meet[ing] with people at the office' correlates directly with the infrequency of experiencing gender cross-examination, including at the toilet. Nevertheless, when inevitably challenged on his choice of toilets, Aarone creates an 'excuse' that the 'correct' toilet—the 'sex-equals-gender' toilet—is 'full'. He also acknowledges that there are occasions whereby 'after a few times', or a series of uncomfortable toilet-related interrogations, he has had to 'remove [him]self' and 'go a different floor' where is unknown. Aarone thus resorts to the fabrication of a (less than truthful) reason and anonymity in order to 'minimise the impact' of gender interrogations, even if they appear in subtle and oblique forms.

Alco does not now experience the unfavourable elements connected with the toilet. For him, the toilet is a site where his self-affirmed gender identity is reinforced:

> I just did not feel complete, you know. Ah, when I speak to someone, they call me '*kakak*' (elder sister), you know. Er, I go to the women's toilet, you know, and things like that. But after I started taking hormones, yeah, people started calling me '*abang*' (elder brother), and when I go to the women's toilet, they look at me funnily, you know, and then I said, 'Oh sorry, sorry, wrong toilet. I'll go to the men's toilet' ... for some people it's small, small things, like when someone calls you '*kakak*', you know, or '*abang*', but to me it's a big thing, and when people starts calling me '*abang*', you know, I'll just turn to look at ... my wife and she goes like, (teasing tone) '*abang*, okay'? (both laugh). So, it may be small, but it, it's important to me. It made me feel great, all those small, small things, to be able to go to a man's toilet ... that's an achievement of its own, you know?

Alco describes the before-and-after experiences of (GAHT) in his life as a trans man in relation to the toilet. Prior to GAHT, he would 'go to the women's toilet' without any opposing reactions. The ease with which he was able to do so indicates that despite his best attempts, he was still hailed as '*kakak*' rather than '*abang*' (elder brother),[14] and hence could not pass successfully as man when he visited the female toilet. This would have been the reason why 'just did not feel complete'. The feeling of gender incompleteness therefore arises from the lack of accomplishing a self-affirmed gender identity in society, whereby the toilet becomes one of the prominent yardsticks of gender 'achievement'. Unsurprisingly therefore, 'the men's room represents the most severe test of [Alco's] ability to pass' (Halberstam 1998, 25).

Conversely, GAHT reverses the experiences of gender incompletion for him. Society 'looks at [him funny]' and turns him away from the women's toilet. A funny look translates as a gaze of doubt, confusion, accusation and even disapproval in discerning that something is amiss in the concatenation of sex and gender. Being welcomed at the women's toilet becomes a mark of gender failure, while being unwelcomed at the same venue becomes the sign of gender success through 'effective' passing. Conventional yet socially endorsed matchings of sex and gender serve as misgendering for Alco, while a self-appointed and an unconventional pairing of 'man' with a female body which society would denounce as disordered becomes for him an accurate interpretation of who he is. As Raine Dozier succinctly asserts, 'being "she'd" [is] a constant reminder of the incongruence between social identity and internal gender identity' (2005, 306).

The journey from being '*kakak*' to '*abang*' is significant. It propels gender affirmation beyond toilets to society at large, and establishes a sense of pride in Alco 'through identifying as male, taking steps in the identity process, and currently living as [himself]' (Budge et al. 2015, 419). The ability 'to go to a man's toilet' without being accosted by disdainful eyes may be considered by some as '[a] small [thing]', but it is 'an achievement'] that '[makes him] feel great'. The power of the quotidian in fortifying the subjectivity of the trans man should not be underestimated.

[14]It is common for Malaysians to address older female and male siblings, and non-siblings of a similar age in Malay as '*kakak*' and '*abang*' respectively.

There are two salient points that can be gleaned from this occurrence. First, the favourable appellation of '*abang*' concurs with Michael G. Peletz's position that 'in the practice of everyday life, certain male relational roles—e.g. ... elder brother—may well dominate the category of "male", and may also inform the meanings of all male relational (and "positional") roles (1995, 100), as well as ground socioculturally sanctioned gender roles. In short, to be '*abang*' is to be man and male. Second, the toilet acts as a microcosm of unquestioned social acceptance and gender achievement. This reality is not exclusively understood and experienced on a deeply bodily level by Alco: it is a shared relational reality. His wife's retort of '*abang*, okay' may appear jocular, but it is in effect a statement of pride and satisfaction of persuasive passing that she shares with Alco.

Conclusion

The interactional and inter-relational processes of gender formation are evident. The subjectivities of Malaysian trans men are heavily influenced by their engagements with society in particular spaces, namely with their immediate family members, cisgender friends, fellow trans men and colleagues. Just as a welcoming environment in these sites of social interaction correlates positively with the mental and emotional well-being of trans men, suspicion and rejection contribute to a sense of gender attrition among them.

Immediate family members often act as gender invigilators that create an atmosphere of surveillance for trans men during both childhood and adulthood. Often, trans men rely on their families as the 'first responders' who will support them in the face of societal dismissiveness and repudiation, but instead experience passivity, embarrassment and exclusion. Similarly, trans men look to both cisgender and transgender friends for affirmation. Although it proves impossible to ascertain if cisgender friends genuinely support their life journeys or are merely exoticising and fetishising them, or perhaps even an entangled interweaving of both attitudes, they continue to play vital roles in the subjectivities of trans men. Friendships are unpredictable because they can potentially harbour rejection and discrimination. Similarly, relationships between trans men themselves can register positive and negative outcomes.

Collegial exchanges also prove to be precarious. Conflicts can challenge and dismantle gender identities, but they can also corroborate and concretise them. Nevertheless, interactions at the workplace sometimes do culminate in a situation of misgendering, possibly due to confusion and/or the lack of gender sensitisation, appropriate language and an obsession with stabilising normative gender categories. In these interactions, particularly ones that involve Malay-Muslim Malaysians, sociocultural, ethnic, religious and nationalistic demands intervene in their gender identities and expressions.

Issues of disclosure and non-disclosure also prove to be highly complex processes. The closet cannot be simplistically interpreted as hiding one's (trans)gender history through stealth. A noteworthy case in point is the closet experience of one trans man in which he feels compelled to present as woman and to obscure man. Stealth is concerned with careful deliberations revolving around the decision to divulge a female or transgender history while presenting as man to people in the present and from the past. Coming out is the revelation of a current self-affirmed gender identity and the disclosure of a previous gender identity which was assigned at birth. As such, closet and stealth cannot be conflated by default.

Public toilets continue to be sites of radical gender contestation for trans men who desire nothing more than to be seen and treated as unnoticeably men. Nevertheless, they still experience these spaces as perilous to their history as individuals who were assigned female at birth. The risk of exposure and disqualification for those who do not quite pass is potentially destructive site for subjectivity, while for those who do pass, it is a site of validation and empowerment.

Bibliography

Abelson, Miriam J. 2019. *Men in Place: Trans Masculinity, Race, and Sexuality in America*. Minneapolis, MN: University of Minnesota Press.

Arneil, Barbara. 2000. 'The Politics of the Breast'. *Canadian Journal of Women & the Law* 12 (2): 345–70.

Bockting, Walter O., Michael H. Miner, Rebecca E. Swinburne Romine, Autumn Hamilton, and Eli Coleman. 2013. 'Stigma, Mental Health, and Resilience in an Online Sample of the US Transgender Population'. *American Journal of Public Health; Washington* 103 (5): 943–51.

Bong, Sharon A. 2011a. 'Beyond Queer: An Epistemology of Bi Choice'. *Journal of Bisexuality* 11 (1): 39–63.

———. 2011b. 'Negotiating Resistance/Resilience through the Nexus of Spirituality-Sexuality of Same-Sex Partnerships in Malaysia and Singapore'. *Marriage & Family Review* 47 (8): 648–65.

Boyer, C. Reyn, and M. Paz Galupo. 2018. 'Transgender Friendship Profiles: Patterns Across Gender Identity and LGBT Affiliation'. *Gender Issues; New York* 35 (3): 236–53.

Brewster, Melanie E., Brandon Velez, Cirleen DeBlaere, and Bonnie Moradi. 2012. 'Transgender Individuals' Workplace Experiences: The Applicability of Sexual Minority Measures and Models.' *Journal of Counseling Psychology* 59 (1): 60–70.

Brown, Michael Eric. 2016. *A Herstory of Transmasculine Identities: An Annotated Anthology*. Miami, FL: Boundless Endeavors, Inc.

Buchbinder, David. 2013. *Studying Men and Masculinities*. New York: Routledge.

Budge, Stephanie L., Joe J. Orovecz, and Jayden L. Thai. 2015. 'Trans Men's Positive Emotions: The Interaction of Gender Identity and Emotion Labels'. *The Counseling Psychologist* 43 (3): 404–34.

Butler, Judith. 1993. *Bodies That Matter: On the Discursive Limits of 'Sex'*. New York: Routledge.

———. 1999. *Gender Trouble: Feminism and the Subversion of Identity*. New York: Routledge.

Chua, Hang Kuen. 2019. '*Malu* Sensitivity and the Identities of Non-Heteronormative Malay Muslim Men in Peninsular Malaysia'. *Kajian Malaysia* 37 (1): 109–30.

Connell, Raewyn. 2005. *Masculinities*. 2nd ed. Cambridge, UK: Polity Press.

Cromwell, Jason. 1999. *Transmen and FTMs: Identities, Bodies, Genders, and Sexualities*. Urbana, IL: University of Illinois Press.

Devor, Aaron. 1993. 'Sexual Orientation Identities, Attractions, and Practices of Female-to-Male Transsexuals'. *The Journal of Sex Research* 30 (4): 303–15.

———. 2016. *FTM: Female-to-Male Transsexuals in Society*. Bloomington, IN: Indiana University Press.

Dozier, Raine. 2005. 'Beards, Breasts, and Bodies: Doing Sex in a Gendered World'. *Gender and Society* 19 (3): 297–316.

Emerton, Robyn. 2006. 'Finding a Voice, Fighting for Rights: The Emergence of the Transgender Movement in Hong Kong'. *Inter-Asia Cultural Studies* 7 (2): 243–69.

Galupo, M. Paz, L. Andrew Bauerband, Kirsten A. Gonzalez, D. Brienne Hagen, Shandelle D. Hether, and Tiana E Krum. 2014a. 'Transgender Friendship Experiences: Benefits and Barriers of Friendships Across Gender Identity and Sexual Orientation'. *Feminism & Psychology* 24 (2): 193–215.

Galupo, M. Paz, Shane B. Henise, and Kyle S. Davis. 2014b. 'Transgender Microaggressions in the Context of Friendship: Patterns of Experience Across Friends' Sexual Orientation and Gender Identity'. *Psychology of Sexual Orientation and Gender Diversity* 1 (4): 461–70.

Galupo, M. Paz, Tiana E. Krum, D. Brienne Hagen, Kirsten A. Gonzalez, and L. A. Bauerband. 2014c. 'Disclosure of Transgender Identity and Status in the Context of Friendship'. *Journal of LGBT Issues in Counseling* 8 (1): 25–42.

Goh, Joseph N. 2014a. 'Transgressive Empowerment: Queering the Spiritualities of the *Mak Nyahs* of PT Foundation'. In *Queering Migrations Towards, from, and Beyond Asia*, edited by Hugo Córdova Quero, Joseph N. Goh, and Michael Sepidoza Campos, 123–37. New York: Palgrave Macmillan.

———. 2014b. 'Fracturing Interwoven Heteronormativities in Malaysian Malay-Muslim Masculinity: A Research Note'. *Sexualities* 17 (5–6): 600–17.

———. 2015. 'Peculiar Politics in Malaysia: A Queer Perspective on Non-Heteronormative Malay-Muslim Men'. In *Ways of Queering, Ways of Seeing*, edited by Jillian E. Cox and Jo Grzelinska, 3–33. Oxford, UK: Inter-Disciplinary Press.

———. 2019. 'God>Cursing>Shaming>Blessing>Pride'. *TSQ: Transgender Studies Quarterly* 6 (3): 435–41.

Goh, Joseph N., and Thaatchaayini Kananatu. 2019. '*Mak Nyahs* and the Dismantling of Dehumanisation: Framing Empowerment Strategies of Malaysian Male-to-Female Transsexuals in the 2000s'. *Sexualities* 22 (1–2): 114–30.

Greatheart, Marcus. 2013. *Transforming Practice: Life Stories of Transgender Men That Change How Health Providers Work*. Toronto, ON: Ethica Press.

Halberstam, Judith. 1998. *Female Masculinity*. Durham, NC: Duke University Press.

heinz, matthew. 2016. *Entering Transmasculinity: The Inevitability of Discourse*. Chicago, IL: Intellect Ltd.

Hines, Sally. 2007. *TransForming Gender: Transgender Practices of Identity, Intimacy and Care*. Bristol, UK: Policy Press.

Ho, Josephine. 2006. 'Embodying Gender: Transgender Body/Subject Formations in Taiwan'. *Inter-Asia Cultural Studies* 7 (2): 228–42.

Horton, Paul, and Helle Rydstrom. 2011. 'Heterosexual Masculinity in Contemporary Vietnam: Privileges, Pleasures, and Protests'. *Men and Masculinities* 14 (5): 542–64.

Ismail Baba. 2001. 'Gay and Lesbian Couples in Malaysia'. In *Gay and Lesbian Asia: Culture, Identity, Community*, edited by Gerard Sullivan and Peter A. Jackson, 143–63. New York: Harrington Park Press.

Izharuddin, Alicia. 2018. '"Free Hair": Narratives of Unveiling and the Reconstruction of Self'. *Signs: Journal of Women in Culture and Society* 44 (1): 155–76.

Khartini Slamah. 2005. 'The Struggle to Be Ourselves, Neither Men nor Women: *Mak Nyahs* in Malaysia'. In *Sexuality, Gender and Rights: Exploring Theory and Practice in South and Southeast Asia*, edited by Geetanjali Misra and Radhika Chandiramani, 98–111. London: Sage.

Kuru-Utumpala, Jayanthi. 2013. 'Butching It Up: An Analysis of Same-Sex Female Masculinity in Sri Lanka'. *Culture, Health & Sexuality* 15 (Suppl. 2): S153–65.

LaSala, Michael C. 2000. 'Lesbians, Gay Men, and Their Parents: Family Therapy for the Coming-Out Crisis'. *Family Process* 39 (1): 67–81.

Lee, Julian C. H. 2011. *Policing Sexuality: Sex, Society and the State*. London: Zed Books.

Lewis, Nathaniel M. 2012. 'Remapping Disclosure: Gay Men's Segmented Journeys of Moving Out and Coming Out'. *Social & Cultural Geography* 13 (3): 211–31.

Li, Lusha, and Myron Orleans. 2001. 'Coming Out Discourses of Asian American Lesbians'. *Sexuality and Culture* 5 (2): 57–78.

Lunceford, Brett. 2012. *Naked Politics: Nudity, Political Action, and the Rhetoric of the Body*. Lanham, MD: Lexington Books.

Mellström, Ulf. 2010. 'The Cultural Construction of Masculinity Among Working-Class Malaysian Chinese in the Intersection of Race, Class and Gender'. In *Gendered Inequalities in Asia: Configuring, Contesting and Recognizing Women and Men*, edited by Helle Rydstrøm, 252–85. Gendering Asia. Copenhagen, Denmark: NIAS Press.

Minter, Shannon, and Christopher Daley. 2003. 'Trans Realities: A Legal Needs Assessment of San Francisco's Transgender Communities'. National Center for Lesbian Rights. http://www.nclrights.org/wp-content/uploads/2013/07/transrealities0803.pdf.

Nadal, Kevin, Kristin Davidoff, Lindsey Davis, and Yinglee Wong. 2014. 'Emotional, Behavioral, and Cognitive Reactions to Microaggressions: Transgender Perspectives'. *Psychology of Sexual Orientation and Gender Diversity* 1 (1): 72–81.

Peletz, Michael G. 1995. 'Neither Reasonable nor Responsible: Contrasting Representations of Masculinity in a Malay Society'. In *Bewitching Women, Pious Men: Gender and Body Politics in Southeast Asia*, edited by Aihwa Ong and Michael G. Peletz. Berkeley, CA: University of California Press.

———. 2002. *Islamic Modern: Religious Courts and Cultural Politics in Malaysia*. Princeton, NJ: Princeton University Press.

Pfeffer, Carla A. 2017. *Queering Families: The Postmodern Partnerships of Cisgender Women and Transgender Men*. New York: Oxford University Press.

Schrock, Douglas, and Michael Schwalbe. 2009. 'Men, Masculinity, and Manhood Acts'. *Annual Review of Sociology* 35 (1): 277–95.

Seamont, Morgan M. H. 2018. 'Becoming "The Man I Want to Be": Transgender Masculinity, Embodiment, and Sexuality'. University of Colorado, Boulder, CO. https://scholar.colorado.edu/anth_gradetds/85.
Sedgwick, Eve Kosofsky. 2008. *Epistemology of the Closet*. 2nd ed. Berkeley, CA: University of California Press.
Seidman, Steven, Chet Meeks, and Francie Traschen. 1999. 'Beyond the Closet? The Changing Social Meaning of Homosexuality in the United States'. *Sexualities* 2 (1): 9–34.
Siti Nor Amalina Ahmad Tajuddin, and Noraini Zulkepli. 2019. 'An Investigation of the Use of Language, Social Identity and Multicultural Values for Nation-Building in Malaysian Outdoor Advertising'. *Social Sciences; Basel* 8 (1): 18.
Swain, Scott. 2003. 'Covert Intimacy: Closeness Men's Friendships'. In *The Gendered Society Reader*, edited by Michael S. Kimmel, 2nd ed., 364–82. New York: Oxford University Press.
tan, beng hui. 2007. 'Time's Up! Moving Sexuality Rights in Malaysia into the New Millennium'. ISIS International. http://www.isiswomen.org/index.php?option=com_content&view=article&id=564:times-up-moving-sexuality-rights-in-malaysia-into-the-new-millennium&catid=132:women-and-sexuality&Itemid=261.
Tan, Chris K. K. 2011. 'Go Home, Gay Boy! Or, Why Do Singaporean Gay Men Prefer to "Go Home" and Not "Come Out"?' *Journal of Homosexuality* 58 (6–7): 865–82.
Teh, Yik Koon. 2001. 'Mak Nyahs (Male Transsexuals) in Malaysia: The Influence of Culture and Religion on Their Identity'. *International Journal of Transgenderism* 5 (3).
Wang, Frank T. Y., Herng-Dar Bih, and David J. Brennan. 2009. 'Have They Really Come Out: Gay Men and Their Parents in Taiwan'. *Culture, Health & Sexuality* 11 (3): 285–96.
Wong, Day. 2007. 'Rethinking the Coming Home Alternative: Hybridization and Coming Out Politics in Hong Kong's Anti-Homophobia Parades'. *Inter-Asia Cultural Studies* 8 (4): 600–16.
Wong, Yuenmei. 2012. 'Islam, Sexuality, and the Marginal Positioning of *Pengkids* and Their Girlfriends in Malaysia'. *Journal of Lesbian Studies* 16 (4): 1–14.
Yee, Jennifer. 2009. 'Ways of Knowing, Feeling, Being, and Doing: Toward an Asian American and Pacific Islander Feminist Epistemology'. *Amerasia Journal* 35 (2): 49–64.
Zimman, Lal. 2009. '"The Other Kind of Coming Out": Transgender People and the Coming Out Narrative Genre'. *Gender and Language* 3 (1): 53–80.

CHAPTER 4

Grappling with Gender Dysphoria

Gender Dysphoria (GD), as described by Marcus Greatheart, is 'the emotional and psychological distress that results from a dissonance between one's affirmed gender … and the sex assigned at birth' (2013, 137–38; see also Byne et al. 2018).[1] This distress 'may be related to the entire body or parts, the genitalia, or secondary sexual characteristics such as the breasts or body hair' (Tellier 2019, 194). GD 'is persistent, continuing over a long period of time … not alleviated by other treatments … and [is] a crisis so profound that it may push a person to suicide' (Tanis 2003, 20). Scholars like Jason Cromwell contend that 'it is nontranspeople who have gender dysphoria' (1999, 25) due to a sense of unease with gender diversity that is then redirected towards transgender people. In their everyday spatial extensions, bodies experience bodily dissatisfaction, and physical and emotional torment. When

[1] 'Gender Dysphoria' is used in the American Psychiatric Association's *Diagnostic and Statistical Manual of Mental Disorders*, 5th Edition (DSM-5). In the World Health Organisation's *International Statistical Classification of Diseases and Related Health Problems* (ICD), 11th Edition (ICD-11), 'Gender Incongruence' is used as a parallel term to 'Gender Dysphoria' (see Beek et al. 2016). An analysis of the numerous debates and complexities surrounding the use of these two terms (for instance, Vargas-Huicochea et al. 2018) is beyond the scope of this volume. Hence, I only employ the term 'Gender Dysphoria' in this monograph, primarily because this term was used by my research participants and despite its contested use (see Drescher 2010).

J. N. Goh, *Becoming a Malaysian Trans Man*,
Gender, Sexualities and Culture in Asia,
https://doi.org/10.1007/978-981-15-4534-4_4

trans men experience, interpret and speak of the anguish that arises from the discordance between their gender identities and anatomical assemblages, they speak from and to deeply grounded embodied epistemologies. In other words, they *speak from* and *speak to their bodies as the loci of knowledge*.

While I agree with scholars that not all trans men experience GD, or that some encounter it minimally (Cromwell 1999; Greatheart 2013; Selvaggi et al. 2018; Vitelli et al. 2017), the majority of those with whom I had conversed expressed grave discontentment with their current corporeal forms as they either lacked crucial characteristics that could contribute to a more cogent gender identity, or provided an excess that threatened this identity. Some trans men, notably those who have never experienced a female or lesbian history, tend to eschew or demonstrate disdain towards terms such as 'female', 'woman' or 'feminine' to describe their past. Nonetheless, none of my research participants displayed any sense of overwhelming aversion when the subject came up, even if some were adamant that they were never acquainted with any experience of being a woman or a lesbian individual.

The concept of GD has seen significant development over the last seven decades, particularly in the *Diagnostic and Statistical Manual of Mental Disorders* (DSM), 'a compendium of all officially recognized diagnoses used in psychiatry and specifies the symptoms that must be present [and] the product of the first systematic effort to create an official classification scheme for psychiatric disorders in the United States' (Black and Grant 2014, xvii) and elsewhere in the world. The notion of 'transsexualism', a purported psychiatric aberration associated with gender identity and expression, debuted in the DSM-III in 1980, even though the pilot versions of the DSM in 1952 and 1968 made no mention of gender diagnosis. Transsexualism was regarded as evident in those who experienced unease with their genitalia and were keen to excise them, and were obsessed with wearing clothes that were more 'appropriate' for the opposite gender. This simplistic pathologisation of transgender lives persisted right through to the DSM-IIIR in 1987. By this time, there was increasing awareness that while the incipience of 'Gender Identity Disorder' (GID) could be traced to, and remain within childhood, it could also continue into adulthood without a desire to appropriate either the biology or appearance of the opposite gender.

This pathologisation persisted in the DSM-IV in 1994, although people were increasingly becoming discontented with the notion of transgender subjectivities as a mental disorder. A dilemma arose.

Despite the fact that experts were eager to dismantle the discrimination and stigma associated with GID, they were also aware that this act of de-pathologisation could preclude access to healthcare that was pertinent for transgender people and entrench an attitude of dismissiveness towards them, particularly by family and friends. The consequent name change from 'Gender Identity Disorder' to 'Gender Dysphoria' in the DSM-5 in 2013 was significant in that that gender dysphoria, not gender identity, became the issue of health concern. Additionally, the formulation of GD is more expansive as it includes any form of non-normative gender identity beyond the transgender subjectivity, such as intersex and genderqueer people (see American Psychiatric Association 2013; Black and Grant 2014; Byne et al. 2018; Kraus 2015; Narrow and Cohen-Kettenis 2010).

All my research participants spoke of GD at various stages in their lives, with the vast majority attesting to its persistent prevalence. While this discontent is often experienced in the form of physical discomfort, a few trans men also mention that they are emotionally afflicted in various ways. In response to such vicissitudes, trans men perform coping strategies that allow them to navigate numerous forces that seek to interrupt their gender identities. In the pages that follow, I first provide a comprehensive overview of the bodily lack and excess that trans men experience in the living out of their gender identity. Then, I provide a detailed disclosure of the emotional turmoil that they undergo due to GD. Finally, I turn my attention to the diverse and creative coping mechanisms that Malaysian trans men appropriate to mitigate such upheavals.

Confronting Corporeal Lack/Excess

The bodily experiences of my research participants underscore 'an unacknowledged understanding of the human body as a completely reliable truth-teller' (Middelthon and Colapietro 2012, 162). Trans men often find themselves at enmity with bodies that are assigned as female and woman by society, and these bodies as counterintuitive to their subjectivities. This sense of corporeal unfamiliarity stems from a deeply intuited cognisance that because 'female bodies' do not cohere with their self-affirmed gender identities, the absence of key anatomies constitutes a form of privation, while the unyielding persistence of others proves to be superfluous and even inhibitive to gender identity.

'The Body Doesn't Tally with the Mind': Rejecting the Female Body

Aarone describes a state of being 'dysphoric' in relation to his body, which he feels necessitates 'surgery' as a certain remedy:

> *Goh*: How do you feel about your body now?
>
> *Aarone*: Er, I still have the dysphoric, so … that's the reason why, er, the planning of surgery is in the pipeline.
>
> *Goh*: Can you say what it means for you to be dysphoric, er, about your body?
>
> *Aarone*: Meaning … the body doesn't tally with the, with the mind, with the self … so it's very stressful. Stressful, because it's not the body that I want. It's not the body that is supposed to tally with what's going on inside myself. And, erm, because of that, I push myself to take up a lot of er, physical activities such as playing sports which is always good. So part of it, because of that. So that I will develop muscles, I would, I will not have so much of the, what do you call that, female figure, kind of thing?

Aarone unpacks his feelings of GD as the state in which his 'body doesn't tally with [his] mind'. For many trans men like Aarone, 'the body is a knower and a producer of knowledge, an inscriber, not only a site of inscription or embodied knowledge' (Middelthon and Colapietro 2012, 162). His use of 'body' refers principally to the anatomical assemblages in which the notion of femaleness is uncritically translated into womanliness. Aarone's parallel use of 'mind' with 'the self' and 'what's going on inside' demonstrates the belief that a self-affirmed gender identity—and by extension, the self-affirmed 'self'—resides in the realm of the mind and emotions that must somehow be somatically translated. While the body may betray and act contradictorily to gender identity, the mind and the emotions manifest uninterrupted fidelity. This act of fracturing himself into three distinct but interrelated categories of body, mind and emotions becomes an important way by which he is able to make sense of his gender identity.

'The incongruities of a mismatched sex and gender' (Brown 2016, 16), indeed between the body and the mind, leads to a 'stressful' stage, or tensions and struggles with his present dysphoria. Aarone's emphatic statement that his current body is undesirable underscores an intense desire to align his physicality with his mental and emotional states. His pursuit of becoming more manly plays out concretely through a self-induced impetus to engage in 'a lot of … physical activities such as playing sports'. The correlation between male (hyper)masculinity, (hyper)muscularity and sports is well documented (Gorely et al. 2003; Hunt et al. 2013; Kidd 2013; Kossakowski et al. 2020; Muir et al. 2020). This is a doing of gender that is at once a survival strategy which enables him to 'develop muscles' and thus mitigate a 'female figure' in accordance with 'discursive formations created by the articulation of degrees of muscularity, sport and gender-appropriate embodiment' (Gorely et al. 2003, 437). Physical activities and sports, which constitute a 'male practice' (Kidd 2013, 554) and contribute to muscular development, are thus conscripted as masculinising mobilisations that simultaneously attenuate his 'womanliness' and accentuate his 'manliness'. He is thus able to excise an excess while building up a lack. Nevertheless, this is a short-term strategy before 'surgery'.

Some trans men like Adam experience GD on a less severe level. The remaining 'twenty per cent' that he feels is due to his 'genitals':

> *Goh*: How do you feel about your body now?
>
> *Adam*: I feel good. I er, of course the surgery is not as beautiful as most of us want it to be. But … I'm reasonably satisfied. Because I like to have erm, bigger dick, longer dick. Then I'm thinking cisgender man also want that, bigger dick (laughs) … I think erm, it's probably eighty percent gone lah this gender dysphoria. But probably the twenty percent because of the genitals. For me, it does not feel or look male enough. Erm, so, but fortunately I'm not naked walking around or looking at my mirror naked all the time, so … it's not in my erm, consciousness most of the time. But sometimes … I feel like, that's not how it's supposed to look like. That's not how it's supposed to feel like, you know. But I would say … live with it lah! (laughs).

What I find noteworthy is that while Adam has undergone phalloplasty, 'the construction of a penis, using tissue from the patient's forearm, groin, or abdomen' (Hansbury 2005, note 6, 254), the surgical procedure does not produce the desired effect in its fullness. He finds himself only 'reasonably satisfied' only because he does not have the desired penis size and length. Adam justifies this desire by making an assumption that a 'cisgender man [would] also want [a] bigger [penis]'. Cromwell's assertion that 'it is a very rare transman or FTM who has never wished he could have a large erection' (1999, 114), and logically, a larger penis, is particularly apt here.

Adam's assumption is important, as it encapsulates an active process of analogy through which a man who was assigned female at birth grows in resemblance to a man. He is, as it were, *putting on* what he sincerely believes as the mind of a cisgender man in order to *become* a cisgender man. The desire for a larger and lengthier appendage stems from a belief that 'it does not feel or look male enough'. The yardstick with which to determine the measure of maleness in any conclusive manner is evidently arbitrary. Yet Adam utilises what he sees as a bodily lack of maleness to achieve maleness. The idealised penis, 'the most powerful signifier of manhood' (Devor 1993, 311)—which I would translate as the most desired signifier of maleness for many trans men— remains unachievable. As I mention elsewhere in relation to the importance of the penis for masculinities:

> the biological-discursive constructions of a penis [act as] *consolidating constitutors* of gender, in that the presence/absence of genital materiality is brought into confluence with pre-existing socio-cultural dictations of gendered categories in order to consolidate and constitute a logical interpretation of the sexual subjectivity (2018, 18; original emphasis)

Hence, maleness is enervated by the absence of the penis. Adam attempts to deflect these feelings of deficiency through a double-layered strategy. First, he avoids performing a protracted gaze at his naked body. In so doing, this deficiency is removed from the forefront of his 'consciousness most of the time'. This distancing holds a malescaped body in suspension as an unfinished project. Adam experiences reasonable satisfaction with an accomplished feat that is concomitantly an unreached goal as his body retains a certain femaleness and is thus 'not how it's supposed to look [and] feel like'. Second, he engages in self-motivation and instructs himself 'live with it', 'it' being the corporeal imperfections that he detects within himself. This seemingly abrupt and callous approach to what he is going through is a method to avoid being submerged under what can develop into petty dissatisfactions. Adam resorts to a qualified acceptance in which he is aware that he does indeed have a manly body, albeit falling short of ideal standards.

While Adam decides not to dwell on his bodily 'shortcomings' and learns to accept what he perceives to be the lack of perfection, Superman devises a strategy in which the 'soul' is accorded a higher status than the body:

Goh: Okay erm, how do you feel about your body right now?

Superman: Er, I feel comfortable, but I will say that only sixty percent level. Erm, because I am moving towards er, you know, my ideal self which is my highest self. So, I'm taking it one day at a time, you know. For me, the body is not as important as my soul.

Goh: You mentioned your ideal self ... What does that mean?

Superman: Basically I'm at that level where I am, I'm really aligned and one with unconditional love. My whole self is alive and living with unconditional love. I don't think I'm there yet, because of ego, I have a fear. So, I feel that is far more important than the physical body, because the heart and the mind can ... determine and change how you see, and how you react to the world. There are people who are paralysed, you know, and yet they can perform things that, that a strong man cannot perform. So it's really about the spirit.

In contrast with Adam who measures his GD at twenty per cent, Superman currently experiences it at forty per cent. The lack of being 'comfortable' with his present body, he muses, holds lesser significance than his 'ideal self', which he designates as his 'highest self'. In 'moving towards' this dimension of who he is, he substitutes the GD connected with his 'physical body' with a quest of the 'spirit'. He thus surmises that the 'soul', which he uses interchangeably with 'ideal self', 'highest self' and 'spirit', deserves more attention than the body.

Superman thus carves out a spirituality, an intangible yet deeply experienced sense of vivacity, to anchor him in self-appreciation despite his dysphoria. Transgender and queer people often co-opt personal spiritualities to invigorate their gender and sexual identities as a hermeneutics of gender and sexual affirmation (for instance, Beardsley and O'Brien 2016; Goh 2017; Tanis 2003; Whitehead and Whitehead 2014; Yip 2010).[2] For Superman, spirituality is constituted of 'the heart and mind', and allows him to become 'alive', 'aligned' and united with 'unconditional love'. Spirituality is a project that harbours greater profundity in meaning and goal, and enables him to be more fully in control of his GD.

Superman's reference to feats of strength by 'people who are paralysed' is an example that he uses to express an interior strength that emanates from his 'highest self' and provides the means to navigate

[2] The importance of spirituality and religiosity in the production of (trans)gender identities is discussed in greater length in 'Performing Faith'.

his body and the realities around him because it is able to assist him in 'determin[ing] and chang[ing]' his 'react[ions]'. Elijah Adiv Edelman and Lal Zimman assert that 'discourse and the body [are] inextricably linked such that discourse does not override the truth of the body but rather brings it into social existence' (2014, 674). The act of bringing the spirituality and the body into convergence is a discursive exercise of gender meaning-making and sense-making for Superman towards 'a greater feeling of wholeness' (Tanis 2003, 158).

I suggest that Superman is actually drawing on the dynamics of the 'highest self' to address his GD. In placing the soul above the body, he is able to exercise greater control over his GD and strive towards 'spiritual health [which] depends on sorting out this disconnect and moving toward integrity in [his] experience of gender identity' (Whitehead and Whitehead 2014, 176). While '[he's] at that level where [he is]' his 'highest self', this pursuit has not reached perfect completion as he is hampered by 'ego' and 'fear'. Nevertheless, the degree of imperfection that he experiences in the soul is lesser than that which he feels in his body. Yet, by designating his body as a project that can never achieve the same level of importance as the soul, any lack of 'success' in transforming himself into a man is compensated with the mounting 'success' of growing into his 'highest self'.

'There's Something Around Your Chest': Binding

In many parts of the world, breasts are expected and accepted as social markers of femininity (Devor 2016; Dozier 2005; La et al. 2019; Summers-Effler 2004), and Malaysia is no exception (Abdullah and Yip 2004). To a certain extent, I agree with Cromwell that 'breasts are hated more than genitals, which the majority of people in one's life do not see' (1999, 106). However, not all my research participants necessarily *hate* their breasts (or their genitals), even if the greater number of them feel estranged from these body parts and see them as foreign appendages that contribute to their GD.

For this very reason, binding, or 'the process of flattening one's breasts to have a more masculine or flat appearing chest' (Brown 2016, 204) through the use of 'elastic bands, belts, or bandages' (Pfeffer 2017, 36) becomes a necessary procedure for many trans men to maintain their gender identities as men, particularly for those who have yet to, or do not wish to undergo 'top' or 'chest reconstructive surgery'

(Marinkovic and Newfield 2017).[3] This practice also provides them with some assurance of public safety (Ekins and King 2006). The fact that binding is a necessity does render this practice as a negative experience, as Pokerface explains:

> I would like live my life as a male, and I wanted to have a family, a kid, with my girlfriend, and I want to be comfortable in my own skin ... and like I can just go out without having the need to bind my chest, and I can just take my shirt off when I'm doing sports, like football, badminton, you know, those things that I like, but for now, I can't do all that ... when females reach puberty have menses right, girls, ugh, dysphoria, because I don't really like having a menses, and it just feels weird. Then when I'm going out, I bind my chest, that's why I feel like, who on earth have to bind your chest?

Pokerface begins with practical social arrangements which contribute directly to what it means for him to 'live [his] life as a male'. His mention of having a 'family' and a 'kid' with his 'girlfriend' denotes the semiotic significance of the nuclear family for the performance of heteronormativity and cisnormativity (Hubbard 2000; Kitzinger 2005; O'Reilly 2004), in which he seems eager to participate. A nuclear family assures an inconspicuous but lauded masculinity in which heteronormativity and cisnormativity are its unspoken but obligatory constituents.

Pokerface also expresses an interest in 'football [and] badminton'—activities which are often associated with masculinity. Nevertheless, his desire to engage in 'sports' extends beyond mere physical activity to the ability and freedom of 'just tak[ing his] shirt off'. Becoming a (trans) man through sports for Pokerface is less a matter of skill and strength than it is an issue of socially acceptable upper body nakedness in which he, like 'many female-bodied transpeople[, desire to] become *invisible* by living as men' (Cromwell 1999, 11; added emphasis). As previously discussed in relation to Aarone, sports and muscularity are inexorably connected to normative performances of male masculinity.

Binding is often an effective method to relieve trans men of GD (Lee et al. 2019), but it does not appear to be the case in its entirety for Pokerface. The doings of 'man' which allow him 'to be comfortable in [his] own skin' are interrupted by 'the need to bind [his] chest'.

[3] For a lengthier discussion, see 'Embarking on Medical Transitioning'.

Although binding enables him to pass as man in society, it is done so in secrecy. The revelation of binding on the torso of a person who was assigned female at birth but now lives as a man compromises on passing. Binding thus acts as a double-edged sword that both conceals and reveals the precariousness of gender identity, and precludes greater bodily exposure and freedom. Although his question, 'who on earth [has] to bind [their] chest?' might seem rhetorical for a trans man at first blush, I would also interpret it as a cry of frustration and exasperation for having to repeatedly engage in a counterintuitive activity.

It is interesting that Pokerface discusses binding at the same time that he expresses his displeasure with 'menses', a 'quintessentially female' (Cromwell 1999, 105) feature which emerges at 'puberty' and makes him feel 'weird'. In addition to binding, Pokerface perceives menstruation as incommensurate with being a man. It is likely that akin to Aaron Devor's research participants, Pokerface's sense of repugnance stems from the reality of being 'subjected to unrelenting social pressures to abandon [his] tomboyish ways and join the ranks of womanhood' and a realisation that '[he was not a boy] and would not grow up to be [a man]' (2016, 193). Therefore, menstrual flow is a reality that invalidates his gender identity as much as does binding.

Aarone's articulation of GD at the outset of this Chapter as 'the body [not] tally[ing] with … the mind' is echoed in Ray's experiences and his desire for Gender Affirming Surgery (GAS)[4] (Selvaggi et al. 2018) due to the discomfort of binding:

Goh: When you say that you want to change your body to sort of coincide with what's in your mind, what's in your mind?

Ray: The body would be more, would cut a more masculine figure definitely. Also the comfort, but for me it's like, because when I bind it's uncomfortable because of my large size, and it's very restrictive because while I know I look down it's more in line with what I want to look, at the same time when I bind I'm reminded that it's there, it's like you know there's something around your chest, that you're pushing it down. So it's not, I don't think it's healthy in the long term, so I'd rather get surgery, and just get it over and done with.

Akin to Adam who has an archetypical image of what a cisgender man 'should' look like, Ray also has an abstract notion of 'a more masculine

[4] See 'Embarking on Medical Transitioning' for a lengthier analysis.

figure'—as opposed to a more feminine figure at present—that would appear when he 'get[s] surgery'. provides an interim solution to GD because it allows him to be 'more in line with [how he] want[s] to look' and accords him the luxury of a more 'manly' presentation, congruent with 'many trans men [who] use binders to give their chests a more male appearance and relieve some of the dysphoria they feel about their bodies' (Seamont 2018, 102). Nevertheless, inasmuch as binders are devices that can affirm his gender identity, binders are also a constant reminder of excess, restraint and repression. Ray looks at binding as an '[un] healthy' practice of 'pushing down … something around [his] chest' and thus less than ideal in the long run. I suggest that the unhealthy dimension of binding is both physical and mental. The act of 'pushing down' or flattening breasts is simultaneously the force to obliterate markers of womanliness and femininity.

Many trans men experience chest binding as inconvenient, unhealthy, painful and even life threatening, but a necessary daily exercise (Fletcher 2020; Marinkovic and Newfield 2017; Peitzmeier et al. 2017; Seamont 2018). Ray realises that surgery will furnish him with better man presentation, and allow him to relinquish the discomfort of binding. He is cognisant that 'because of [his] large size', or the bigger proportions of his breasts, binding becomes a 'restrictive' experience. It is particularly noteworthy that 'larger chest sizes [have] primarily [been] associated with self-reported skin and soft tissue health outcomes' (Peitzmeier et al. 2017, 73). This restriction is not only an allusion to obvious physical constraints and possible health risks that come with binding— it is also indicative of the gender restrictions that come with having to bind his chest, even if they bring temporary relief for GD. Surgery will 'get [these quandaries] over and done with'.

Pokerface's and Ray's sentiments are echoed in Axman's impression of binding, which include economic and hygienic aspects:

Goh: How do you feel about your body?

Axman: I like it a lot less now because I'm not able to work out, because given that I'm driving full time, I need the money. I need to pay my bills … But of course I'm looking at other ways to gradually ease out of it and still be able to make my financial commitments. And of course I want to be able to afford back my, you know, the fitness whole thing, the whole fitness life. Because if you really want to delve into it, the level that I've been to before, it can be very costly, you know.

Goh: And how do you view binding?

Axman: I don't like it (laughs). Because binders are expensive for one thing, and … you have to wash them pretty much on a daily basis. And when you don't have, you can't go out, that sort of thing. And it would be nice if I already had top surgery. If I want to go, just go down and get something from my car, I can just go without a shirt.

Upon my enquiry on how he 'feel[s] about [his] body', Axman quips that he 'likes it a lot less' because of his inability to 'work out'—a masculinising practice not unlike the one envisioned by Aarone. A 'full time' job as a Grab Car rideshare driver (2018) prevents him from performing exercises at the gym that can masculinise his body, thus reducing the GD that he feels. The job is currently essential and thus a non-negotiable feature in his life, as it 'need[s] to pay [his] bills'. Torn between the demands of 'financial commitments' that requires him to give up the gym, and the lure of 'work[ing] out' in order to become 'manlier', Axman chooses the first option. He is, however, strategising ways in which he can be financially stable while appropriating 'the whole fitness [way of] life'.

Axman and Pokerface share a similar proclivity to appear unclad from the waist up in public. While Pokerface expresses a desire to be topless during sporting activities, Axman speaks of simple acts of 'go[ing] out' or 'get[ting] something from [his] car … without a shirt [on]'. This act appears to be trivial, but the seeming banality of it can propel him into the realm of manness. It is for this purpose that Axman aspires towards 'top surgery'.

Meanwhile, he relies on binders, although he expresses a dislike for using them as these devices are 'expensive'. Moreover, binders require laundering 'on a daily basis' as they have been known to cause hygiene-related skin issues (Peitzmeier et al. 2017). His reference to the high costs of binders could possibly be a reference to those that are 'specially made of dense, minimally stretchy material in a tank top style garment' (Seamont 2018, 102), although binders also comprise 'commercially available sports bras, layering shirts, compression bandages or even tape' (Lee et al. 2019, 969; see also Peitzmeier et al. 2017). While both binders and his desired 'level' of gym patronage 'can be very costly', he seems to express a preference for the latter. This preference, I submit, emerges from what I see having to choose between one practice that allows him to pass in a limited manner by concealing his breasts, to another practice that provides a more expansive method of passing as man through a bulkier, manlier frame before ultimately moving to 'top surgery'. The construction of a masculine appearance through exercise seemingly sits squarely between the use of binders and chest reconstructive surgery.

'This Is Not the Body': Dictating Bodily Contact

Some trans men avoid bodily contact with women, owing to the fact that close proximity serves as a reminder of the biological similarities that they continue to share with women. Jon provides insights into the complexities of contact that permeate his life by comparing himself with a 'lesbian woman':

> For me the lesbian woman, they identify … as a woman, they like to dress, they like to make up, they have no … struggle with them as a woman, they will feel comfortable as a woman, and they attract in woman … I don't like, even I feel their lifestyle with me is totally different … let's say … they're two womans with hug by themselves, they can hold hand … but I'm not, I'm not comfortable a woman hug me a lot … only my partner.

Although he was assigned female at birth, and despite the fact that some trans men have a lesbian history (Brown 2016; Cromwell 1999), Jon distances himself from any similarities with lesbian women. Lesbian individuals, he surmises, do not 'struggle … as [women]' who are 'attract[ed to] wo[men]'. In this context, Jon is implying that his attraction to women as a man does not unsettle him as would being attracted to women as a woman. He certainly 'feel[s that the] lifestyle' of lesbian women who are inclined to 'dress [and] make up … is totally different' to his, yet it is not only their presentation as women loving women that he feels at odds with.

In this respect, Jon's narrative brings to mind relationships between trans men and cis women (Devor 2016; Pfeffer 2017), and/or Megan Sinnott's description of the Thai butch-femme relationships between a *tom* and a *dee*. *Toms* are both 'masculine beings, who express their masculinity in their personality, dress, and sexual attraction to females' and 'transgendered female[s], with a core, inborn masculine soul' (2008, 134). *Dees*, conversely, are '"ordinary women" … who [are] normatively attracted to a masculine partner who could either be male or female bodied' (Sinnott 2008, 134).

Jon notes that lesbian lovers are comfortable with bodily contact with each other, including 'hug[ging]'and hand-holding. Conversely, he discovers that he is 'not comfortable' with being embraced by a woman, except for his 'partner', whose presentation and demeanour as he describes to me over the course of our conversation mirrors that of a *dee*'s. Jon's sense of unease is typical of *toms* who are 'unwilling to be touched sexually by their partners or to remove their clothes during sex' (Sinnott 2008, 140). While this 'untouchability' (Sinnott 2008, 140) emerges from a proactive sexual approach by *toms* to pleasure *dees*, it could also 'stem from insecurity and embarrassment over their female bodies and fear that their lovers do not want to be reminded that they are not with real men' (Sinnott 2004, 147). The exception he makes in regard to his partner could be due to the latter's unconditional acceptance of his subjectivity.

There are, however, several layers of complexity pertaining to this alienation from his body:

> Even my cousin is a ladies, yes of course from young I saw her as a baby, I raise her up, is very close to me; even she hug me I also feel uncomfortable, because she is a lady. I no problem be hug with a man, a guy, but I got problem hug with another girl. Then this is why I feel that I am not a lesbian, because lesbian will then, two ladies open their clothes face to face is nothing problem. They love each other body, themselves and the opposite. But for me, I don't love my body. I even don't want my partner touch my body. Because this is not the body suppose belong to me.

The discomfort that Jon experiences through bodily contact with a woman extends even to a lady 'cousin' with whom he shares a closeness and whom he 'raise[d] … as a baby'. The reference to this cousin is significant, as it buttresses the uneasiness he experiences in being physically close with a woman as a man, even someone with whom he is deeply familiar and towards whom he harbours no romantic attraction. His earlier mention that his 'partner' was the only exception in this regard is contradicted by a subsequent statement that he 'do[esn't] even want [his] partner to touch [his] body'.

What emerges to the fore is the reality that as a man who was assigned female at birth, he feels conflicted about sharing his body—on numerous levels—with a woman who was assigned female at birth. Jon's experiences correspond to other findings in which 'it was only after [trans men] had manly bodies that they were first able to enjoy looking at themselves in mirrors when naked, allowing others to look at them naked, permitting others to touch their bodies freely, and taking pleasure in solo sexuality' (Devor 2016, 491).

He finally reveals the source of his discomfort as the inability to 'love [his] body' as a man who continues to bear female characteristics. In its current form, 'this is not the body [that is] suppose[d to] belong to [him]'. I am convinced that bodily contact with a woman—either a relative or his own partner—unleashes an unbearable reminder of an unresolved 'womanliness' that resides in his body, the risk of a lack of manliness that resonates with Sinnott's findings (2004, 2008). Bodily contact propels him to see, as it were, a reflection of his own body that pronounces him as woman, not man.

These feelings of being estranged from his body reinstate him as a man who is attracted to women and a non-lesbian, because he is not comfortable to 'open [his] clothes' in the presence of a woman. Moreover, while lesbians revel in their own bodies as women, and in the bodies of other women, he 'do[esn't] love [his] body'. As such, although he is attracted to women, a pursuance of this attraction through physical intimacy repels and distances him from himself. Ironically, that which makes him feel 'truly manly' is also that which makes him feel 'less manly'.

Jon's idea that he does not bear 'the body [that is] suppose[d] to belong to [him]' is shared by Braveheart who also feels that his 'body is something that is not [his] to begin [with]'. There is no reluctance on his part in being physically intimate with women, but he resists any form of bodily contact in which he finds himself a passive recipient:

> Trans guys are guys who are in the wrong body. The body is something that is not ours to begin, and anything remotely in relation to sex for pleasure is a taboo like penetrative sex. If that's the case, I might as well be the other gender. No penetration, no oral thing on me, yucks! As a cis guy, since I don't have a dick I use the strap-on for those who want it, but some gals who are still virgins then the oral sex comes to play. But I will not allow any woman to perform on me like oral or penetration as how I would on them. No way! I'm not a lesbian.

Braveheart's sense of alienation from his body stems from his overarching belief that 'trans guys' like himself—although he also sees himself as a 'cis guy'—'are in the wrong body', even though not all trans men agree with the notion, or share the same experience of being born into an erroneous corporeality (Cromwell 1999; heinz 2016). These actualities aside, it is imperative to note that 'the phrase *wrong body* inadequately describes the feeling that one's body is not a part of one's self' (Cromwell 1999, 105; original emphasis).

That which constitutes the most poignant feature of bodily misregistration is the fact 'anything [related] to sex for pleasure', namely being at the receiving end of 'penetrative sex', is interpreted as 'a taboo'. Braveheart's interpretation of 'taboo' in this context, I suggest, is not a matter of forbidden sex. By retorting that he 'might as well be the other gender', he unpacks the notion of taboo as a self-imposed prohibition of being penetrated like a woman. He thus forbids himself to experience 'sex for pleasure' if he is to play a passive role in its execution, either in terms of vaginal or oral penetration'. Braveheart, like 'most gender and sex dyphoric females [and] unlike most lesbian women, have been found to generally prefer that their sexual partners not touch them on their breasts *or manually penetrate their genitals*, as *this would call attention to their persistent femaleness*' (Devor 2016, 188; added emphasis).

Braveheart's exclamation of 'yucks!' denotes a sense of disgust in being sexually *acted upon* as a 'lesbian [woman]' rather than sexually *acting upon* a woman as a 'cis guy'. Active sexual roles for Braveheart require him to resort to devices such as a 'strap-on' with which to penetrate women 'who want it'. Braveheart seems unfazed by the fact that he does not have a penis as he is still able to engage in penetration through 'packing', or the act of 'wearing a phallic device on the groin and under clothing' (Brown 2016, 207) specifically for penetration in this context, although whether he is referring to vaginal, anal and/or oral penetration is undetermined. Alternatively, the possibility of engaging in 'oral' sex with 'gals who are still virgins' hints at the heterosexist notion of proving male masculinity through sexual conquests.

By reinstating his role as an active sex partner and interpreting it as a 'manly' position, Braveheart shares with many other trans men the experience that 'in spite of transpeople's female bodies, which society insists means that they are women, they become men and in many ways behave like other men in their respective communities' (Cromwell 1999, 12). It is evident that Braveheart is really giving voice to his sexual prowess and experience as man, not woman, to dissipate his gender dysphoria. By boasting of his skilful exploits and time-tested sexual practices with women as compensation for the lack of a penis, Braveheart presents man.

Experiencing Emotional Pain

The GD that trans men experience often manifests itself in extreme emotional turmoil and unbearable pain, such as depression and suicidal ideation (DiStefano 2008; Kohlbrenner et al. 2016; Tucker et al. 2018). Some of my research participants speak of such struggles voluminously, while others mention them casually and briefly. Although numerous intersectional issues are often implicated in suicide attempts (Cole 2009), this section concentrates on the role of GD in suicidal ideation.

'Very Emotional and Stressful': Continuing Struggle

For Pokerface, GD emerges due to a lack of 'freedom' to live as man at a desired, but presently unattainable level:

> *Goh*: What ... do you mean by dysphoria?
> *Pokerface*: When something will make you feel very emotional, and stressful, to the extent that you feel like, why me, why not others? ... every time I see something in the cis male that I like wanted so much, but I can't have it ... to be able to like have kids, get married legally, and when they have like, not to say male privilege lah, just to say they have more freedom, they can do whatever stuff they want, but not everything like for example, male can go shirtless if they want, impossible I go shirtless out there.

In response to my enquiry about his interpretation of GD, Pokerface speaks about feelings of being 'very emotional' and 'stressful' situations due to the inability to comprehend why he, and 'not others', is subjected to a mismatch between his anatomical structure and gender identity as a 'cis male'. He realises that due to this discrepancy, he is excluded from socioculturally accepted norms of 'hav[ing] kids [and] get[ting] married legally' as well as— similar to Axman as previously discussed— 'go[ing] shirtless' in public.

While Pokerface hesitatingly refers to these pursuits as 'male privilege', or the privilege 'to be seen as males on a social level' (Brown 2016, 65), I contend that he does indeed see them as privileges that are accorded to men who are assigned male at birth, and deeply desired by men who are assigned female at birth (heinz 2016). 'Why me' is thus a cry of dysphoric anguish that is fraught with emotions and stressfulness due to an acute cognisance of the unattainability of such pursuits in his current physical form.

This anguish, as I see it, is echoed in Warp's frustration at not being as fully understood as he would like to be in his struggles as a trans man:

> I think people don't realise that it's hard to be with a trans person... for a trans person to tell a cis person, you can empathise, but you will never be able to understand what it's like to be in that situation. Because you can know the things that we tell you, but in reality there's so much more and that includes your own mental state and it is indescribable and so that causes a lot of problems for partners ... Like, for my partner ... I told her, because that is what I assumed, that after my top surgery I will stop having chest dysphoria, but that's not true. I still do have it because of the experiences that I've experienced in relation to having breasts. You know, like all the sexual harassment that I've been through, all the sexual abuse like that, also weighs in a lot with the dysphoria and everything like that.

Warp lays claim to an unbridgeable chasm between the experiences of 'a trans person' and 'a cis person', even if the latter is capable of empathising with the former. While true of all human experiences, and 'while each transmasculine individual's life experience will be a unique phenomenon' (heinz 2016, 12), the ownership of trans experiences that are simultaneously unique and irreproducible for Warp locates him in a position of particular loneliness. Hence, 'when an individual experiences himself as a man but continues to have body processes that are inconsistent with his perceived gender, that causes another kind of emotional and, perhaps, psychic pain' (Greatheart 2013, 91) that can never be truly understood by those 'whose assigned birth sex matches the gender with which they identify' (heinz 2016, 8).

Warp provides an example in relation to his 'top surgery', in which his assumption that the surgical removal of breasts would dissipate his GD is proven wrong. Instead, he continues to experiences a sort of persistent multifaceted dysphoria in which the absence of breasts does not uproot traumatic encounters associated with breasts. Such realities are evidently not solely connected to a transgender subjectivity as they interlock with 'indescribable' forms of his 'mental state' that are related to harrowing experiences in the past.

The indescribability of which he speaks, which refers to the immense difficulty of effectively communicating the inner convolutions and conflicts he experiences in relation to his diverse interior upheavals, are consistent with the symptoms of Post-Traumatic Stress Disorder (PTSD) that are experienced by transgender and queer people who experience sexual violence (DiStefano 2008). Consequently, although Warp's 'offending' body parts have been removed, re-collections of 'sexual harassment' and 'sexual abuse' that are connected with them continue to linger.

The ravages of sexual abuse which he had experienced due to the presence of breasts may be a factor that persistently contributes to his disdain for any semblance of womanliness or femininity. The emotional pain and struggle Warp experiences may be mitigated by a mastectomy, but this procedure does not lead to a total diminishment of either GD or the distress that is associated with having breasts in the past. It is important for me to clarify at this juncture that I am not simplistically attributing a transgender subjectivity to sexual abuse as evident in some literature (Amran and Suriati 2013). What I am saying is that sexual abuse adds an additional layer of complexity to Warp's GD and that GD cannot be simplistically understood in terms of a one-dimensional reality.

'Battling with What Society Wants': Suicidal Ideation

The emotional pain that many trans men experience in resisting assimilation to cisnormativity, or 'the assumption that all those born male will naturally become men, and all those born female will naturally become women' (Pyne 2011, 131) in this context often prompts suicidal ideation. Suicidal thoughts among transgender people are not uncommon (Greatheart 2013; Hendricks and Testa 2012; Maguen and Shipherd 2010; Toomey et al. 2018) and official religiosity plays an important role in the processes of gender and sexual validation (Bong 2020; Goh 2018; van Klinken 2019). My focus here is on the manner in which religion contributes to suicidal ideation while personal spirituality ameliorates suicidal ideation. Warp, for example, divulges that his suicidal thoughts were connected to a fear of 'the Christian hell':

Goh: You also mentioned that you tried to commit suicide more than once.

Warp: Erm, it was mostly the stress … that religion was placing upon me at that time. Erm, well rather my belief. And I was constantly under the impression I would go to hell.

Goh: The Christian hell or the Hindu hell?

> *Warp*: Erm, the Christian one (laughs). I don't know if Hinduism has a hell to be honest, I think the Hinduism for hell, is life. Because your rebirth is like hell and *moksha* is the destiny, the destination. So I find that very interesting. As a trans person especially I find that very interesting.

Warp's current fusion of with personal spiritual insights is gender self-affirming but his initial subscription to Christianity, albeit brief, proved to be an unsettling experience.[5] He confesses to numerous suicidal attempts primarily due to the 'stress' that he experienced as a consequence of his 'belief' in Christianity and the ensuing 'impression [that he] would go to [the Christian] hell' due to his gender identity. The 'difficult relationship' (Isherwood and Stuart 1998, 52–77) between Christianity and transgender and gender-variant people continues to be the focus of much contemporary religious scholarship (Campos 2012; Cornwall 2013; Goh 2020; Watts 2002).

The thought that he would spend eternity in utter misery and agony—a terror shared by many transgender Christians globally (Tanis 2003)—is sufficient to prompt him to contemplate ending his own life, even if he ironically does not consider how suicide would actually expedite his journey towards the damnation that awaits him in everlasting existence. It is unsurprising therefore, that Warp no longer practises Christianity due to such bleak prospects.

The contrast that he paints between a 'Christian hell' and a 'Hindu hell' is significant. While the former awaits him at the end of life, the latter is what he is currently experiencing because '[hell] for [Hinduism], is life'. By stating that 'rebirth is hell', Warp seems to suggest that his gender identity and its attendant sufferings are predestined and to be encountered in the present material life, not in a later spiritual realm. The prospect of living out hell on earth and achieving '*moksha*' or 'removing suffering and attaining a state of eternal bliss' (Mohapatra 2019, 50) becomes more appealing than an eternity of suffering. One religion prompts him towards suicide due to a dreary immortality while another seems to nullify it due to the promise of ultimate liberation and perpetual happiness. These ideas are possibly what he refers to as 'very interesting [for] a trans person'.

[5] See a detailed analysis of Warp's spirituality in 'Performing Faith'.

Superman also reels from religion-induced GD:

> My psychologist gave me coping techniques for my anxieties, 'cause after a while I developed anxiety attacks and panic attacks. I was a bit suicidal as well. Erm, so she told me things about breathing. She introduced me to see and learn about cognitive behaviour therapy. That helped a lot. Erm, she introduced me to concepts that were very helpful lah, lifelong concepts. So I'd say she helped a lot. It was just that I realised that I couldn't connect with her ... because I'm just on a ... different plane of consciousness, I connect with spirit more.

Superman's GD manifests as 'anxiety attacks' and suicidal inclinations. Initially, he seeks assistance and support from a psychologist who equips him with 'lifelong concepts' and 'coping techniques' that range from 'things about breathing'—which suggest strategies to counter hyperventilation during 'panic attacks'—to 'cognitive behavioural therapy', or a treatment that involves the transformation of mindsets to achieve mental wellbeing. Researchers note the pivotal role that healthcare professionals play 'to provide competent mental health services to trans clients' (Hendricks and Testa 2012, 466), and Superman's experiences demonstrate the immense significance of such services.

While these measures 'helped a lot' in keeping his tensions and suicidal thoughts at bay, Superman senses an inability to 'connect with [his psychologist]' as they are both 'on a ... different plane of consciousness'. What he appears to mean is that while he appreciates and has benefitted from the diversity of these taught skills, 'he connect[s] with [the] spirit more'. I suggest that this spiritual dimension is a deepening of personal discernment, which 'leads to a peaceful decision and a mood of consolation' (Whitehead and Whitehead 2014, 183), and which buoys him through GD. What I perceive as especially significant here is that the complementarity of psychological treatment and the formulation of a personal spirituality forms a double-charged strategy of empowerment to relieve GD. As Cromwell aptly articulates in relation to transgender people, 'all things carry equal value: body, identity (spiritual, as well as personal and social) [as it through] the reconstruction – reassociation and reconnection with the body [that] a transperson becomes a whole person' (1999, 135).

Adopting Coping Mechanisms

Although the modified body can be a source of affirmation for gender identity and mitigate gender dysphoria, trans men are aware that it can also betray them in situations where they 'fail' to pass, thus positioning them in precarious situations of scrutiny and judgement. Some transgender people resort to 'drugs, alcohol, and other high-risk behaviours … as coping strategies in reaction to stigma' (Maguen and Shipherd 2010, 35; see also DiStefano 2008).

Many speak of Gender-Affirming Hormone Therapy (GAHT) (McFarlane et al. 2018) as a coping mechanism to deal with such vicissitudes that is at once a strategy of gender invisibility by which they can assimilate into society and escape inquisitive and condemnatory eyes. Others speak candidly of rejecting mainstream gender expectations by devising creative channels to confront challenges. Both approaches showcase ways in which trans men draw on bodily experiences in order to navigate and cope with the world around them, even if 'these reprieves and access are … tenuous, context-specific, and revocable' (Pfeffer 2017, 39).

'Blend into Society': Assimilation

Braveheart shares his story of how he underwent GAHT as a means of pleasing a former love interest who was willing to pledge her affection for him only if he 'fit into society' by passing as man:

Goh: So, am I right to say that the reason why you went for hormone therapy was because there was somebody who would love you if you fit into society … because your wife then said 'I can't be with you because society would not accept you in Malaysia', so that's why you decided to blend in?

Braveheart: Yes … Actually I didn't know there was such a therapy, that I could actually blend into society because being the way I am was also painful … It may look like she was the reason, which in a way was. If she had not insisted for proof, I may have not known of … treatment and began reading about the subject of gender reassignment through pamphlets and the support group which I attended regularly … It was a blessing in disguise.

What piques my interest here is that while Braveheart is cognisant that his ex-wife's[6] investment in their relationship is reliant on his ability to 'blend into society' as 'proof' that he is a man despite being assigned female at birth, he also harbours a desire to embark on GAHT due to personal reasons. In contrast with Carla A. Pfeffer's findings, Braveheart and his previous female companion are resistant towards '*not* wanting to be (mis) recognized by others as traditional or unremarkably heterosexual' (2017, 50). Instead, they are impassioned about 'acting in ways that might seem normative' and 'blending seamlessly into the social status quo' (Pfeffer 2017, 50). He acknowledges that 'being the way [he was] was also painful', a clear indication of the GD that emerges from the inability to pass and '[fit] into society', and thus preserves him as a gender outlier.

The 'insiste[nce]' that he proves himself as a man by winning societal approval in gender norms at the behest of his erstwhile lover becomes a 'blessing in disguise' as it acts as a catalyst for Braveheart's own self-enlightenment and subsequent self-transformation. Through perusing 'pamphlets' and regular participation in a 'support group'—possibly the Transmen of Malaysia (2018)[7]—he learns of 'gender reassignment' procedures. An exogenous demand for a trans man to assimilate in society is concomitantly an endogenous desire to fulfil what appears to be a long-held personal wish to overcome emotional pain by passing 'successfully' as man.

Bottle discovers however that there are severe limits to passing, particularly in situations that demand the perpetuation of the gender binary:

> And then I tried to wear without any bras, or whatever supports, just a plain singlet at the gym. The reaction given is really havoc. Okay, I'd prefer them to actually walk direct to me, and tell me, could you please wear on your bra. I can accept that better than they tell to the gym owner and indirectly asking to feedback to me. So to me, that is a coward action … the gym owner actually did tell me that, because of my … action, it affects the business, and then, maybe I can't join the gym anymore … I don't feel sad because I understand that this is the male situation because when I look into the mirror, doesn't look good as well. So, I've no choice at the moment I just follow whatever they say.

[6]The term 'ex-wife' is not meant to imply that same-sex marriages are legally permissible in Malaysia. Instead, it is used here to honour Braveheart's own description of his female companion.

[7]See 'Appendix 2: Interviewing Dorian Wilde' for more information.

Bottle recollects an incident at the gym in which his donning of a 'singlet' without a brassiere or 'whatever supports' caused a certain degree of consternation among the gym users. I suggest that this deliberately bold act on his part was not only an attempt to exercise his identity as a man, but to explore—perhaps even experiment with—the degree of 'success' with which he passes as such in a public hypermasculine and hypermuscular space. Trans men, as Miriam J. Abelson observes, 'encounter different spatially based situated knowledges that shape recognition as men in social interaction' (2019, 86). Physical exercises with man clothes thus act as the ultimate litmus test for the acceptance and approval of Bottle's gender identity. The gym, like the office and the beach for Pokerface in Chapter 3, parallels Judith Halberstam's trope of the bathroom and proves to be well and truly the curtailment or 'limit of gender identification' (1998, 23).

Nonetheless, Bottle's bold gesture broadly misses the sense of liberation experienced by one of Greatheart's (2013, 95) research participants when he took off his shirt in public and experienced 'a newfound comfort with his body, an integration of body and self, and a satisfaction of both being accepted as a man and not being exposed as trans'. Owing to the fact that the 'gym owner' approaches Bottle to admonish him on 'this action', Bottle surmises that it is his 'havoc'-causing brazen appearance that 'affects the business' and which may possibly disentitle him from 'join[ing] the gym' in the future.

That he does not 'feel sad' despite having 'no choice [but to] follow whatever [the gym owner] say[s]' suggests that Bottle admits to the reality of not being 'sufficiently man' in appearance within this space. 'The male situation' alludes to an interior assent on his part to the sense of unease with which the other gym users approach his gender presentation, and which reflects his own self-perception of not properly 'look[ing] good' in the 'mirror'. The self-acceptance and social endorsement that he longs for but which remains beyond his reach is reproduced in the attitudes of other gym users towards him.

Nevertheless, Bottle expresses his displeasure at being chided by the proprietor rather than by the patrons who are directly affected by his brazen display of gender confidence. By accusing them of performing 'a coward[ly] action', I propose that he is strategically shifting the idea of inappropriateness from not wearing a brassiere in the gym as a non-'"chest-passed"' (Greatheart 2013, 95) trans man to the inability of gym users to 'walk direct[ly] to [him]' to express their discomfort with him. I further propose that Bottle is indirectly re-constructing his maleness that suffered a blow at the gym by implying that the gym users were not, using a colloquial term, 'man enough'—their actual gender identities notwithstanding—to speak directly to him although he was 'man enough' to be a man at the gym. As such, while gym dynamics threaten to diminish Bottle's subjectivity, they can also be personally recast to elevate it.

'Sticky Situation': Disassociation

Some trans men take great pains to assimilate and thus be undifferentiated from cis men. Others engage in deliberate strategies of disassociation by challenging gender norms and expectations at workplaces and in social circles (see Cromwell 1999). In so doing, trans men are able to cope with sociocultural challenges to their gender identities. Schulz, for instance, remains unyielding in his insistence on not being identified as a woman in official work-related matters:

> I joined this place very recently ... I specifically mentioned that I wanted the 'A/P' which stands for *anak perempuan* (daughter of)[8] to be removed from my emails, er, name, signature ... When the IT (information technology) guy came in ... he gave my superior a statement saying that HR (human resources) management didn't allow for that (laughs) ... My question back to him is I'll be dealing with a lot of customers ... they're gonna question me. And sure enough, er, at the third month, someone questioned me ... People started questioning ... why does your name have an 'A/P'? I said, er, I mean, the only way I can joke about it and push it off because ... I'm sick and tired of explaining myself to people of what I am ... how many people do you want me to explain myself to? So, I told them look, IT has made a mistake (laughs), I've told them, it should be 'A/L' (*anak lelaki*, or son of) not 'A/P', and I can't do anything about it. I've told IT, they haven't done anything about it ... that's how I deal with ... this erm, very sticky situation if you can call it that.

'A/P', as does 'A/L', bridges an individual's name with that of her or his father within a patronymic name, and invariably exposes the gender of that individual. Schulz's insistence on the 'remov[al]' of 'A/P' is thus understandable as he is 'sick and tired of explaining [him]self to people'

[8] As mentioned in 'Prologue', many Malaysian Indians have patronymic names and thus lack surnames.

in relation to his subjectivity and because 'A/P' can become indisputable evidence of the gender assigned to him at birth as a Malaysian woman/female of Indian descent.

Similar to official documents such as birth certificates, driver's licenses and passports (Adair 2019; Bishop and Myricks 2004; Taylor et al. 2015), an email signature serves as 'an effective system of identification [which] depends on a stabilizing personal identity ... between a person and a set of signs' (Caplan 2001, 50). I suggest that the annoyance, weariness and frustration that accompanies the act of having to repeatedly 'explain [him]self' has less to do with an inconvenience than it does with the prospect of having to justify his gender identity in a discursive loop through electronic communication, with the possibility of being exposed as a trans man.

The anticipation of being interrogated by customers which eventually transpires, his eventual powerlessness to remedy his fears, and his unwillingness to engage with any individual who is flummoxed by the discrepancy between his appearance and official identity proves to be a 'very sticky situation'—complicated, awkward and embarrassing—for Schulz. A blame-humour-resignation confluence, namely the act of publicly naming 'IT' as responsible for this 'mistake', joking about it, and subsequently acknowledging an inability to '[do] anything about it' becomes a coping strategy of disassociation to 'deal with' the matter.

For Hadi, constant interrogations on 'gett[ing] married' and generating offspring becomes an oppressive heteronormative imposition that he addresses through various techniques of disassociation.

Hadi: When people say, no you have to get married, have a child. No that's for women, not for me ... I don't care what you say. You want ***beranak*** (to bear children) you go lah, don't ask me (laughs) ... ***mesti ada lelaki nak dengan kau*** (there must be men who would want to be with you).

Goh: ***Bila dia orang cakap macam tu***, you ***rasa macam mana***? (when they talk to you like this, how do you feel?)

Hadi: I feel very uncomfortable. I just, sometimes I want to say, 'no, no, don't talk to me like that ... just talk to others' ... Sometimes I just make jokes and say, 'okay, can, I will get married this Sunday, because everybody off' (laughs).

Goh: Okay, so in a way, when you are in front of people, you know, you just allow them to call you whatever they want.

Hadi: Yes.

Goh: But inside your heart you know you are a man.
Hadi: Yeah.

The pressure that is placed on Hadi 'to get married [and] have a child' by 'people'—alluding to acquaintances, friends and family—makes him 'feel very uncomfortable' as sociocultural expectations of marriage and progeny are intimately linked to cisgender roles and norms as a form of 'reproductive heterogenitality' (Huang 2011, 25). In a similar fashion to SR in Chapter 2, and reminiscent of his own experiences with wearing the *tudung* in the same Chapter, Hadi blatantly experiences how family and offspring are particularly imperative for the ethnic, religious and nationalistic identities of Malay-Muslims (see Siti Nor Amalina and Noraini 2019). That he does not want them to converse with him but 'to others' in this respect points to an unwillingness to engage with those who intend on steering him away from his self-affirmed gender identity.

The resoluteness of their intentions for Hadi to be married and bear children is concomitantly a forced reiteration of his identity as a woman that can potentially disqualify any attempts he makes to become a (trans)man. He recalls fragments from conversations with 'people' who assure him that 'there must be men who would want to be with [him]'. I suggest that this could be an allusion to his manly demeanour that is perceived by 'people' as detrimental to prospects of being in a relationship with a man, as well as an exhortation on their part for him to find a male companion and produce offspring.

The insistence for Hadi to be heterosexually married and 'bear children' leads him to 'feel very uncomfortable', which then prompts him to engage in various disassociative strategies to relieve this anxiety. The first strategy is to erect an interior bulwark to fend off unsympathetic remarks about his unmarried state of life from heteronormative perspectives, which takes the form of a detached attitude and deciding to '[not] care [about] what [they] say'. Hence, nonchalance acts as a form of disassociation in which 'the phenomenological body [becomes] a site of resistance to sex and gender ideologies'(Cromwell 1999, 42).

Hadi's second strategy builds on the first, in which he adopts a more truculent attitude. He reprimands those who insist that he engages in a heterosexual marriage and bears children by recasting the burden of these responsibilities on to them. If they are so adamant on having children, they should proceed without recruiting him in their personal project. Third, Hadi also 'make[s] jokes' as a strategy to dispel further questioning. By announcing that he 'will get married this Sunday, because everybody [has a day] off', he provides both a distraction and a subterfuge. Evocative of Schulz's methods, a convergence of nonchalance, indignation and hilarity helps to alleviate the heteronormative and cisnormative arsenal levelled at him.

Conclusion

The becomings of Malaysian trans men are often marked by profound experiences of bodily ambivalence and dissatisfaction. Trans men are often distressed by the dissonance they see between a masculine identity and a perceived female body. They identify these misplacements and displacements of their bodies as GD, which manifests itself in an array of emotions as well as suicidal ideation. Some see an intolerable physical deficiency in themselves while others experience an unbearable sense of bodily excess, particularly as the subjectivity that they experience cerebrally and emotionally often meets with somatic untranslatability in the Malaysian society. The strong emotional perturbations that emanate from GD are intersectional in nature. In the case of one trans man, the experience of sexual abuse in the past continues to galvanise and complicate GD despite his having undergone chest reconstructive surgery.

Although trans men speak of the inconvenience and discomfort of chest binding, they are more troubled by the risk of being publicly exposed as transgender individuals from wearing binders, a risk which effectively restricts their spatial mobility. Binders also prove to be artefacts of anxiety that unrelentingly alert trans men to the mismatch between their bodies and their self-affirmed gender identities. Some trans men recoil at the prospect of intimate touching, even by their female partners, due to the possibility of being disregarded as unreal men when their physical bodies appear in plain sight. The attainment of manness which can materialise through clothed physicality can also be its undoing through unclothed physicality. Clearly, a strong correlation between anatomy and gender persists for trans men in the pursuit of their self-affirmed gender identities.

Malaysian trans men confront and negotiate GD through a variety of strategic associations and diassociations. One method of association is to '[blend] in and [become as] unnoticeable and unremarkable' (Cromwell 1999, 39) as possible. In so doing, trans men invisibilise themselves in order to circumvent any possibility of dispute regarding their gender identities. Techniques of disassociation include the conscription of blame, umbrage, humour, nonchalance and acquiescence to situations beyond personal control. One particularly important finding is the role that formal religion plays in the deterioration of mental and emotional health among trans men, including suicidal ideation. Contrarily, personal spirituality prompts the formulation and deployment of subjective empowerment and affirmation, notably when spirituality is coupled with psychological care. In Southeast Asian countries like Malaysia where socio-political structures and population demographics *both* powerfully condition *and* are heavily influenced by faith systems, the role of religiosity and spirituality must be acknowledged and suitably considered in the dynamics of GD among trans men.

Bibliography

Abdullah N. Hisham, and Cheng-Har Yip. 2004. 'Overview of Breast Cancer in Malaysian Women: A Problem with Late Diagnosis'. *Asian Journal of Surgery* 27 (2): 130–33.

Abelson, Miriam J. 2019. *Men in Place: Trans Masculinity, Race, and Sexuality in America*. Minneapolis, MN: University of Minnesota Press.

Adair, Cassius. 2019. 'Licensing Citizenship: Anti-Blackness, Identification Documents, and Transgender Studies'. *American Quarterly* 71 (2): 569–94.

American Psychiatric Association. 2013. *¿: DSM-5*. Arlington, VA: American Psychiatric Association.

Amran Hassan, and Suriati Ghazali. 2013. 'Sexual Abuse and Childhood Traumatic Experience: A Case Study on the Psychological Health of Transsexuals in Malaysia'. *International Journal of Environment, Society and Space* 1 (1): 33–42.

Beardsley, Christina, and Michelle O'Brien. 2016. *This Is My Body: Hearing the Theology of Transgender Christians*. London: Darton, Longman & Todd.

Beek, Titia F., Peggy T. Cohen-Kettenis, and Baudewijntje P. C. Kreukels. 2016. 'Gender Incongruence/Gender Dysphoria and Its Classification History'. *International Review of Psychiatry* 28 (1): 5–12.

Bishop, Elena P., and Noel Myricks. 2004. 'Sex Reassignment Surgery: When Is a "He" a "She" for the Purpose of Marriage in the United States?' *American Journal of Family Law* 18 (1): 30–35.

Black, Donald W., and Jon E. Grant. 2014. *DSM-5 Guidebook: The Essential Companion to the Diagnostic and Statistical Manual of Mental Disorders*. Arlington, VA: American Psychiatric Publishing.

Bong, Sharon A. 2020. *Becoming Queer and Religious in Malaysia and Singapore*. New York: Bloomsbury Academic.

Brown, Michael Eric. 2016. *A Herstory of Transmasculine Identities: An Annotated Anthology*. Miami, FL: Boundless Endeavors, Inc.
Byne, William, Dan H. Karasic, Eli Coleman, A. Evan Eyler, Jeremy D. Kidd, Heino F. L. Meyer-Bahlburg, Richard R. Pleak, and Jack Pula. 2018. 'Gender Dysphoria in Adults: An Overview and Primer for Psychiatrists'. *Transgender Health* 3 (1): 57–70.
Campos, Michael Sepidoza. 2012. 'The Baklâ: Gendered Religious Performance in Filipino Cultural Spaces'. In *Queer Religion*, edited by Donald L. Boisvert and Jay Emerson Johnson, 2:2: 167–91. Santa Barbara, CA: Praeger.
Caplan, Jane. 2001. '"This or That Particular Person": Protocols of Identification in Nineteenth-Century Europe'. In *Documenting Individual Identity: The Development of State Practices in the Modern World*, edited by Jane Caplan and John Torpey, 49–66. Princeton, NJ: Princeton University Press.
Cole, Elizabeth R. 2009. 'Intersectionality and Research in Psychology'. *American Psychologist* 64 (3): 170–80.
Cornwall, Susannah. 2013. 'British Intersex Christians' Accounts of Intersex Identity, Christian Identity and Church Experience'. *Practical Theology* 6 (2): 220–36.
Cromwell, Jason. 1999. *Transmen and FTMs: Identities, Bodies, Genders, and Sexualities*. Urbana, IL: University of Illinois Press.
Devor, Aaron. 1993. 'Sexual Orientation Identities, Attractions, and Practices of Female-to-Male Transsexuals'. *The Journal of Sex Research* 30 (4): 303–15.
———. 2016. *FTM: Female-to-Male Transsexuals in Society*. Bloomington, IN: Indiana University Press.
DiStefano, Anthony S. 2008. 'Suicidality and Self-Harm Among Sexual Minorities in Japan'. *Qualitative Health Research* 18 (10): 1429–41.
Dozier, Raine. 2005. 'Beards, Breasts, and Bodies: Doing Sex in a Gendered World'. *Gender and Society* 19 (3): 297–316.
Drescher, Jack. 2010. 'Queer Diagnoses: Parallels and Contrasts in the History of Homosexuality, Gender Variance, and the Diagnostic and Statistical Manual'. *Archives of Sexual Behavior* 39 (2): 427–60.
Edelman, Elijah Adiv, and Lal Zimman. 2014. 'Boycunts and Bonus Holes: Trans Men's Bodies, Neoliberalism, and the Sexual Productivity of Genitals'. *Journal of Homosexuality* 61 (5): 673–90.
Ekins, Richard, and Dave King. 2006. *The Transgender Phenomenon*. London: Sage.
Fletcher, Dawn. 2020. 'The Positive Impact of Trans Inclusion in Team Sports: Men's Roller Derby'. In *The Palgrave Handbook of Masculinity and Sport*, edited by Rory Magrath, Jamie Cleland, and Eric Anderson, 171–87. Cham, Switzerland: Palgrave Macmillan.

Goh, Joseph N. 2017. 'Bridging Benedictions, Enlightening Embodiment: Interpretations of Spirit through Desire among Gay and Bisexual Malaysian Men'. *Journal for the Study of Spirituality* 7 (2): 128–41.
Goh, Joseph N. 2018. *Living Out Sexuality and Faith: Body Admissions of Malaysian Gay and Bisexual Men*. London: Routledge.
Goh, Joseph N. 2020. 'Trans/Forming Church in the Asia Pacific Region: Narratives of Hospitable Ecclesiology by Philippine and Tongan Transgender Women'. *QUEST: Studies on Religion & Culture in Asia* 4: 1–17.
Gorely, Trish, Rachel Holroyd, and David Kirk. 2003. 'Muscularity, the Habitus and the Social Construction of Gender: Towards a Gender-Relevant Physical Education'. *British Journal of Sociology of Education* 24 (4): 429–48.
Grab. 2018. 'GrabCar'. Grab MY. https://www.grab.com/my/car/.
Greatheart, Marcus. 2013. *Transforming Practice: Life Stories of Transgender Men That Change How Health Providers Work*. Toronto, Canada: Ethica Press.
Halberstam, Judith. 1998. *Female Masculinity*. Durham, NC: Duke University Press.
Hansbury, Griffin. 2005. 'The Middle Men: An Introduction to the Transmasculine Identities'. *Studies in Gender and Sexuality* 6 (3): 241–64.
heinz, matthew. 2016. *Entering Transmasculinity: The Inevitability of Discourse*. Chicago, IL: Intellect Ltd.
Hendricks, Michael L., and Rylan J. Testa. 2012. 'A Conceptual Framework for Clinical Work with Transgender and Gender Nonconforming Clients: An Adaptation of the Minority Stress Model'. *Professional Psychology: Research and Practice* 43 (5): 460–67.
Huang, Hans Tao-Ming. 2011. *Queer Politics and Sexual Modernity in Taiwan*. Hong Kong: Hong Kong University Press.
Hubbard, Philip. 2000. 'Desire/Disgust: Mapping the Moral Contours of Heterosexuality'. *Progress in Human Geography* 24 (2): 191–217.
Hunt, Christopher John, Karen Gonsalkorale, and Stuart B. Murray. 2013. 'Threatened Masculinity and Muscularity: An Experimental Examination of Multiple Aspects of Muscularity in Men'. *Body Image* 10 (3): 290–99.
Isherwood, Lisa, and Elizabeth Stuart, eds. 1998. *Introducing Body Theology*. Sheffield, UK: Sheffield Academic Press.
Kidd, Bruce. 2013. 'Sports and Masculinity'. *Sport in Society* 16 (4): 553–64.
Kitzinger, Celia. 2005. 'Heteronormativity in Action: Reproducing the Heterosexual Nuclear Family in After-Hours Medical Calls'. *Social Problems* 52 (4): 477–98.
Kohlbrenner, Verena, Keshab Deuba, Deepak Kumar Karki, and Gaetano Marrone. 2016. 'Perceived Discrimination Is an Independent Risk Factor for Suicidal Ideation Among Sexual and Gender Minorities in Nepal'. *PLoS ONE* 11 (7).
Kossakowski, Radosław, Dominik Antonowicz, and Honorata Jakubowska. 2020. 'The Reproduction of Hegemonic Masculinity in Football Fandom:

An Analysis of the Performance of Polish Ultras'. In *The Palgrave Handbook of Masculinity and Sport*, edited by Rory Magrath, Jamie Cleland, and Eric Anderson, 517–36. Cham, Switzerland: Palgrave Macmillan.

Kraus, Cynthia. 2015. 'Classifying Intersex in DSM-5: Critical Reflections on Gender Dysphoria'. *Archives of Sexual Behavior* 44 (5): 1147–63.

La, Jessica, Sue Jackson, and Rhonda Shaw. 2019. '"Flat and Fabulous": Women's Breast Reconstruction Refusals Post-Mastectomy and the Negotiation of Normative Femininity'. *Journal of Gender Studies* 28 (5): 603–16.

Lee, Alexander, Paul Simpson, and Bridget Haire. 2019. 'The Binding Practices of Transgender and Gender-Diverse Adults in Sydney, Australia'. *Culture, Health & Sexuality* 21 (9): 969–84.

Maguen, Shira, and Jillian C. Shipherd. 2010. 'Suicide Risk Among Transgender Individuals'. *Psychology & Sexuality* 1 (1): 34–43.

Marinkovic, Maja, and Ron S. Newfield. 2017. 'Chest Reconstructive Surgeries in Transmasculine Youth: Experience from One Pediatric Center'. *International Journal of Transgenderism* 18 (4): 376–81.

McFarlane, Thomas, Jeffrey D. Zajac, and Ada S. Cheung. 2018. 'Gender-Affirming Hormone Therapy and the Risk of Sex Hormone-Dependent Tumours in Transgender Individuals—A Systematic Review'. *Clinical Endocrinology* 89 (6): 700–11.

Middelthon, Anne-Lise, and Vincent Colapietro. 2012. 'Bodies and Their Signs: Acknowledging and Interpreting Erotic Responses'. In *Understanding Global Sexualities: New Frontiers*, edited by Peter Aggleton, Paul Boyce, Henrietta L. Moore, and Richard Parker, 153–68. New York: Routledge.

Mohapatra, P. K. 2019. *An Applied Perspective on Indian Ethics*. Singapore: Springer.

Muir, Ken, Keth D. Parry, and Eric Anderson. 2020. 'Masculinity and Inclusive Rugby in the United Kingdom'. In *The Palgrave Handbook of Masculinity and Sport*, edited by Rory Magrath, Jamie Cleland, and Eric Anderson, 323–40. Cham, Switzerland: Palgrave Macmillan.

Narrow, William E., and Peggy Cohen-Kettenis. 2010. 'The Revision of Gender Identitiy Disorder: DSM-5 Principles and Progress'. *Journal of Gay & Lesbian Mental Health* 14 (2): 123–29.

O'Reilly, Andrea. 2004. *From Motherhood to Mothering: The Legacy of Adrienne Rich's* Of Woman Born. Ithaca, NY: State University of New York Press.

Peitzmeier, Sarah, Ivy Gardner, Jamie Weinand, Alexandra Corbet, and Kimberlynn Acevedo. 2017. 'Health Impact of Chest Binding Among Transgender Adults: A Community-Engaged, Cross-Sectional Study'. *Culture, Health & Sexuality* 19 (1): 64–75.

Pfeffer, Carla A. 2017. *Queering Families: The Postmodern Partnerships of Cisgender Women and Transgender Men*. New York: Oxford University Press.

Pyne, Jake. 2011. 'Unsuitable Bodies: Trans People and Cisnormativity in Shelter Services'. *Canadian Social Work Review; Ottawa* 28 (1): 129–37.

Seamont, Morgan M. H. 2018. 'Becoming "The Man I Want to Be": Transgender Masculinity, Embodiment, and Sexuality'. Boulder, CO: University of Colorado. https://scholar.colorado.edu/anth_gradetds/85.

Selvaggi, Gennaro, Christopher J. Salgado, Stan Monstrey, and Miroslav Djordevic. 2018. 'Gender Affirmation Surgery'. *BioMed Research International* 2018: 1–2.

Sinnott, Megan. 2004. Toms *and* Dees*: Transgender Identity and Female Same-Sex Relationships in Thailand.* Honolulu, HI: University of Hawaii Press.

———. 2008. 'The Romance of the Queer: The Sexual and Gender Norms of *Tom* and *Dee* in Thailand'. In *AsiaPacifiQueer: Rethinking Genders and Sexualities*, edited by Fran Martin, Peter A. Jackson, Mark McLelland, and Audrey Yue, 131–45. Urbana, IL: University of Illinois Press.

Siti Nor Amalina Ahmad Tajuddin, and Noraini Zulkepli. 2019. 'An Investigation of the Use of Language, Social Identity and Multicultural Values for Nation-Building in Malaysian Outdoor Advertising'. *Social Sciences; Basel* 8 (1): 18.

Summers-Effler, Erika. 2004. 'Little Girls in Women's Bodies: Social Interaction and the Strategizing of Early Breast Development'. *Sex Roles* 51 (1/2): 29–44.

Tanis, Justin Edward. 2003. *Trans-Gendered: Theology, Ministry, and Communities of Faith.* Cleveland, OH: Pilgrim Press.

Taylor, Jami K., Barry L. Tadlock, and Sarah J. Poggione. 2015. 'Birth Certificate Amendment Laws and Morality Politics'. In *Transgender Rights and Politics: Groups, Issue Framing, and Policy Adoption*, edited by Jami K. Taylor and Donald P. Haider-Markel, 252–72. Ann Arbor, MI: University of Michigan Press.

Tellier, Pierre-Paul. 2019. 'Improving Health Access for Gender Diverse Children, Youth, and Emerging Adults?' *Clinical Child Psychology and Psychiatry* 24 (2): 193–98.

Toomey, Russell B., Amy K. Syvertsen, and Maura Shramko. 2018. 'Transgender Adolescent Suicide Behavior'. *Pediatrics* 142 (4): e20174218.

Transmen of Malaysia. 2018. 'Transmen of Malaysia'. Facebook. https://www.facebook.com/TransmenofMalaysia/?ref=br_rs.

Tucker, Raymond P., Rylan J. Testa, Tracy L. Simpson, Jillian C. Shipherd, John R. Blosnich, and Keren Lehavot. 2018. 'Hormone Therapy, Gender Affirmation Surgery, and Their Association with Recent Suicidal Ideation and Depression Symptoms in Transgender Veterans'. *Psychological Medicine* 48 (14): 2329–36.

van Klinken, Adriaan. 2019. *Kenyan, Christian, Queer: Religion, LGBT Activism, and Arts of Resistance in Africa*. University Park, PA: Penn State University Press.
Vargas-Huicochea, Ingrid, Rebeca Robles, Tania Real, Ana Fresán, Jeremy Cruz-Islas, Hamid Vega-Ramírez, and María Elena Medina-Mora. 2018. 'A Qualitative Study of the Acceptability of the Proposed ICD-11 Gender Incongruence of Childhood Diagnosis Among Transgender Adults Who Were Labeled Due to Their Gender Identity Since Childhood'. *Archives of Sexual Behavior* 47 (8): 2363–74.
Vitelli, R., C. Scandurra, R. Pacifico, M. S. Selvino, S. Picariello, A. L. Amodeo, P. Valerio, and A. Giami. 2017. 'Trans Identities and Medical Practice in Italy: Self-Positioning Towards Gender Affirmation Surgery'. *Sexologies* 26 (4): e43–e51.
Watts, Fraser. 2002. 'Transsexualism and the Church'. *Theology & Sexuality* 9 (1): 63–85.
Whitehead, James D., and Evelyn Eaton Whitehead. 2014. 'Transgender Lives: From Bewilderment to God's Extravagance'. *Pastoral Psychology* 63 (2): 171–84.
Yip, Andrew K. T. 2010. 'Coming Home from the Wilderness: An Overview of Recent Scholarly Research on LGBTQI Religiosity/Spirituality in the West'. In *Queer Spiritual Spaces: Sexuality and Sacred Places*, edited by Kath Browne, Sally Munt, and Andrew K. T. Yip, 35–50. Surrey, UK: Ashgate.

CHAPTER 5

Embarking on Medical Transitioning

In many parts of the world, transgender people are subjected to the dehumanising horrors of pathologisation, which is 'often used interchangeably with the term "medicalization"' (Liebert 2014, 1327) or 'defining a problem in medical terms, usually as an illness or disorder, or using a medical intervention to treat it' (Conrad 2005, 3; cited in Liebert 2014). Understandably therefore, the very word 'medical' evokes undesirable images of abject abnormality and coerced therapy for many transgender people. This chapter, however, employs the term 'medical' and its cognates in a non-pathological sense.

My use of 'medical transitioning' refers to the diverse methods of gender-affirming medical treatments and procedures to address Gender Dysphoria[1] (GD) or 'the condition where individuals have a marked incongruence between their experienced or expressed gender and the one they are assigned at birth [and] have persistent discomfort with their anatomical sex' (Nanda et al. 2017, 185). As GD is experienced only minimally by some trans men, or sometimes not at all (Cromwell 1999; Greatheart 2013; Selvaggi et al. 2018; Vitelli et al. 2017), medical transitioning—principally Gender Affirmation Surgery (GAS)[2] and

[1] I explain my use of 'Gender Dysphoria' in 'Grappling with Gender Dysphoria'.

[2] Aren Aizura 'question[s] whether the language of affirmation/confirmation invests in the idea that everyone has a "true" gender identity that has always been, and that surgery merely reflects that inner, lifelong identity' (2018, 13). Nonetheless, and while cognisant

J. N. Goh, *Becoming a Malaysian Trans Man*,
Gender, Sexualities and Culture in Asia,
https://doi.org/10.1007/978-981-15-4534-4_5

Gender-Affirming Hormone Therapy (GAHT)[3]—is neither a mandatory process nor a guarantee of the dissipation of GD.[4] Transitioning is a more general description of

> The time when a person begins to living as the gender with which they identify rather than the gender they were assigned at birth, which often, but not always, includes changing one's name, and perhaps dressing or expressing their outward presentation differently. Transitioning may or may not also include medical and legal aspects, including taking hormones, having surgery, or changing identity documents … to reflect one's gender identity. (Brown 2016, 209)

'Medical transitioning' foregrounds the medical aspect of transitioning.

In my conversation with trans activist Dorian Wilde prior to fieldwork, I had initially broached the subject of trans men's subjectivities in binary terms of 'pre-operative' and 'post-operative' surgeries, a common approach in studies on Malaysian trans women or *mak nyah* (Teh 2001, 2002). Almost as though he were echoing Jason Cromwell's (1999) stand, Wilde quickly amended my trajectory, as the following narrative divulges:

> Physically we exist in so many different forms. There are some who are non-op, non-transition, which means that they don't want to transition. Minority mostly. *We don't believe in this pre-op, post-op thing.* Because that defines a sort of a designated journey that you need to be on, a start and an end. For a lot of trans people, there is no start and there is no end. The start can be anywhere from, starting with hormone shots or starting by presenting yourself as male. (Appendix 2: Interviewing Dorian Wilde, para. 17; added emphasis)

Despite a widespread notion in many societies that transitioning necessarily implies 'a social, medical, and surgical component' (Tellier 2019, 194),

of the debates surrounding notions of 'true gender identity', 'affirmation' and 'affirming' remain as my preferred terms to recognise and respect the interiority and exteriority of gender identities and expressions.

[3] During fieldwork, I used the term 'hormone replacement therapy', a term which seemed to command popular—but not absolute—currency among Malaysian trans men. Other popular terms include 'testosterone', 'T', 'hormone injection' or simply 'hormone'. Like 'GAS', my preference for 'GAHT' stems from my desire to honour gender-affirmation efforts among my research participants.

[4] For instance, see Warp's experience in 'Grappling with Gender Dysphoria'.

not all transgender people are keen on surgery or anchor their gender identities exclusively in genitalia (Abelson 2019; Aizura 2018; Burke 2011; Goh 2014; Khartini 2005). Moreover, surgeries always comprise multiple operations rather than a single procedure (Cromwell 1999). Nonetheless, very few transgender research participants whom I encounter express the intense disinclination as articulated by Wilde. In fact, almost all the trans men I interviewed express a keen willingness to undergo multifarious forms of gender-affirming transitioning.

Medical issues are ordinarily magnified in extant literature on transgender people (Gibson et al. 2016; Pearce 2018; Rowniak et al. 2011; Selvaggi et al. 2018; Teh 2008; Tucker et al. 2018). Studies on health issues pertaining to trans men include various forms of GAS and GAHT (Marinkovic and Newfield 2017; Selvaggi et al. 2018; Vitelli et al. 2017) or at least mention them (Abelson 2019; Barcelos 2019; Brown 2016; Devor 2016; heinz 2016). GAS consists of 'the whole genital, facial, and body procedures required to create a body phenotype that best represents one's own identity' (Selvaggi et al. 2018, 1; see also Aizura 2018). While GAS involves both non-genital and genital procedures, therapies involving the sexual organs are known as 'gender assignment', 'gender reassignment', 'gender confirmation', 'genital reassignment', 'sex confirmation' or 'sex reassignment' surgeries (Cromwell 1999, 20) with different emphases on the procedure involved. Some experts suggest that they typically involve 'five processes: diagnostic assessment, psychotherapy or counseling, RLE [or Real-Life Experience],[5] hormone therapy, and surgical therapy' (Hembree et al. 2009, 3136).

'Top' surgery or 'chest reconstructive surgery' (Marinkovic and Newfield 2017) is 'a form of mastectomy with chest contouring' (Greatheart 2013, 14) that is regarded as a non-genital procedure. 'Bottom' surgeries are genital procedures that include, but are not limited to hysterectomy, oophorectomy, phalloplasty, metoidioplasty and scrotoplasty (Greatheart 2013; Nanda et al. 2017). They often rank lower in the hierarchy of transitioning processes among Malaysian trans men, often due to the exorbitant costs that they incur, disproportionate health risks, and the dearth of holistic surgical expertise and post-surgical care in Malaysian healthcare facilities.

[5] RLE is a duration of time whereby 'while on hormones people present as their desired gender for a significant period before being eligible for surgery' (Hines 2007, 69). However, none of my research participants speak of RLE.

GAHT (McFarlane et al. 2018), also described as hormone replacement therapy (HRT) or 'gender-affirming testosterone therapy' (Moravek 2018) is an ongoing non-genital procedure that is popular among many trans men to 'induce secondary sex characteristics more typical of males, and … diminish female secondary sex characteristics' (Moravek 2018, 690). Some, however, do not feel the need to invest in GAHT, either due to financial constraints, apprehensions in relation to the proper procedures, or because they find themselves in spaces where their everyday interior performances as men have surpassed and nullified the need to conform to socio-cultural expectations of physical maleness in appearance. From among these men, some are ostensibly contented with just changing their names, and realigning their attire and demeanour to conform to their self-affirmed gender identities.

Among my research participants, four are neither on GAHT nor opt for any surgical procedures (Hadi, Jon, Pokerface, Ray), eight are exclusively on GAHT (Aarone, Alco, Axman, Braveheart, Michael, Schulz, SR, Superman), two embrace GAHT and have completed top surgery (Bottle, Warp), and one has undergone top and bottom surgery and is concurrently on GAHT (Adam). There is however a greater proclivity towards GAHT in contrast with GAS among Malaysian trans men who embark on gender-affirming transitioning. The experiences of each research participant inform me of how 'access to the appropriate financial and/or social resources typically have more options for negotiating physical transition, be this through private providers or self-medication' (Pearce 2018, 203).

Despite the fact that health care is state-subsidised, funded by general taxation and generally available to all Malaysians, a majority of trans men do not have access to health care that is apropos to their gender identity, and often are unable to access adequate medical counsel and support, least of all in issues of medical transitioning. There are no formalised or systematic state-sanctioned procedures or insurance schemes to assist trans men *specifically* towards gender-affirming transitioning processes, such as counselling, diagnoses and referrals for GAS and GAHT, as transgender subjectivities are legally and religiously criminalised, and transgender women or *mak nyah* in particular are often regarded as justifiably meriting physical brutality as a consequence (Goh 2019; Justice for Sisters 2014; Khartini 2005).[6] Wilde also observes female-related

[6] See 'Prologue' as well.

health issues that trans men avoid, due to the potential awkwardness of a physical appearance that is incongruent with a gender assigned at birth such 'going to the clinic with a beard, looking like a man and asking for a pap smear' (Appendix 2: Interviewing Dorian Wilde, para. 24).

Additionally, any medical interest in transgender Malaysians, particularly *mak nyah*, usually focuses on issues of sexual health (Gibson et al. 2016; Teh 2008). Those who do receive proper professional guidance in undergoing GAS or GAHT find that such opportunities are serendipitous because of chance connections with sympathetic healthcare professionals, community-based organisations and/or health-related programmes.[7] In this respect, some discover to their frustration that they need to act surreptitiously and sometimes at great risk to themselves, often without the knowledge or consent of family members or religious authorities who ordinarily play significantly active roles in the lives of these individuals.

This chapter aims to investigate the nuanced negotiations of medical transitioning in the lived experiences of Malaysian trans men, rather than delve into intricate medical methods (as seen, for instance, in Djordjevic et al. 2019; Jeftovic et al. 2018; Moravek 2018; Nanda et al. 2017; Qvistgaard 2018). I foreground the objectives, considerations and consequences of GAHT, the purpose and precariousness of GAS, the role of peer support and the monetary complexities connected to medical transitioning. This chapter intends to show how the convoluted and frequently conflictual negotiations with gender-affirming medical procedures are crucially constitutive of trans man subjectivities.

Bodyscaping: Gender Affirmation Surgery

Aren Z. Aizura aptly notes that 'dominant understandings of surgical reassignment slide between the assumption that surgically modified bodies are always mutilated, abject, and monstrous, and the equally problematic and utopic expectation that [GAS] renders the trans body whole or properly gendered' (2018, 204). Although occurring less frequently as a method of gender-affirming transitioning, Malaysian trans men do participate in, or aspire towards myriad forms of GAS in hopes of securing

[7] This is a de-identified, general description to protect the privacy, confidentiality and security of actual people, organisations and programmes that often operate with discretion.

modifications that will indisputably speak truth to gender for them. Others actively resist GAS, and designate it as either an exercise in futility or view it with doubt and trepidation.

'Born Again': Reshaping for Congruence

Some trans men are interested to undergo GAS as it holds a similar, if not higher value to GAHT for them in the pursuit of gender congruence, which I interpret in this chapter as the pursuit of a harmonious compatibility between a self-affirmed gender identity and a more permanent bodily presentation. Braveheart, for example, shares heartfelt meanings of the surgical procedures that occurred '27 years ago' outside Malaysia:

> I actually want to do the bottom surgery as well. The bottom surgery at the time, back 27 years ago, was very crude. Even the top was crude … as though somebody just slashed me across my chest like that. I am horribly disfigured. But I am still happy. Then the bottom surgery was … not very perfected you know, and they told me the pros and cons, so I said to myself, 'I'm going to go in and out of hospital, is that what I want'? So never mind, this top surgery was enough and maybe if I want to go for the bottom surgery there I'll think about it later. And the top, once the surgery was done, you know, and it was like I was at peace, honestly. It was a tremendous release of pressure for me (chuckles). It was as though (tears up) I'm born again. For the first time in thirty years I saw myself in the mirror.

Braveheart's decision to embark on 'chest contouring' (Greatheart 2013, 14) seems to be based on an awareness of the possibility that 'with hormone therapy there is hypertrophy of breast tissue but they never reach the desired shape and volume' (Nanda et al. 2017, 189). He recounts his experiences of 'top surgery' that did not yield the results that he had expected, 'as though somebody [had] just slashed [him] across [his] chest'. The aim of the procedure which was 'to provide [a] male chest with minimal scars' (Nanda et al. 2017, 187) was unmet, and the quality of the surgery was so dire that he refers to himself as being 'horribly disfigured'. His experience illuminates how GAS is frequently 'inadequate no matter what techniques are used [and that] there is at least one or more physical reminder of once being female in body[, such as] scars …' (Cromwell 1999, 29).

Braveheart's musings indicate that he is not pleased with the 'crude' quality of surgery from more than two decades ago, but this situation did not hinder him from feeling 'happy' and 'at peace', which he further explains as 'a tremendous release of pressure'. Visibly moved by this recollection during our conversation, the pressure of which he speaks is indisputably GD, and mastectomy—understood in a general sense as 'the surgical removal of part or all of a breast' (Fallon and Alic 2015, 3214) or usually both breasts—has dissipated this anxiety. The joy and tranquillity that GAS generates, no matter how imperfect, manifests 'the relationship between gendered and sexual embodiment and recognition' (Abelson 2019, 71). It is through this experience that Braveheart is finally able to '[see him]self in the mirror'.

GAS enables an embodied confirmation of self-recognition, a congruity between a self-affirmed gender identity and its corporeal signification. Braveheart conscripts the Christian parlance of being 'born again', an allusion to Christian gospel of John (3.3-5) to articulate the immense significance of a mastectomy in his life as an intensely pivotal, life-changing and cathartic event. For Arthur D. Canales, 'becoming "born-again" is a significant attribute of personal encounter with God' (2002, 99). In my esteem, top surgery is not only a godly experience for Braveheart who identifies as a devout Roman Catholic, but a renewal and transformation of his very createdness that somehow continues to be divinely endorsed.[8]

Braveheart was duly informed of the 'pros and cons', or advantages and disadvantages of 'bottom surgery' as a procedure that had yet to be 'perfected'. The prospect of 'go[ing] in and out of hospital' for a procedure that was still 'crude', under-developed and risky—derisively labelled by some trans men as '"frankendicks", a term that conjures up an image of foreign parts attached to one's body, with resultant scarring and ugliness' (Cromwell 1999, 113–14)—did not appeal to him. The decision against 'bottom surgery' was thus deferred at that point in time, but Braveheart continues to ponder on its potential.

The deployment of surgical changes for gender affirmation is undeniably important for trans men. Yet there appears to be a hierarchy of importance in which top surgery, which more conspicuously attenuates societal perceptions of a feminine form, ranks higher than bottom surgery which some perceive as harbouring higher health risks and less

[8]'Performing Faith' contains a fuller discussion of the role of faith in the subjective production of Malaysian trans men.

visible to the public compared to amendments to the upper torso. Adam is one of the few who have undergone both 'top surgery and bottom surgery':

> *Goh*: So you've gone through top surgery and bottom surgery?
>
> *Adam*: Metoidioplasty ... Because after hormones, the clit actually grows longer. So they can make it a bit longer, and thicker a bit more. But basically you'll be intact, which means they don't cut that off. So I thought that was safer. And I know that phalloplasty I'd do it in Bangkok. Erm, there's a bit of a problem with ... having an erection. So I'm er, I do not want to have a flaccid penis (laughs) that I can't hardly feel... never mind mine is small ... but it's my thing, and it can stand (laughs).

Adam intimates the relief he feels in not having his clitoris surgically removed during metoidioplasty or the procedure of 'creating a phallus from surgically manipulated enlarged clitoris' (Nanda et al. 2017, 187). That this appendage remains 'intact' is perceived as a 'safer' decision. Hence, although some trans men embrace genital-focused GAS in a bid to appear and feel more manly, and thus project a more 'convincing' gender identity, their decisions to undertake such treatments are steered by matters of overall physical well-being.

Adam appears to have mixed feelings about his new endowment. On the one hand, he seems to be satisfied as the penis is constructed from his clitoris and thus '[his] thing'. Despite its diminutive size, 'it can stand', which probably implies the capacity for an erection. In the same breath, Adam relates problems with 'having an erection' and a lack of sensation, and is thus considering 'phalloplasty ... in Bangkok'—Thailand being an incontestably popular global destination for GAS (Aizura 2010, 2018; Khartini 2005)—to remedy a situation which he perceives as less than ideal. Phalloplasty refers to 'the surgical construction of a penis [to create] a functional and esthetic neophallus that provides tactile and erogenous sensation and the ability to void while standing' (Kim et al. 2018, 181). For trans, the decision to undergo GAS is driven by, and decided upon in accordance with the probability of, and yearning towards even fuller functionality.

Adam's 'flaccid penis' that '[can] hardly feel' may be the upshot of a 'safer' bodily decision and embraced as a personal appendage, but its lack of effectiveness evokes feelings of dissatisfaction. While surgical technologies, coupled with GAHT have constructed the desired bodily effects, their flaws and limitations somewhat leave trans men with feelings of incongruence between their self-affirmed gender identity and their corporeality. Any measure of congruence achieved through GAS and GAHT is ironically at the same time an interminable and unresolved project of subjective incongruity.

Not all trans men necessarily feel that their manliness is defined by GAS. Alco speaks of the absence of 'top surgery' that was an initial challenge to his self-affirmed gender identity before gleaning an insight that makes him comfortable as he is:

> There were times when I am with, with some trans men who have maybe gone through their top surgery ... they have gone through certain transition that I may not have gone through ... maybe I felt incomplete at that point in time, but ... the brain is a powerful tool. It's how I'm able to shift one, at that moment in time, to, to motivate myself and speak to myself to say that, you know what, it's not about the body, it's about how you feel. People may have gone and done whatever transitioning that they may have gone through, but you are no less a man than others.

The contrast that Alco draws between trans men who have undergone mastectomy and his own non-surgically modified body is one that had initially led him to feel 'incomplete', possibly due to an entrenched belief in 'a logic of essentialized biological gender difference' (Abelson 2019, 190). Moreover, as seen in Chapter 2, he speaks of a certain gender ambivalence due to the absence of a penis. While there is admittedly no explicit mention of it, there appears to be a sort of rivalry among trans men to 'outman' each other through surgical procedures. In this seeming unspoken competition for 'successful' passing, Alco experiences feelings of being 'less a man than others' and thus falls short of gender congruence.

In the face of such perceived shortcomings, he devises a method to 'motivate' himself by assuring himself that becoming man is 'not about the body [but] how [he] feel[s]'. Alco's privileging of feelings is simultaneously his recourse to 'the brain [as] a powerful tool', in which the brain acts as the repository of intellect and seat of emotions, particularly in gender identity. As such, to appear outwardly as man is not as important as thinking and feeling inwardly as man. Alco's statement sheds light on how some trans men see manness as comprising discrete but interconnecting elements of mind, feeling and bodily appearance, yet assign a higher meaning to manness as an intellectual and emotional ensemble of gender conviction. Such self-devised taxonomies are necessary strategies to deal with feelings of inadequacy that may emerge when trans men compare their feats of surgical transitioning. The anchoring of masculine congruence is thus relocated from sheer physicality to intellectual and emotional spaces, within which a personalised manner of being man surfaces, albeit unstable and shifting.

'Natural Tendency': Defectiveness and Risks

Some trans men actively and deliberately eschew any form of GAS due to a firm belief that such surgical procedures will either be defective or pose risks that they do not discern as worth taking. Bottle, who has undergone chest reconstructive surgery and is on GAHT expresses his apprehensions of 'bottom surgery' owing to the fact that he perceives a prosthetic penis as less than functional:

> So far whatever research that I get, the feeling of, your man-made penis, doesn't really feel that strong, and then, the success rate is very low … which means, you have to go through four surgery, four major surgery in order to get a successful bottom surgery to be done, and then, it's about four years … anyone can remove any parts, and put it back, but it could be, but the recovery period and the feeling period, it takes time to actually come back. And then some unlucky chap, they don't even feel anything. It just like you have a hand, without the nerves, so when you touch on something hot, you won't feel hot … Natural tendency is not there. … In order to have erections, you need to actually pump it physically, it's just like they insert one reservoir, okay, and a tube. So when you need it to be in, in an erect mode, you have to press on the reservoir for the fluid to flow through the tube, and to create that false erections.

Bottle's own initiative in undertaking 'research' on phalloplasty, possibly from online resources and conversations with other trans men, adopts a sharply realistic approach which leads him to believe that while a '[hu]man-made' anatomy may resemble its biological counterpart in appearance, it is unlikely to deliver full functionality. He is cognisant of the fact that 'four major surger[ies]' over 'four years'—a nod to the awareness that GAS comprises multiple operations (Cromwell 1999)—with a long 'recovery period' may still eventuate in a 'success rate [that is] very low', which he subsequently defines as the absence of a 'strong' penis and the probability of delayed or absent sensations. Bottle feels disinclined to undergo major 'bottom surger[ies]' over a protracted period of time with considerable health risks to produce form but not function. His pragmatic approach to GAS dispels the any illusion that trans men readily throw caution to the wind in favour of fulfilling bodyscaping aspirations and fantasies.

The penile turgidity and sensation of which Bottle speaks hold special gravitas for him in terms of achieving 'erections' like other men who were assigned male at birth, not unlike Adam's own beliefs as previously discussed. Although he details the somewhat complex processes in which phalloplasty enables him to achieve an erection through various mechanisms, such processes merely 'create … false erections', rather than a 'natural tendency'. These processes cannot deliver 'natural' strength and 'natural' sensation, which he likens to touching 'something hot' without 'feel[ing] hot', and which are testimonies to the frequent inadequacies and inefficacies of GAS that include 'an inability to have spontaneous erections, and (for most) a lack of sensation in the penile shaft, the insertion of a prosthetic device for intercourse, and an inability to urinate through the penis' (Cromwell 1999, 29)

Bottle demonstrates how gender identity cannot solely be the mere pursuit of romanticised aesthetics, and his reference to 'natural tendency' suggests a heartfelt longing among trans men to live out their gender identities with as much biological 'authenticity' and 'integrity' as possible. The desire to become man is not to simply look like man: it is also the ability to perform as effectively as a man who was assigned male at birth in order to achieve the sexual congruence of masculinity. Such congruence, as previously mentioned, often eludes the grasp of the trans man.

While sharing reservations that are similar to Bottle's, Superman also divulges why GAS bears significance for him:

> At the moment I'm watching technology, and watching the news around technology. Er, it's not yet guarantee, commonly guaranteed that I will retain my sensations when I become, you know, phallic-abled. So, at the moment it's fine 'cause not yet a, you know, it's a go or miss kind of thing situation. Not, not artificially phallic-able (laughs) … I feel like I'm missing my dick … I always feel it.

Superman responds to my enquiry on the importance of phalloplasty for him by intimating that he is currently 'watching technology' or monitoring the development of 'somatechnologies' (Aizura 2018, 13) in relation to this surgical procedure. His apprehension lies in the fact that the construction of a penis cannot 'guarantee' ensuing 'sensations', as such a procedure can be a '[hit] or miss' in terms of effectiveness. While projecting the semblance of a penis, one that is incapable of 'sensations' renders the trans man 'artificially phallic-able', which he may translate as owning a counterfeit appendage and constructing a counterfeit sense of manness. In this sense, Superman is lamenting the lack of—borrowing from Bottle's words—'natural tendency', in which both the form and functionality of a penis must, as far as possible, draw on the body itself.

The uncertainty of a functional penis is a matter of concern that Superman shares with Bottle, and he explains it in terms of someone who 'feels like [he is] missing [his] dick'. Superman may be alluding to what is popularly touted as 'penis envy', or a sense of unease and unhappiness with being deprived of an anatomy that in this case contributes to the full realisation of man. It is the presence of a fully operational penis that can make him 'phallic-abled', which I suggest is an analogy for the ability to perform sexually as a biological male with satisfactory effectiveness, and can augment his manness.

Cromwell writes that the demand of transsexuals for the rectification of a 'wrong body [as] a biophysical entity of sex' is concomitantly an insistence 'on the right to declare a gender, thus *overruling* and *subverting* society's biological designation of sex' (1999, 104; added emphasis). Based on Superman's narrative, and hearkening back to Braveheart's and Bottle's experiences, I argue instead that the compelling logic behind corporeal modification is less a matter of veto or subversion than it is the comforting galvanisation and sedimentation of a chosen gender-sex matrix, the validation of a gender that is premised on biology as its main signifier. The declaration of gender is thus reliant on the cogency of anatomy to the trans man himself.

Injecting Identity: Gender-Affirming Hormone Therapy

GAHT is often either the most basic or sole form of gender transitioning that Malaysian trans men undergo. By injecting themselves regularly with testosterone,[9] trans men discover with immense delight that they are able

[9]None of my research participants mention any subcutaneous means of GAHT. For more information on this procedure, see Pfeffer (2017).

to grow outwardly into the individuals that they have always felt—and continue to feel—inwardly.

'Grounded': Aspiring Towards Gender Congruence

For Adam, GAHT is a means to be 'grounded' in his identity as man, thus allowing him to grow towards greater self-affirmation:

> When I took my first shot, you know how I felt? I felt so warm, like a RUSH (raises voice). Abrupt, like a rush. I don't know if other guys tell you that warmth, and I felt grounded for the first time. I felt like I'm standing, and I'm sprinting at my own space. And just the first shot I knew, this is what I need. This is correct. This is the right decision. The first shot, because of how it makes you feel. Grounded … I felt, it suddenly felt like I was floating before. I was struggling … it's not correct. But I took it, I felt the warmth, the RUSH (raises voice again), I feel grounded. I feel a relief, that first shot. Like my body needed this. It didn't have enough of this. It needed testosterone to feel grounded … I never felt so happy in my life to be who I am … If it's for you, it is for you.

Adam divulges intimate vignettes from a previous period of life as a pre-GAHT trans man. He describes feelings of 'floating' and 'struggling' prior to GAHT, which represent instability, uncertainty and inner conflict. Yet with the 'first shot' of testosterone, Adam experiences sensations of 'warmth', 'rush' and 'relief', which convince him that GAHT was the 'correct [and] right decision'. The repeated mentions of 'warm', 'warmth' and 'rush' may simply be a reference to the physiological effects of being injected with testosterone. I am more inclined to believe Adam's experiences are similar to those of a research participant in Ruth Pearce's study whose joy was 'grounded not simply in the initial physical changes and biochemical rush of hormone administration, but also in the certainty of hormone time[, thus effecting a migration] from a discourse of difficulty, towards a discourse of hope' (2018, 146; added emphasis). GAHT provides Adam with a sense of personal control over his self-affirmed gender identity.

I further suggest that Adam is also attempting to explain the intensity of the experience for him. To be 'grounded' in Adam's words is to feel like he is 'standing' and 'sprinting at [his] own space'. His animated description here is the antonym of the idiom 'running in one place', which conveys the experience of not making satisfactory progress in what one is doing. Instead, Adam uses this description to express 'relief' that he is able to make substantial progress in terms of his self-affirmed gender identity. The 'floating' and 'struggling' volatilities of life which eventually yield to a 'grounded' steadfastness in gender identity display a growing inner self-conviction and 'the concreteness of [a] projected "better" future as transition progresses and possibility turns into reality' (Pearce 2018, 146). Adam's oft-repeated use of the word 'grounded' demonstrates the gravitas of experience 'as the uncertain transitional futurity of waiting and anticipation is replaced with the grounded certainty of a physical transition that is definitely underway' (Pearce 2018, 146).

Through GAHT, he is happiest than he has ever been 'to be who [he is]', as his 'body needed this' and 'it is for [him]'. Adam's gender identity achieves its apex from a profound embodied perspective through testosterone. In other words, the 'correct' interior cohesiveness as man which a trans man experiences and wishes to express outwardly becomes 'enough' or achieves a greater sense of congruence with hormonal injection. It is this congruence that makes him grounded.

Adam's sense of gender congruence through GAHT is reflected in an ascription of 'hormone' and 'surgery' as the means to 'be … a better package' by Bottle, whose experiences show that 'while transgender people who have phalloplasty … are also likely to modify their bodies through hormones (testosterone for transgender men …), many people transition using only hormones and/or non-genital surgeries (such as double mastectomies for transgender men …)' (Currah and Moore 2009, 125). He discloses his thoughts in the following narrative:

Bottle: For my case, I take hormone and I go for surgery … I want it to be like a better package.

Goh: Can you explain … what you mean by better package?

Bottle: It's like, if what you want falls into this category, please look like one. Okay, I'm not saying that those who mention that they are trans men who don't go for hormone, who don't go for this operation, they are not trans men, they can be trans men as long as they feel that 'This is what I am', but to me, if I don't go for hormone, I don't go for operation, I don't feel like this is what I am. I still feel like lack of something, and I, this one doesn't belong to my body, and there's a certain period which I have this thought, just very fast once thought that, I would like to injured my body because this is not my body … I've done … er mastectomy and hystero.

Bottle is keenly aware that the basis of gender identity is mental certitude rather than mere bodily disposition, and respects trans men 'who don't go for hormone [or] operation' as a method of gender affirmation. Nonetheless, he discovers that 'go[ing] for hormone [and] operation' is imperative for him to 'feel like this is what [he is]'. The absence of GAS and GAHT makes him 'feel like [he] lack[s …] something', because 'access to a variety of medical procedures [is] absolutely crucial [for trans men to live] in their bodies and everyday social worlds in a way that line[s] up with their gender identity' (Abelson 2019, 174) This 'lack' forms an embodied disassociation which even justifies a consideration on his part, albeit briefly, to do harm to his body.

Bottle looks to a personal self-definition as well as bodily alterations in order to identify as a 'better package' of manliness. In this regard, he is cognisant of the socio-culturally defined 'category' of man with its attendant expectations, and his ability to enter into and appropriate such a category through GAHT as well as surgery, chiefly 'mastectomy' and 'hyster[ectomy]', the latter being 'the surgical removal of all or part of the uterus' (Gordon and Sherk 2015, 2610) in the general sense. By manipulating existing taxonomies of anatomy and gender to his advantage instead challenging them, Bottle seems to uphold mainstream ideas of sex as inevitably and resolutely determinative of gender.

Corporeal amendments are thus indispensable for men who were assigned female at birth such as Bottle in order to overcome feelings of 'lack'. Such feelings of deficiency can be overwhelming, as attested to by Bottle in the sense of a dysphoric disconnectedness from his body and a proclivity to '[injure his] body' due precisely to this dissonance. Both GAHT and GAS are procedures which he has undergone to 'remedy' the sense of incongruity that he feels and which thus can foster a greater sense of embodied avowal and ease.

My conversations with Malaysian trans men however, suggest that a combination of GAHT and GAS is uncommon among them. A preference for GAHT over GAS is often dictated by financial feasibility, as well as the accessibility to and mistrust of surgical procedures, a matter which I will discuss further in the final section of this chapter. Bottle's case, as such, is more of an exception than the norm. What is noteworthy in Bottle's experiences is that the multiple layers of gender-affirming transitioning, through which he is able to 'look like' and pass 'successfully' as man, is imperative for him to feel more 'grounded' and 'complete' as man.

The sense of groundedness which GAHT provides to Adam and Bottle is also a factor that propels Michael towards greater self-assurance:

> When I was eighteen, that's when I found out about the testosterones, what it can do to ... your body, what it can make you look like and stuff like that, so ... I was like blown away ... I was like super stoked, I was thinking I should, you know, like come out to my parents, like to my mum as soon as possible, and then I was thinking, let's not come out to her now, because ... I think at that time I was only like, nineteen, I was thinking let's wait until I'm twenty-one, because I don't want them to think that ... I'm making a decision without thinking rationally, and they might think that I'm too young to make this kind of decisions, and they might just think that it's just a phase.

Michael's learning of GAHT when he was 'eighteen' or 'nineteen' bespeaks a growing recognition of personal agency in relation to gender affirmation and attendant opportunities that is simultaneously a rite of passage into early adulthood for him. The awareness of the potential effects of testosterone leads to the experience of being 'blown away' and 'super stoked', or being immensely impressed by and excited at the prospect of having the means of self-transformation at his disposal. Like Braveheart and Adam, Michael experiences the exhilaration which emanates from a serendipitous awareness that it is possible for one to be in control of one's own gender destiny by virtue of endocrinal injections.

This exhilaration is extended to a newly acquired sense of self-confidence that prompts him to consider 'com[ing] out to [his] parents ... as soon as possible', particularly to his mother. The awareness that GAHT can deliver a concrete possibility of gender-affirming transitioning provides Michael with the impetus to disclose his self-affirmed gender identity as man to his family. GAHT is thus not only indispensable for attaining personal gender congruence that is concomitantly gender 'groundedness': it allows the transitioning individual to include the revelation of his self-affirmed gender identity to his family as constitutive of this notion of congruence. GAHT underscores the fact that transitioning is an inter-relational process, rather than a purely privatised project of ongoing self-construction, as discussed variously in this volume. Michael's experiences reveal how 'men's expressions of masculinity and experiences as men [depend] on the spaces and places they [live] in and [move] through during their everyday lives' (Abelson 2019, 194).

For some Malaysian trans men, coming out is incomplete if their families are not enlightened in regard to their gender identities.[10]

This potential that GAHT holds is not without its limitations. Michael is aware that he may be accused of not 'thinking rationally', or that his zeal may 'just [be] a phase' due to his youth. Owing to the possibility of an adverse reaction to his disclosure, he decides to withhold coming out to his family and 'wait until [he's] twenty-one', which he seemingly perceives as the age of legal adulthood even though the age of majority in Malaysia is 18 (The Commissioner of Law Revision, Malaysia 2006). Therefore, while GAHT and family awareness can act as con-constructors of a valid self-affirmed gender identity, this validity is perceived as attaining credibility only when it is seen as embodied by a 'rationally' mature adult.

'Health Risk Seem Quite High': Impeded by Health Concerns

Many trans men whom I interviewed explained that their plans for transitioning were often interrupted or occluded by health risks. Such concerns become a disincentive for these men to resort to hormonal injections. For Pokerface, the prospect of being saddled with 'male-related sickness[es]' becomes one of two deterrents in embarking on GAHT:

> *Goh*: You said that … you don't want to do hormone replacement therapy now because of health issues and legal issues.
>
> *Pokerface*: For health issue, it's because my family have like high blood pressure, cancer, yeah, so … if you take hormone … you will develop erm, more like male-related sickness, such as er, high blood pressure, heart disease, and stuff. So that's what I'm considering because my family have this background, so that's why I'm thinking whether I should take or shouldn't take.

Pokerface furnishes a 'background' of hereditary health issues, including 'cancer', 'high blood pressure' and 'heart disease', which cast doubt and uncertainty on his plan to embrace GAHT. In Malaysia, '115,238 new cancer cases were registered for the period of 2012–2016 [in which] 44.7% were among males and 55.3% were among females' (National Cancer

[10] I discuss the complexities of coming out in more detail in 'Engaging with Society'.

Institute 2019, 1). Pokerface neither masculinises nor feminises cancer, and only names it as a hereditary medical trait. Nevertheless, he assigns heart diseases as 'male-related sickness[es]'. This declaration resonates with the fact that 'ischaemic heart diseases [remain] as the principal causes of death for males (17.8%)' (Department of Statistics, Malaysia 2019, 2), although there is no significant difference in cases of hypertension between men and women in the country (Institute for Public Health 2015).

Contrary to a widespread acknowledgement by trans men themselves that 'women's health issues often are transmens health issues as well' (heinz 2016, 204), including 'gynaecological problems [such as] cysts[,] ovarian cancer an [c]ervical cancer' (Appendix 2: Interviewing Dorian Wilde, para. 26), Pokerface chooses to foreground diseases that he perceives as male-related ailments and which should be eschewed. It is unclear as to whether the masculinisation of cardiovascular disease and hypertension is based on reliable statistics or simply anecdotal, or if he holds the view that to embrace the subjectivity of manness is also to embrace the possibilities of contracting illnesses that he sees as typically plaguing men who were assigned male at birth.

Whichever the case may be, GAHT bears the insidious threat of damaging his health in terms of exacerbating 'male-related sickness[es]'. As such, GAHT does not render itself as an indispensable element of gender-affirming transitioning, as trans men prioritise physical health within a negotiation of factors that contribute directly to their overall quality of life. For Pokerface, the risk of compromising his health surpasses the desire to alter his physicality through hormonal injections, and physical well-being is prioritised over corporeal reconstruction. Specifically, Pokerface reflexively surmises that the appropriation of man does not oblige one to succumb to expectations of what constitutes man in terms of popular assumptions, chiefly GAHT and 'male-related sickness[es]'.

Ray also shares some of Pokerface's concerns with GAHT and health:

Goh: Are you undergoing hormone replacement therapy?

Ray: Currently not really … the health risk seem quite high, and … because of my family history medically … I don't think it's suitable, just not something I want to take lah, because I'm concerned about the health reason than anything else. If there's a way to take hormones where it's safer to me, where I won't get like high blood pressure, or immune system getting weaker because of the hormone replacement therapy then I'd probably take HRT.

Ray's response to my question as 'not really' suggests that he has attempted GAHT before, but now finds himself more disinclined because of the 'health risk[s that] seem quite high'. Not unlike Pokerface, he is keenly aware of his family's medical history as well as the potential health hazards that hormonal injections may bring. Ray counts 'high blood pressure' and a compromised 'immune system' as two of such health risks. Consequently, GAHT is 'not something [he] want[s] to take' as it is no longer 'suitable' for him at this juncture of his life. Yet, his present decision is not irrevocable. Ray is willing to undergo GAHT should there emerge 'a way to take hormones [that is] safer'. The decision not to be on GAHT, however, does not cause an attenuation of his masculinity:

Goh: Do you feel less masculine because you don't take GAHT?

Ray: Not really I mean, I am who I am honestly so it's like, so if you don't see that way that's your problem not mine ... I think the need to not shave facial hair is just one thing that I'm enjoying for now, but the thing is like, yeah that's not really a big concern of mine ... it doesn't really matter to me because I feel myself as a male person, so I don't really care about that.

Ray's description of 'shav[ing] facial hair' as something that he is denied at present due to the absence of GAHT evinces 'the significance of growing facial hair as an unambiguous marker of masculinity' (Greatheart 2013, 78) for trans men. Nevertheless, he does not 'feel less masculine' and is thus unperturbed. His identity as '[he is] who [he is]' as man is not exclusively dependent on GAHT. As is the case with many other trans men, manness is a deep conviction of '[one]self as a male person' or an acute sense of authenticity as 'the discursive construction of self-representation and self-determination in the becoming of one's subjectivity in messy and indeterminate ways' (Goh 2016, 64). The unruliness and evolutionary instabilities of authenticity as 'a verb rather than a noun' (Goh 2016, 63) emerge from within Ray's emotional certitude, and locate him in the self-assurance of his subjectivity. The self-confidence that enables him to adopt a nonchalant and dismissive attitude towards those who do not acknowledge him as man because he is not on GAHT destabilises the conviction of some trans men that GAHT is imperative in order to be 'successful' as man.

'Male Period': Physical Discomfort

While some trans men discuss GAHT in terms of substantial health risks and thus avoid it, others speak of physical discomfort that they are willing to tolerate in order to attain their bodyscaping goals. In candid fashion, Michael relates experiences of side effects after a 'testosterone shot', which he refers to as the 'male period':

> I just get my testosterone shots from [a local hospital][11] and er, they inject this testosterone in me … for a few weeks I'll be like a bit cranky, not to say cranky, but everything seems to be heightened, like I get like this hunger feeling for at least like a week, and, and dissolve, that kind of thing. It's basically like, er, I would say, er, I call it like male, male period (chuckles), so like sometimes my friends call me er, like I'll be, probably like a day after my testosterone shot, and, 'You wanna go out'? 'No, I'm on my male period, I can't go out'. That kind of thing, because I'll actually be in pain, because they kinda inject it in my butt, so it feels uncomfortable sitting down too long, and all that.

The assistance that Michael receives from '[a local hospital]' for GAHT is a departure from the norm among many trans men such as Bottle who resort to self-administration based on anecdotal advice from other trans men and/or personal research. Although personal initiatives taken by trans men in relation to gender-affirming transitioning are laudable, genuine medical care is of supreme importance to their health as Malaysians who are summarily spurned as abnormal, ill and iniquitous in their gender and sexual subjectivities are often excluded from critical health care.

Michael's narrative reinforces the statement I made at the outset of this chapter that while medical assistance for Malaysian trans men is often sporadic and clandestine, it exists and is available. Michael admits that he feels 'cranky' or irritable after a hormonal injection, and unpacks this experience as that of 'heightened' sensations, such as feeling hunger pangs which last 'a week'. Due to the fact that 'testosterone shots' are administered in his buttocks, he feels physical pain and discomfort if he '[sits] down [for] too long'.

The effects of GAHT on the emotions of trans men remain largely academically inconclusive, but clinical experience among experts suggest that 'transmen who begin testosterone therapy may experience

[11] The actual hospital has been de-identified for privacy, confidentiality and security.

increased energy and psychomotor agitation' (Elizondo et al. 2012, 17). Carla A. Pfeffer enumerates a range of emotions experienced by trans men on GAHT even though 'it is difficult to assess whether these perceived changes are largely physiologically or socioculturally motivated, and some trans men assert that these changes are often overstated or even mythical' (2017, 103). Her findings bear resonance with Miriam J. Abelson's claim that 'cultural scripts about testosterone also have a permissive effect for men to enact particular expressions … people who believe testosterone causes certain aggressive and antisocial behaviors are more likely to enact those behaviors when they think they have been injected with it, even if they were actually injected with a neutral saline solution' (2019, 102).

The 'crank[iness]' or 'male period' brought on by GAHT is worth discussing here. Over a prolonged period of time, GAHT is capable of ending menstruation due to cessation in oestrogen production (Hembree et al. 2009; Moravek 2018). I suggest that as Michael is undergoing or looking forward to such a situation, his use of 'period' carries particular import for a man who was assigned female at birth. Although this expression may appear whimsical or even endearing, it belies a gender stereotype that women who are assigned female at birth and who are menstruating are cantankerous due to their bodily pain and discomfort. Michael may even be drawing on personal experiences from his past. Thus, while Michael may de-identify as woman, he continues to conscript a term that is stereotypically associated with undesirable female traits in order to distance himself from any form of womanliness.

Akin to Michael, Axman also experiences 'crank[iness]' in the use of GAHT:

Goh: Let's talk about hormones first, hormone injections … Are you guided by a medical professional in your jabs?

Axman: Supposedly … it's actually at [a local hospital] but, I realised that it's very much trial and error, the doctor, how [the local hospital is][12] doing it, you see. So that was why I, there's plenty of research on the internet … For me I generally do three weeks, every three weeks. Even though there was one time I really forgot, I dragged it to more than four weeks (laughs). And I was like, why am I feeling so cranky? And then when I checked my reminder I was like, oh no (laughs) … Because

[12] The actual hospital has been de-identified for privacy, confidentiality and security.

> you can see, when the hormone is first administered, in the beginning, maybe for the first few days there will be sometimes some mood swings or sporadically it pops up. As in sometimes I get more irritable. Alright? Then when I know it's actually low, I also will get irritable … my temper has improved a lot. As in I'm actually a lot more patient, now that it's more, you know? I found something that is more suitable for me.

Axman's retort that he 'supposedly' receives assistance from a health professional for testosterone injections stands in marked contrast with Michael's experience of professional guidance from '[a local hospital]'. As variously discussed in this chapter, the 'trial and error' approach to GAHT that Axman undergoes at a 'government facility' articulates a general lack of expertise on—perhaps even a hesitance or an unwillingness to engage with—gender transitioning in Malaysia. Consequently, like Bottle, Axman has had to be proactive by researching GAHT procedures and developing a privately crafted schedule of injecting himself with testosterone 'every three weeks' that he determines as 'more suitable for [himself]'.

While this modus operandi is the fruit of his own 'trial and error', which is not vastly different to the experimental processes of '[a local hospital]', Axman appears to place greater trust in his experience-based techniques. This situation is arguably unsurprising as 'having less power in … institutional contexts and the focus on their bodies [make] trans men particularly vulnerable in these settings' (Abelson 2019, 173). In this context, the attenuation of power does not lie in the confusion, condescension and condemnation that often typify Malaysian healthcare attitudes pertaining to transgender people, but the inadequacy, inefficiency and ignorance of medical professionals that could potentially harm the physical well-being of a trans man. This vulnerability compels many trans men to rely greatly on what I refer to elsewhere in relation to gay and bisexual men's sexualities as a form of '*somatic wisdom*' (Goh 2018, 58; original emphasis) that is cultivated from actual experiences. The 'crank[iness]' from GAHT that Axman experiences echoes those of Michael's as he 'sporadically' experiences 'mood swings', irritability and even bad 'temper'. Axman's embodied wisdom, which has been translated to a self-devised regularity of GAHT, contributes positively to a more even keel in his temperament.

Negotiating Social Support and Financial Means

Not unlike what I had discussed earlier pertaining to coming out for trans men as both a personal and public endeavour, I contend here that gender-affirming transitioning is as much an intensely personal enterprise as it is a project of social support in which trans men journey with other trans men, as well as with sympathetic medical professionals who are directly involved in their transformations. Transitioning is also an undertaking of substantial monetary means, and trans men soon discover that their pursuits of self-realisation require them to contemplate deeply and pragmatically on available financial resources.

'Showing Some Love': Peer Support

SR expresses an appreciation for the 'help' that he receives from his 'trans men friends' while he is undergoing GAHT:

> *Goh*: In what way have your trans men friends been helpful, and supportive to you?
>
> *SR*: I strongly believe, that they're gonna help me the same way for example, probably not in terms of money, but in terms of … motivation. Like, I'm telling them, 'guys, I'm taking this hormone, so I'm quite worried now'. 'Okay, don't worry'. So they were giving like moral support, they were giving like a lot of thing, advice. They always there … Even though at 3 o'clock in the morning. Doesn't matter what time, they will still reply … they were showing some love.

By 'help', SR is not referring to monetary assistance. Instead, he explains that he is appreciative of the ways in which trans men furnish him with 'motivation', which he unpacks as the comfort, 'moral support' and 'advice' during moments when he experiences doubts and worries in relation to hormonal injections. SR's resolute belief that other trans men will come to his aid irrespective of the time of day, even at unorthodox hours such as '3 o'clock in the morning', attests to his explicit experience of, and firm conviction in the support of other trans men.

SR interprets their 'help' as assistance, and further elucidates it as their way of 'showing some love'. For some trans men, the journey of transitioning is often one that is bewildering and lonely, and there are very few mentors or confidantes. In SR's case, this predicament is somewhat assuaged by the accompaniment of others who are embarking on similar journeys. Although SR may be using the term 'showing some love' in a casual manner, it is possible that his interactions with other trans men have galvanised a deeper sense of identification and solidarity with fellow trans men. I further suggest that this quip may also induce feelings of well-being that Stephanie L. Budge et al. express as 'positive feelings through community, feelings of belonging, love, and a process of feeling for others' (2015, 416; original emphasis) as a consequence of camaraderie among trans men. In this regard, 'social recognition as a man', specifically social support from other trans men, 'can further legitimize the internal sense of being a man' (Abelson 2019, 62).

The sense of co-journeying is also experienced through online means, which may in turn provide a link to actual interaction with other trans men, as in the case of Schulz:

> I told myself, okay if I ever were to do it, maybe not at that age, because I still wasn't financially supporting myself and there were no available clinics around or anything. So I just let it, you know, let the whole depression sink in and … at the age of 19, the curiosity began again, you know, finding for hormones and people like me, trans men like me, in Malaysia. Er, I saw a lot of videos of trans men from US and overseas and all that, but, I couldn't find a trans man in Malaysia. Erm, at the year of 2012, I saw this video of, a trans man, Malaysian trans man on YouTube, and managed to contact him, meet him up, and erm, he told me, he enlightened me, he told me that these are gonna be the side effects, and there's gonna be a lot of changes in you physically and all that.

Schulz recalls the 'depression' that assailed him at an earlier period of his life, presumably before he turned 19, when financial independence was out of his reach and he was unable to find any 'available clinics' that could aid him in gender transitioning. His failed recourse to medical assistance, similar to Michael's experience, may indicate that 'an appeal to medical expertise is effectively an appeal to a higher discursive authority' (Pearce 2018, 99) but it is also a cri de cœur for help in his subjective production. The unavailability of avenues that could provide some relief to his GD, and the reality that he 'still wasn't [capable of] financially supporting [him]self' are factors that contributed to Schulz's sense of lingering sadness. Gender-affirming transitioning is thus not only a matter of physical and hormonal transformation, or an inter-relational process, or the availability of medical expertise and facilities: it is also a matter of financial stability.

Upon reaching 19 years of age, Schulz regains his 'curiosity' to source avenues for GAHT and also to meet other 'trans men like [him]'. That these pursuits are a matter of *rekindled* interest suggests that his earlier bout of 'depression' was an incapacitating condition that originally prevented him from further exploring his self-affirmed gender identity. Schulz's desire to locate fellow trans men indicates an acute aloneness and loneliness in transitioning. Both his and SR's experiences suggest a profound desire for the journey of gender transformation to be one that is ideally undertaken with communal support.

While this initial solitary venture prompts Schulz to watch 'a lot of videos of trans men from US and overseas', it does not alleviate his sense of isolation as they are geographically and socio-culturally removed from his own realities. It is only when he watches 'this video of a … Malaysian trans man on YouTube'—possibly Wilde's (2010) transition weblog—that Schulz discovers a fellow trans man whose own experiences can contextualise and inform his gender-affirming transitioning, particularly in terms of 'changes' and 'side effects'. For Schulz, watching a video of, and eventually meeting another trans man in person constitutes 'enlighten[ment]', or a process of moving from ignorance to knowledge in terms of gender determination. While a trans man's own body epistemology contributes to his own self-affirmed gender identity, peer support, even in media representation, is often vital to guide and enhance this self-knowledge.

Braveheart recounts interactions with other trans men during which he longs to play a primary role of providing 'feedback' to others who are less knowledgeable in matters of gender-affirming transitioning:

Goh: So when you are among them, what do you feel? With the other trans men?

Braveheart: It's just a chat group of trans men … we talk about issues we face as trans men. A support group, it's like men's group you know, that's what I meant … I gave my feedback as I was probably the only one under proper authoritative supervision who were experts in the transgender field unlike in Malaysia where the expertise lack and the doctors are treating transmen as how they would treat cis men. So this area is very new. I believe you can't treat trans men like cis men in terms of healthwise … most trans men are getting the T without being diagnosed as trans men. We know who we are but to get proper medical treatment it is the requirement to be verified as sound mind … I'm in Malaysia, I don't know where I can get resources.

Braveheart's mention of the 'chat group' of trans men is very probably a reference to the Transmen of Malaysia (2018), which mitigates the aloneness and loneliness of transitioning by providing opportunities for trans men to 'talk about issues' and support each other through an online forum. It is within such a 'support group' that he presents himself as the sole trans man who was 'under proper authoritative supervision' in gender-affirming transitioning and thus an authority to [give] his feedback' to other trans men, owing to the reality that he had benefitted from professional medical 'experts in the transgender field' outside Malaysia.

The authority which he claims is not merely what appears to be a badge of pride that he wears in contrast with his experiences of non-Malaysian health care. It is also a general distrust of the medical 'expertise' in his own country as transgender health is an 'area [that] is very new', not unlike Bottle's and Axman's scepticism with medical professionals who are ignorant of gender-affirming transitioning issues. Wilde himself laments the fact that 'ninety-nine percent [of medical doctors] have no idea [of] what [he is] talking about' (Appendix 2: Interviewing Dorian Wilde, para. 22) in terms of transitioning.

Braveheart is concerned that many trans men self-administer 'the T' or testosterone shots without any medical referrals, a situation which Wilde admits is 'very harmful' (Appendix 2: Interviewing Dorian Wilde, para. 22). Braveheart's main grouse that 'doctors are treating trans men as … they would treat cis men' implies, as I understand it, two key issues in relation to trans men. First, as some Malaysian physicians are uninitiated in matters pertaining to transgender people, they do not make important distinctions between men who were assigned male at birth and men who were assigned female at birth, which are crucial for the physical well-being of trans men who embark on GAHT.

Second, the 'diagnos[is]' of local medical professionals which proves necessary for trans men to access 'proper medical treatment' is often unavailable. The diagnosis of which Braveheart speaks is imperative for a referral for medical transitioning—the shape and form of which remains uncertain—undertaken by trans men who are 'verified as [being of] sound mind' and who 'know who [they] are', rather than deranged victims of a gender-related pathology and thus viewed by Malaysian health professionals as 'oddities, attention seekers, mentally ill, or perhaps duplicitous' (Abelson 2019, 172). As such, Braveheart emblemises many trans men who do not look to local medical professionals as validators of their gender identity, but strategic individuals who can facilitate the process of gender-affirming transitioning.

Braveheart's expression of concern serves to buttress his sense of authority in terms of the proper procedures and standards of gender-affirming transitioning. In a sense, he shows how 'gendered knowledge and expertise resides within the individual and with trans communities, rather than with health professionals' (Pearce 2018, 103). Yet, despite demonstrating a command of trans men's issues, he still is unaware of 'where [he] can get resources', or health services that can directly benefit trans men. Braveheart's willingness and eagerness to provide support to his peers is thus limited, possibly due to the dearth of sympathetic medical professionals in the country and/or his own lack of knowledge of such 'resources'.

'I Can't Afford That': Medical Mentoring

The absence of dedicated official medical mentoring, which I define as a sustained, non-judgemental and unconditional state-sanctioned commitment to providing reliable counsel on health matters for trans men in relation to their self-affirmed gender identities, is an issue that many trans men encounter and find irresolvable. The concern I wish to raise here is the costs of medical assistance which prove to lie beyond the reach of many Malaysian trans men and which Wilde refers to as 'really, really expensive' (Appendix 2: Interviewing Dorian Wilde, para. 18). Aizura observes how 'questions of economic access to health care also throw into relief [GAS] as a comparatively privileged resource' (2018, 14), to which I would also add GAHT for some trans men. As was previously discussed, financial constraints and the sparse availability of adequate health services propel a number of trans men to turn to other trans men for advice. Aarone explains how he 'initially' proceeded with GAHT:

Goh: And for your hormone therapy … Do you have medical assistance or are you doing it on your own or?

Aarone: Er, initially, was via medical assistance because I first went through the proper way, via what do you call this, erm, psychological assessment. Because I was at, almost like a, break down at one point. I've been keeping everything inside for so long. So … I was lucky I have this friend who is a doctor … My first few injections I went er,

> properly to a doctor, to a hospital … they … make me go through all the medical, what do you call this, blood test, to ensure that my body is healthy, especially the liver and the kidney … so from then on they helped me with the monitoring. So, and then after that, erm, because it's a little bit expensive going through the hospital, so then I decided to learn how to do the injection myself. And now I do it myself … In a year … I will always go … for a check-up … I did recently, er, about three weeks ago.

The magnitude of Aarone's GD, which reached an overwhelming level at which he was on the verge of a 'break down', was due to the fact that he had 'been keeping everything inside for so long', or a prolonged repression of feelings related to his self-affirmed gender identity. The loneliness of transitioning which I discussed previously is also evident here.

In a serendipitous turn of events, he was able to seek recourse from a 'friend who is a doctor'—a stark contrast with the 'feeling of vulnerability [which] is especially heightened for trans people trying to access medical care [and where] medical contexts [are] also often the sites of more subtle forms of violence that [cause] small, often psychological, injuries that [have] a large cumulative negative effect over time' (Abelson 2019, 172–74). It is this physician-friend who guides Aarone in the direction of a 'psychological assessment' prior to receiving hormonal injections 'properly' at the hands of 'a doctor'. A psychological evaluation is accompanied by a 'blood test' to ascertain the health of his internal organs. Eventually, Aarone is placed on GAHT, and receives assistance 'with the monitoring'.

'Proper' health care as medical mentoring which involves the direct intervention of supportive and affirming healthcare professionals is one that many trans men aspire towards, but few achieve due to financial limitations or lack of knowledge. What Aarone is explaining is a fortuitous occurrence, as a personal relationship with a friend who is also a medical professional allowed him to make inroads with gender-affirming transitioning. As mentioned variously in this monograph, few trans men in Malaysia have access to such opportune connections and consequences.

Nevertheless, Aarone finds that he needs to discontinue medical mentoring as it is 'expensive'. This decision sheds light on the reality that he had more than likely been personally financing his transitioning in the past before finally 'decid[ing]' to learn how to do the injection

[him]self'. At the time of the interview, Aarone admitted that he was unemployed, but he observes a regularity in an annual 'check-up'. Nevertheless, I feel that the long-term financial feasibility of such health projects is questionable.

Alco, who is undergoing GAHT, finds that he does not have the financial means for GAS due to what he understands as more pressing priorities:

> I'm taking hormones at the moment. Erm, operation is not important because … I am comfortable with myself … if I have the extra money, I would go for it. I would go for my top surgery and even the … sexual reassignment surgery … I think as a husband and as a father, I have my priorities, and my children are my priorities. So, you know what, if I'm going to spend fourteen thousand ringgit, you know, just to have my top surgery, might as well I keep the money for their education. So, those are the things that I'm happy balanced, and for me my children, my children are priorities … So, I would put that money aside for them first.

Alco expresses feelings of being 'comfortable with [him]self' that enable him to undervalue GAS. Yet he seemingly contradicts himself by affirming that he 'would go for … top surgery and [GAS]' if he were in possession of 'extra money'. The issue at hand is not an aversion to GAS, but a decision to channel funds to his family. In the face of such a dilemma, Alco chooses his family, particularly his children whom he mentions several times. I suggest that the prioritisation of family over GAS is concomitantly the formulation of a coping strategy to address the unattainability of GAS for him. By undervaluing GAS, foregrounding a personal sense of ease and balance, and prioritising the needs of his wife[13] and children in his financial mappings at the same time, Alco pursues a path of self-acceptance that allows him to reach towards 'a desirable model of masculinity' by being a 'caring, sharing, and present partner, provider, and father' (Johnson 2016, 61) on his own terms as a trans man.

Thus, in 'put[ting] money aside' for his family instead of for surgical procedures, Alco recruits the notion of being 'a husband and … father' to construct and augment his personal conceptualisation of manliness. In so doing, he interrogates prevalent assumptions pertaining to (trans)gender identities and expressions 'by bringing into question

[13]Trans men refer to their female life partners as girlfriends, partners and in Alco's case, wife.

what it means to be a man or masculine [and becoming] more fluid in [his] identifications with the signs or props of masculinity and maleness' (Cromwell 1999, 109). In this respect, manness for the Malaysian trans man is constituted by a posture of contentment, level-headedness, practicality and family-centredness rather than an unproblematic striving for bodily modification via surgical procedures.

Conclusion

This chapter has shown that there are multifaceted issues surrounding various forms of medical transitioning, namely GAS and GAHT. For some trans men, the bodyscaping procedures of GAS serve as a valuable means to accomplish a sense of congruence between a self-affirmed gender identity and material corporeality. This desired consonance is nonetheless fraught with instability and uncertainty as GAS procedures can be imperfectly executed. Trans men speak of the lack of aesthetics in chest reconstructive surgeries and the unpredictability of penile function through phalloplasty and metoidioplasty. Such experiences do not only render a certain sense of artificiality to the subjectivities of trans men: they are forces which foster a keen awareness among trans men that medical transitioning comprises a diverse series of endocrinal and/or surgical procedures which deliver a melange of success, failure, pauses and interruptions. Trans men realise that despite an imagined promise of perfection, medical transitioning can never be the ultimate measure of success for manness.

Many men also undergo GAHT to ameliorate their dysphoric dissonance and fortify their self-affirmed gender identities. Considerably less invasive and more accessible and affordable than GAS, GAHT renders a sense of gender-affirming groundedness to trans men. Therefore, despite a keen awareness of the lack of consistent and reliable medical availability and guidance, and physical discomforts that ensue from endocrinal therapy, many trans men consciously elect to undergo GAHT. Among those who do are individuals who embark on personal projects to equip themselves with the necessary knowledge pertaining to the self-administration of GAHT, and who rely on the experience-based expertise and peer support of other trans men. Conversely, there are trans men who resist any form of hormonal intervention due to concerns with the possibility that hereditary health issues may be exacerbated by GAHT. Although many enthuse over the possibilities that GAS holds, the reality of financial constraint remains a primary deterrent. In such situations, some trans men devise strategies that allow them to affirm their subjectivities sans recourse to expensive surgical and/or endocrinal treatments.

To a major extent, the journeys of becoming Malaysian trans men are conditioned by medical interventions that serve to anchor gender identity in reconstructed corporealities via GAS and/or GAHT. This 'reembodiment of gender through physical sex changes raises again the spectre of biological determinism' (Hollway 2014, 773), which is unsurprising as 'bodies that deviate from a gender-as-genitals configuration are subject to hyper-embodiment' (Edelman and Zimman 2014, 675). The material body thus acts as a panopticon of interminable gender surveillance, which simultaneously qualifies and disqualifies the subjectivities of trans men as dictated by local spatial and temporal contexts. The deeper question here however, is if their desire to conform to cisnormative and heteronormative notions of sexual difference, as well as to sociocultural segregations of manness and womanness, belie a simplistic acceptance of biology and gender as mutually, perhaps even inevitably constitutive of their self-affirmed gender identities.

Bibliography

Abelson, Miriam J. 2019. *Men in Place: Trans Masculinity, Race, and Sexuality in America*. Minneapolis, MN: University of Minnesota Press.

Aizura, Aren Z. 2010. 'Feminine Transformations: Gender Reassignment Surgical Tourism in Thailand'. *Medical Anthropology* 29 (4): 424–43.

Aizura, Aren Z. 2018. *Mobile Subjects: Transnational Imaginaries of Gender Reassignment*. Durham, NC: Duke University Press.

Barcelos, Chris A. 2019. '"Bye-Bye Boobies": Normativity, Deservingness and Medicalisation in Transgender Medical Crowdfunding'. *Culture, Health & Sexuality* 21 (12): 1394–408.

Brown, Michael Eric. 2016. *A Herstory of Transmasculine Identities: An Annotated Anthology*. Miami, FL: Boundless Endeavors, Inc.

Budge, Stephanie L., Joe J. Orovecz, and Jayden L. Thai. 2015. 'Trans Men's Positive Emotions: The Interaction of Gender Identity and Emotion Labels'. *The Counseling Psychologist* 43 (3): 404–34.

Burke, Mary C. 2011. 'Resisting Pathology: GID and the Contested Terrain of Diagnosis in the Transgender Rights Movement'. In *Sociology of Diagnosis*, edited by P. J. McGann and David J. Hutson, 183–210. Bingley, UK: Emerald Group Publishing Limited.

Canales, Arthur. 2002. 'A Rebirth of Being "Born Again": Theological, Sacramental and Pastoral Reflections From a Roman Catholic Perspective'. *Journal of Pentecostal Theology* 11 (1): 98–119.

Conrad, Peter. 2005. 'The Shifting Engines of Medicalization'. *Journal of Health and Social Behavior* 46 (1): 3–14.

Cromwell, Jason. 1999. *Transmen and FTMs: Identities, Bodies, Genders, and Sexualities*. Urbana, IL: University of Illinois Press.

Currah, Paisley, and Lisa Jean Moore. 2009. '"We Won't Know Who You Are": Contesting Sex Designations in New York City Birth Certificates'. *Hypatia* 24 (3): 113–35.

Department of Statistics, Malaysia. 2019. 'Statistics on Causes of Death, Malaysia'. Putrajaya, Malaysia: Department of Statistics, Malaysia. https://www.dosm.gov.my/v1/index.php?r=column/pdfPrev&id=RUxlSDNkcnRVazJnakNCNVN2VGgrdz09.

Devor, Aaron. 2016. *FTM: Female-to-Male Transsexuals in Society*. Bloomington, IN: Indiana University Press.

Djordjevic, Miroslav L., Marko Bencic, Vladimir Kojovic, Borko Stojanovic, Marta Bizic, Sinisa Kojic, Zoran Krstic, and Gradimir Korac. 2019. 'Musculocutaneous Latissimus Dorsi Flap for Phalloplasty in Female to Male Gender Affirmation Surgery'. *World Journal of Urology* 37 (4): 631–37.

Edelman, Elijah Adiv, and Lal Zimman. 2014. 'Boycunts and Bonus Holes: Trans Men's Bodies, Neoliberalism, and the Sexual Productivity of Genitals'. *Journal of Homosexuality* 61 (5): 673–90.

Elizondo, Paul M., Willy Wilkinson, and Christopher Daley. 2012. 'Working With Transgender Persons'. *Psychiatric Times* 29 (9): 16–18.

Fallon, L. Fleming, and Margaret Alic. 2015. 'Mastectomy'. In *The Gale Encyclopedia of Medicine*, edited by Jacqueline L. Longe, 5th ed., 3214. Farmington Hills, MI: Gale, Cengage Learning.

Gibson, Britton A., Shan-Estelle Brown, Ronnye Rutledge, Jeffrey A. Wickersham, Adeeba Kamarulzaman, and Frederick L. Altice. 2016. 'Gender Identity, Healthcare Access, and Risk Reduction Among Malaysia's *Mak Nyah* Community'. *Global Public Health* 11 (7–8): 1010–25.

Goh, Joseph N. 2014. 'Transgressive Empowerment: Queering the Spiritualities of the *Mak Nyahs* of PT Foundation'. In *Queering Migrations Towards, From, and Beyond Asia*, edited by Hugo Córdova Quero, Joseph N. Goh, and Michael Sepidoza Campos, 123–37. New York: Palgrave Macmillan.

———. 2016. 'Close Encounters of the Authentic Kind: Exploring the Meaning-Making of Love, Sex and Intimacy Among Gay-Identifying Malaysian Men'. In *Punks, Monks and Politics: Authenticity in Thailand, Indonesia and Malaysia*, edited by Julian C. H. Lee and Marco Ferrarese, 47–64. London: Rowman & Littlefield International.

———. 2018. *Living Out Sexuality and Faith: Body Admissions of Malaysian Gay and Bisexual Men*. London: Routledge.
———. 2019. 'Untying Tongues: Negotiations and Innovations of Faith and Gender Among Malaysian Christian Trans Men'. *Culture and Religion* 20 (1): 1–20.
Gordon, Debra, and Stephanie Dionne Sherk. 2015. 'Hysterectomy'. In *The Gale Encyclopedia of Medicine*, edited by Jacqueline L. Longe, 5th ed., 2610. Farmington Hills, MI: Gale, Cengage Learning.
Greatheart, Marcus. 2013. *Transforming Practice: Life Stories of Transgender Men That Change How Health Providers Work*. Toronto, Canada: Ethica Press.
heinz, matthew. 2016. *Entering Transmasculinity: The Inevitability of Discourse*. Chicago, IL: Intellect Ltd.
Hembree, Wylie C., Peggy Cohen-Kettenis, Henriette A. Delemarre-van de Waal, Louis J. Gooren, Walter J. Meyer, Norman P. Spack, Vin Tangpricha, and Victor M. Montori. 2009. 'Endocrine Treatment of Transsexual Persons: An Endocrine Society Clinical Practice Guideline'. *The Journal of Clinical Endocrinology & Metabolism* 94 (9): 3132–54.
Hines, Sally. 2007. *TransForming Gender: Transgender Practices of Identity, Intimacy and Care*. Bristol, UK: Policy Press.
Hollway, Wendy. 2014. 'Gendered Subjectivity'. In *Encyclopedia of Critical Psychology*, edited by Thomas Teo, 771–73. New York: Springer.
Institute for Public Health. 2015. 'National Health and Morbidity Survey 2015 (NHMS 2015). Vol. II: Non-Communicable Diseases, Risk Factors & Other Health Problems'. Kuala Lumpur, Malaysia.
Jeftovic, M., B. Stojanovic, M. Bizic, D. Stanojevic, J. Kisic, M. Bencic, and M. L. Djordjevic. 2018. 'Hysterectomy with Bilateral Salpingo-Oophorectomy in Female-to-Male Gender Affirmation Surgery: Comparison of Two Methods'. *BioMed Research International* 2018: 1–5.
Johnson, Katherine. 2016. 'Changing Sex, Changing Self: Theorizing Transitions in Embodied Subjectivity'. *Men and Masculinities* 10 (1): 54–70.
Justice for Sisters. 2014. 'Reported Murders of Transgender Persons in Malaysia 2007–2013'. *Justice for Sisters* (blog), 19 November 2014. https://justiceforsisters.wordpress.com/2014/11/19/reported-murders-of-transgender-persons-in-malaysia/.
Khartini Slamah. 2005. 'The Struggle to Be Ourselves, Neither Men Nor Women: *Mak Nyahs* in Malaysia'. In *Sexuality, Gender and Rights: Exploring Theory and Practice in South and Southeast Asia*, edited by Geetanjali Misra and Radhika Chandiramani, 98–111. London: Sage.
Kim, Seunghwan, Margeaux Dennis, Jessica Holland, Mark Terrell, Marios Loukas, and Justine Schober. 2018. 'The Anatomy of Abdominal Flap Phalloplasty for Transgender Surgery'. *Clinical Anatomy* 31 (2): 181–86.
Liebert, Rachel. 2014. 'Pathologization'. In *Encyclopedia of Critical Psychology*, edited by Thomas Teo, 1327–33. New York: Springer.

Marinkovic, Maja, and Ron S. Newfield. 2017. 'Chest Reconstructive Surgeries in Transmasculine Youth: Experience from One Pediatric Center'. *International Journal of Transgenderism* 18 (4): 376–81.

McFarlane, Thomas, Jeffrey D. Zajac, and Ada S. Cheung. 2018. 'Gender-Affirming Hormone Therapy and the Risk of Sex Hormone-Dependent Tumours in Transgender Individuals—A Systematic Review'. *Clinical Endocrinology* 89 (6): 700–11.

Moravek, Molly B. 2018. 'Gender-Affirming Hormone Therapy for Transgender Men'. *Clinical Obstetrics and Gynecology* 61 (4): 687–704.

Nanda, Bheem Singh, Anubhav Gupta, Sasidhar Reddy J, Mahesh Mangal, S. S. Gambhir, and Sanjibani Sudha. 2017. 'Current Concepts in Gender Affirmation Surgery'. *Current Medicine Research and Practice* 7 (5): 184–90.

National Cancer Institute. 2019. 'Malaysia National Cancer Registry Report (MNCR) 2012–2016'. Ministry of Health Malaysia. https://drive.google.com/file/d/1BuPWrb05N2Jez6sEP8VM5r6JtJtlPN5W/view?usp=sharing.

Pearce, Ruth. 2018. *Understanding Trans Health: Discourse, Power and Possibility*. Bristol, UK: Policy Press.

Pfeffer, Carla A. 2017. *Queering Families: The Postmodern Partnerships of Cisgender Women and Transgender Men*. New York: Oxford University Press.

Qvistgaard, Skailer R. 2018. 'Testosterone and Transgender Men: The Discriminatory Impact of Testosterone's Schedule III Designation on Transgender Men Seeking Medical Care Notes'. *Journal of Health & Biomedical Law* 13 (2): 289–322.

Rowniak, Stefan, Catherine Chesla, Carol Dawson Rose, and William L. Holzemer. 2011. 'Transmen: The HIV Risk of Gay Identity'. *AIDS Education and Prevention* 23 (6): 508–20.

Selvaggi, Gennaro, Christopher J. Salgado, Stan Monstrey, and Miroslav Djordevic. 2018. 'Gender Affirmation Surgery'. *BioMed Research International* 2018: 1–2.

Teh, Yik Koon. 2001. 'Mak Nyahs (Male Transsexuals) in Malaysia: The Influence of Culture and Religion on Their Identity'. *International Journal of Transgenderism* 5 (3). https://www.atria.nl/ezines/web/IJT/97-03/numbers/symposion/ijtvo05no03_04.htm.

———. 2002. *The Mak Nyahs: Malaysian Male to Female Transsexuals*. Singapore: Eastern Universities Press.

———. 2008. 'HIV-Related Needs for Safety Among Male-to-Female Transsexuals (Mak Nyah) in Malaysia'. *SAHARA J: Journal of Social Aspects of HIV/AIDS* 5 (4): 178–85.

Tellier, Pierre-Paul. 2019. 'Improving Health Access for Gender Diverse Children, Youth, and Emerging Adults?' *Clinical Child Psychology and Psychiatry* 24 (2): 193–98.

The Commissioner of Law Revision, Malaysia. 2006. *Age of Majority Act 1971*. http://www.agc.gov.my/agcportal/uploads/files/Publications/LOM/EN/Act%2021.pdf.

Transmen of Malaysia. 2018. 'Transmen of Malaysia'. Facebook. https://www.facebook.com/TransmenofMalaysia/?ref=br_rs.

Tucker, Raymond P., Rylan J. Testa, Tracy L. Simpson, Jillian C. Shipherd, John R. Blosnich, and Keren Lehavot. 2018. 'Hormone Therapy, Gender Affirmation Surgery, and Their Association with Recent Suicidal Ideation and Depression Symptoms in Transgender Veterans'. *Psychological Medicine* 48 (14): 2329–36.

Vitelli, R., C. Scandurra, R. Pacifico, M. S. Selvino, S. Picariello, A. L. Amodeo, P. Valerio, and A. Giami. 2017. 'Trans Identities and Medical Practice in Italy: Self-Positioning Towards Gender Affirmation Surgery'. *Sexologies* 26 (4): e43–e51.

Wilde, Dorian. 2010. *Dorian's Transition Weblog*. https://www.youtube.com/channel/UCk8EJRJyV_k7_KMJVICR7sg.

CHAPTER 6

Performing Faith

This chapter is predicated on the understanding that faith is central to the becomings of many Malaysian trans men. My main aim here is to uncover how the doings of faith impact the construction and sustenance of (trans) gender identities in 'a country that historically embraced gender diversity but discarded this stance for an exclusive interpretation of Islamic modernity' (Goh 2019b, 436). Currently, state-sanctioned measures to censure, penalise and erase transgender and gender nonconforming subjectivities through religious frameworks such as reparative therapy, repentance and counselling are proliferating (Chim 2012; See 2019; Tham 2018).

Malaysian transgender Muslims 'are overwhelmingly *fiqh* oriented [or] oriented to the Muslim jurisprudential tradition [which] sometimes seem[s] to have a stronger grip upon the Muslim mind than the underlying principles of the Qur'an' (Muzaffar 2011, 25–26). Many live with the fear of '*kubur tak terima* (literally, "the grave will not receive", or complications pertaining to burial rites that are specific to gender identities assigned at birth)' (Appendix 2: Interviewing Dorian Wilde, para. 42), thus implying their trepidation at the thought of being refused burial due to their incongruity with the gender assigned to them at birth (see also Khartini 2005) and/or God's rejection of them as trans people at death, particularly if they have undergone bodily modifications. Malaysian transgender Christians are not only admonished for defying God, but accused of usurping the role of God through perverse acts of self-creation (Goh 2013).

J. N. Goh, *Becoming a Malaysian Trans Man*,
Gender, Sexualities and Culture in Asia,
https://doi.org/10.1007/978-981-15-4534-4_6

The concept of faith borrows from, but extends beyond Patrick S. Cheng's articulation of spirituality as 'any practice – whether public or private, formal or informal, praxis-oriented or theoretical – that brings an individual closer to ultimate reality, regardless of the monotheistic, dualistic, polytheistic, or non-theistic nature of that reality' (2006, 235). 'Ultimate reality' is fundamentally the sense and meaning which cradle the visible materiality of human existence, and individuals hold the prerogative to conceptualise and personalise ultimate reality as befitting their lives.

Andrew K. T. Yip notes that spirituality is often interpreted as 'a subjective, reflexive and critical exploration of flexible and fluid meanings and practices devoid of institutional control and surveillance' while religiosity 'denote[s] an individual's habitual – and uncritical – deference to, and observance of, institution-led religious proscriptions, teachings, and rituals' (2010, 35, note 1). Yet he also posits that a clear distinction between religiosity and spirituality is 'rigid and unhelpful, because it constructs "religiosity" and "spirituality" as bipolar opposites' (2010, 35, note 1). Yip thus decries a forced compartmentalisation of the various facets of faith as artificially discrete categories in favour of a standpoint that acknowledges the inextricable interrelatedness of these facets. I agree with Yip as the distinction between personalised spirituality and official religiosity is often ambiguous or undefined among trans men, a reality which fosters my keenness to trace these complex operations that unravel in their lives.

Hence in this chapter, faith refers to tenuous, inconsistent, fluid and situated performances of religion, ethics, life philosophy, spirituality, theology and scriptural inspiration in everyday life that are often partial, situated, interpenetrating, modified and amalgamated. My research findings suggest that Malaysian trans men are keen to validate their customisations of faith in relation to their self-affirmed gender identities against the dominant transnegative legislations and discourses of religious hierarchies and individuals who are communally sanctioned as legitimate and 'worthier' conduits of the sacred. In Malaysia, pastors, priests, monks, *'ulemā*[1] and other religious literati are endowed with undisputed authority to arbitrate in matters of the divine or of human conduct, including gender and sexuality.

Scholars who work at the intersection of gender, sexuality and faith note the vast number of transgender and queer people who approach

[1] *'ulemā'* is also spelled and pronounced as *'ulama'* or *'ulamak'* in Malaysia.

religion with varying measures of scepticism, loathing and/or trepidation due to religious disapprobation and hostility (Bong 2020; Geissinger 2012; Goh 2015b; Sweasey 1997; Wu 2000). Yet many refuse to alienate themselves from their faith systems which have become for them *sine qua non* constituents of self-coherence and purposeful existence. Subsequently, they construct radically affirming and even 'scandalous' or 'heretical' faith perspectives that affirm and sustain their gender and sexual identities (Goh 2018; Harper 2010; Hendricks 2011; Li 2007; Luk 2015; Robinson 2017; Vanita 2012; Yip with Khalid 2010).

There is an increasing corpus of dedicated transgender studies that intersects with Christian scriptures (Burke 2013; Hornsby and Guest 2016), Christian ethics (Childs 2009; Kolakowski 1997), Christian theologies and spiritualities (Althaus-Reid and Isherwood 2009; Beardsley and O'Brien 2016; Cornwall 2009, 2012; Goh 2012a, b, 2019b; Hero 2012; Hipsher 2009; Lowe 2017; Reay 2009; Tanis 2003; Whitehead and Whitehead 2014), Islamic texts (Kamali 2009, 2011; Kugle 2010), Muslim complexities (Goh 2012c; Teh 2008), Buddhist insights (Maggard 2014), Hindu beliefs (Agoramoorthy and Hsu 2015; Hossain 2012; Reddy 2005) and studies on comparative religion (Maggard 2014). Many of these works utilise transgender lived realities as starting points for biblical and Qur'ānic interpretation, theological construction, spiritual, philosophical and ethical reflection, and religious ratification.

Yip observes that for many lesbian, gay and bisexual people, 'sexuality and spirituality are flip sides of each other – to be sexual is to be spiritual; and to be spiritual is to be sexual' (2005a, 276). I expand Yip's insight by offering parallel ideas that gender and faith are flip sides of each other—to be truthful to one's gender is to embrace oneself as a person of faith; and to embrace oneself as a person of faith prompts one to be truthful to one's gender. In other terms, some encounter a fuller sense of their gender identity through heartfelt adherences to faith, and some experience greater degrees of godliness, holiness and/or human fulfilment when they embrace their self-affirmed gender identities.

Recognising Divine Endorsements

In many instances, affirming and supportive Abrahamic faith-based notions of transgender embodiment depend on an intensely unnegotiable recognition of the pivotal role of a supreme, benign divine being (Goh 2012b; Hero 2012; Tanis 2003; Yip and Keenan 2009). In this regard, Malaysian trans men of faith differ very little. Their becomings as trans men rely on divine validations of their self-affirmed gender identities, including the attribution of gender identity to God, the gift of meaningful relationships, the pursuit of self-realisation that are divinely mandated and godly biddings to communicate positive messages on trans men to others.

'Born This Way': Godly Origins

Several trans men trace their self-affirmed gender identities to a divine genesis. For Alco, the nexus that he carves out between his subjectivity and sense of faith is expressed by acknowledging the role of divine ordinance in his life. He recalls the following exchange with his mother, when he came out to her as a trans man before he began medically transitioning:

> I told my mum … before I started my transition … I see myself as a man … she started going … oh my God … is this my fault … why are you like this … I said, 'Mum, you have always taught me to say that God is almighty … and God doesn't make mistakes. So do you think that by me being like this, he[2] made a mistake'? Then my mum started going, you know, being this pious Muslim that she is, 'Oh no, no, no, God never makes mistakes, God don't make mistake'! … I said 'Okay, if God doesn't make mistake, then I am not a mistake. I'm here for a reason, and I don't know what that reason is, but we believe in "*qaḍā'*" and "*qadar*". Why must the "*qaḍā'*" and "*qadar*" be only for specific things, and not for everything? If I am born this way … can't you define it as"'*qaḍā*" and "*qadar*" also'?[3]

The doubts in the mind of Alco's mother are based on Qur'ānic verses that purportedly support the notion of gender as divinely ordained at birth. The Sūrah ar-Rūm, for instance, calls upon humankind to 'set [its] face steadily and truly to the Faith: God's handiwork according to the

[2]Both Muslim and Christian research participants use male pronouns for Allah and/or God, which is consistent with popular patriarchal and androcentric visualisations of the divine in Malaysian Islam and Christianity. Some interesting discussions can be found in Norani and Ng (1995).

[3]Generally, I find that Muslim trans men tend to use the term 'God' more frequently than 'Allah' during interviews in English.

pattern on which [God] has made [hu]mankind: no change (let there be) in the work (wrought) by God' (Qur'ān 30.30).[4] Furthermore, as Scott Kugle (2010, 244) posits, a divinely dictated, clearly delineated gender difference in the Qur'ān demonstrates 'a kind of pairing through which God's will plays out in the world'. Among Malaysian Malay-Muslim communities, gender complementarity is prized highly as the basis of God's plan for the nuclear family (Kalthom et al. 2008). Absolute adherence to one's gender identity thus facilitates divine operations on earth.

Yet when Alco's mother begins to question his self-affirmed gender identity and blame herself for who he is becoming, he appeals to the omnipotence and perfection that characterise God (see, for instance, Qur'ān 59.23), and which filter down to, and are reflected in Alco's own createdness. Alco's idea of being 'born this way' as designated by God resonates with Yip's (2005b) research findings among British lesbian, gay and bisexual Christians and Muslims who attempt to make sense of their sexualities by attributing them to divine creation. Through this appeal to God, Alco understands that he is 'not a mistake' as a trans man because 'God never makes mistakes'. To suggest otherwise is tantamount to suggesting that God is not 'almighty' and capable of error, an idea which is anathema to both these Muslim interlocutors. In other words, he is who he is because he is purposefully created by God to be this way.

Alco then draws a logical connection between divine creation and divine decree. He makes reference to the Islamic concept of '*qaḍā'*' and '*qadar*', which can be understood as references to divine dictate and determination. For Alco, the entirety of life, and not just 'specific things', is *qaḍā* and *qadar*. I further suggest that his understanding of the manner in which God has created him is not to be understood as passive submission to a divine will. To live as a trans man is to be recognised, accepted and executed in sincerity according to God's ordinance, or God's decree and mandate. Corresponding to the idea that '*qaḍā*' is fate and *qadar* is destiny as articulated by M. Khairul Naim et al. (2016), Alco is acutely aware that he is 'here for a reason', even if that reason has not been clearly established or defined. To become a trans man is to adopt a pliability to divine decree, determination and destiny in the active 'doings' of a self-affirmed gender identity. It is to

[4]All English translations of the Qur'ān are taken from Abdullah Yusuf Ali (2013).

'confront the unexpected richness and endless variation of nature, as the Qur'an urges [human beings] to examine God's signs on the horizons and *within the selves*' (Q. 41:53)' (Kugle 2010, 267; added emphasis).

Similar to Alco, Superman avers that who he is actually 'come[s] from God':

> *Goh*: Who is this God to you?
>
> *Superman*: He is the source of creation. The source of love, the source of life. And the source of all … He's the source of love … I cannot detach myself from God … I can detach myself from everything. From my partner, from children. I can't detach myself from God. I am linked to God, and God is in me. I'm just, an extension, a being of God. If I'm a God being. Okay. Because I come from God … And why was I created, I was created out of love … He wanted me to experience just a little joy. Which is this life. I get to experience growth. To experience pain. 'Cause if I don't experience all these things, I'm just a walking zombie …

Superman understands his gender identity to be intrinsically linked and inextricably bound to God. The measure of godliness that is inherent in him appears as profound. While he is able to 'detach [him]self from everything', including his 'partner' and 'children', he finds that he 'cannot detach [him]self from God' who is present within him. Superman pursues the depth of this 'spiritual hunger' (Shallenberger 1996, 211) even more radically by seeing himself as 'a God being', or 'an extension … of God'. In so doing, he seemingly blurs the distinction between the creator and the created, and suggests a radical intimacy between him and God.

I suggest that as a trans man of faith who is true to himself, Superman becomes a living semiotic of an ongoing interpenetrating relationship between a human being and God in the pursuit of greater gender meaning-making. By naming God as the 'source' of who he is and embodying this naming with sincerity and integrity, Superman shatters cisnormative theological formulations that are forcefully foisted on human persons as exclusive conditions for theologically approved human validity (Goh 2014b). In response to my question about the relationship between his gender identity and his faith, Superman invokes the notion of God as the omnisource of 'creation', 'life' and 'love', the reason for his existence and his capacity to express emotions. Superman sees his manliness as a deliberate initiative on the part of God that enables him to experience love, life, 'growth' and 'pain' through 'a continual process of transformation' (Hero 2012, 156) and an ongoing 'personal revelation' (Tanis 2003, 129) which he experiences within himself.

There is possibly a deeper layer to Superman's convictions beyond a God who disrupts rigid normative expectations of who God is. It may well be the case that he is hinting at his ability to incarnate trans-divinity through his own embodied existence as a trans man. Trans-divinity echoes B. K. Hipsher's somewhat controversial theological idea of a God who can be imagined as transgender, 'who has the capacity to move fluidly between gender identities and sexualities' (2009, 100), who resists the restrictions of normative gender and sexuality boundaries, and whose unconstrained personhood in this respect is bestowed upon human persons. Hipsher's ideas are no different to various theological imaginings of God as man, woman, Black, Asian, disabled and queer. If these are indeed his thoughts, to become a trans man is to embrace and mirror the plenitude of the divine gift of human diversity without which Superman is merely 'a walking zombie', or a lifeless entity.

'Truly Blessed': Loving Relationships

The person of God who is deemed responsible for a self-affirmed gender identity is also experienced through loving familial and romantic relationships that are construed as divine benedictions. For Muslim SR, the interplay between his gender identity and faith is manifested in the experience of fulfilling life encounters, particularly through 'wonderful parents', surviving the vicissitudes of life and having sufficient financial resources. He shares the following insights:

> *Goh*: How do you think Allah looks at you?
>
> *SR*: … He created women and men. Adam and Eve … There is no other gender. For me, like, I don't know how he look at me … because … I am not him, but I have faith in him … Doesn't matter who I am, I'm a trans, I'm a man … Allah still loves me. You know why? I'm so grateful, I'm so thankful to him … I have … wonderful parents. I have a wonderful life. Yeah, in life we have ups and down life, this and that. I'm not very rich, I'm not very poor, in the middle. But anyhow … I survive a lot of things. I live, I learn, I love …

I interpret SR's response that he is ignorant of Allah's impression of him because of his inability to position himself in place of the divine as an admission of doubt as to whether he is completely acceptable to Allah.

For most trans men, belief in a Higher Power mitigates rather than obliterates a sense of guilt associated with their gender identities that have long been condemned as deviant and iniquitous. To address this doubt, SR constructs two strategies of self-assurance that are founded on his faith in Islam as 'a canopy of meaning [and] an embracing referential framework' (Yip with Khalid 2010, 94) to decipher his (trans)gender embodiment.

In the first strategy, SR makes a link between his self-affirmed gender identity and divine creation by drawing the conclusion that being a trans man is an intentional act of God. Similar to Alco, SR understands that he is who he is because of God who created him that way, or what Yip (2005a) refers to as the ontogeneric strategy that is co-opted by many of his lesbian, gay and bisexual research participants. What I find particularly noteworthy is SR's recourse to 'Adam and Eve' (Qur'ān 2.30–39) as the first progenitors of the human race to describe the male/man/masculine and female/woman/feminine binary, and to affirm that 'there is no other gender'. Instead of allowing this imagery to undergird a theologically and biologically founded gender dichotomy in which he falls short, or dismantling this dichotomy altogether, he recasts it as an emphatic declaration of his createdness as a man. In other words, he is man—and can only be man—because he is not woman, and this reality is made possible only through divine ordinance. The strict preservation of a gender binary notwithstanding, he appeals to a divinely charged sanctioning of a gender-spirituality nexus with which he is able to concretise his self-identification as man.

The second strategy involves a resolute 'faith' in Allah and the love that Allah bears for him, a loving acceptance that encompasses his subjectivity (Yip with Khalid 2010). Ironically, SR does not portray this personal human–divine relationship as total altruism on the part of Allah. Instead, that 'Allah still loves him' is dependent on his unending gratitude for two particular realities in which Allah plays an important role. The first is the presence of 'wonderful parents', or as he explains elsewhere, parents who are accepting of his gender identity. The second is the cognisance that he is living 'a wonderful life' despite an average income and having to 'survive' the 'ups and down[s]' of life. An acute recognition of one's own ability '[to] live, [to] learn[and to] love' from life as a trans man effectively seals a loving and affirming connection between him and Allah, and the consequent manageability of his gender identity.

Alco also experiences the validating presence of God in his life through loving relationships. In response to my enquiry about how

God 'looks at' and 'feels about' him as a trans man, he provides a rapid response by referring to his family and 'home':

> *Goh*: How do you think God looks at you? How do you think God feels about you?
>
> *Alco*: For ... nineteen over years, I've been with my partner. We've been through ... lots of ups, lots of downs, but we have been blessed. I have been blessed with the most beautiful woman who stand by me to walk with me. She stood behind me to push me up, and sometimes she would stand in front of me to pull me up. I have been blessed with two beautiful children, adopted yes, but they are my children. And to wake up in the morning, to see their smile, to feel their hugs, to be able to feel their kisses, and their 'I love you dada! I love you'! you know, and all that. We have a home, we may not be rich, but we have enough. So, all those things, I am, I feel like I'm truly blessed.

Unlike Superman who can be separated from a partner and children, Alco appeals to an indispensable relationship with a 'partner' who stands 'behind' and 'in front of' him, and 'pushes' and 'pulls [him] up' in the 'ups [and] downs' of life as evidence of God's approval of his self-actualisation as a trans man. The abiding presence of a supportive partner is simultaneously an experience of the abiding presence and steady support of God in a partnered trans man's gender identity.

Although conservative Malaysian Islamic authorities may uncritically disqualify and condemn Alco's relationship with his female 'partner' as little more than a butch–femme lesbian relationship (Jabatan Mufti Kerajaan Negeri Sembilan 2008), Alco's own self-identification as a man who is in a relationship with a woman actually authenticates Islamic 'theological beliefs in Man and Woman as a divine pair' (Kelly 2010, 227). Alco's partnership with 'the most beautiful woman' which is considered illicit by state and religion is concomitantly an act of corroborating religiously mandated gender complementarity and sustaining the gender binary, yet with critically transgressive differences.

Furthermore, Alco speaks enthusiastically of his adopted children, whose 'smile[s]', 'hugs' and 'kisses' are indicative of their loving acceptance of him. Their willing and effusive expressions of love to him as their 'dada'—an affectionate and informal term for 'father'—is particularly crucial for his notion of divine acceptance. It reflects Neil Pembroke's claim that 'when a father cares deeply about his children, there is a spiritual dimension in his relationship with them' (2008, 82). Alco's undertaking of a paternal role in the family and his children's acknowledgement of him as their 'dada' is concurrently God's blessing and acceptance of him as a male parent. Alco's position as the father of the family within 'a home', rather than 'be[ing] rich', is the ultimate measure of being 'truly blessed'.

Alco's formulation of 'home' echoes what Jeffrey Weeks et al. posit as 'doing family', or techniques with which individuals 'perform gender, sexuality, work, caring and other activities that make up the totality of life experiences' (2001, 38). By assembling a 'home' comprising two adopted children, a cisgender, heterosexual 'wife' and 'mother', and himself as a trans man and 'dada', Alco demonstrates that becoming a trans man involves both the doing and undoing of cisnormative and heteronormative[5] notions of family that '[commit] to looking at [a family's] inner content[,] not its external form' (Sweasey 1997, 116).

'Be Our Own Person': Self-Actualisation

As explained in Chapter 2, my use of 'self-actualisation' refers to 'an awareness of the self that facilitates a process of self-determination, self-creation or self-definition as a recognisable subject in the world'. This process galvanises 'a deeper sense of oneself, addressing the whole of life, and a connection with something bigger' (Sweasey 1997, 12). While SR and Alco appear to *actively reap* divine lavishness, Aarone *actively collaborates* with the creator by striving towards self-realisation as both a Muslim and a trans man. The following exchange reveals his inner processes in this regard:

> *Goh*: As a Muslim, would you also believe that … God created you?
> *Aarone*: Yes, of course.
> *Goh*: Then, how does … that idea of God creating you, the idea of God as a creator, relate to your … changes[?]
> *Aarone*: Okay, there is this one …verse in the Qur'ān … about your life. Meaning, I can't remember the name of the verse, but it says that … whatever you do … you take responsibility of your actions. Secondly … if you decide to be successful, you get up and be successful … Even in … the call for prayers. It's *ha ya 'alal falah*, means let's go on towards success. So it's up to you, yourself, what you want to be.

[5] See explanations of 'heteronormativity' and 'cisnormativity' in 'Prologue'.

Similar to SR and Alco, Aarone also understands his gender identity as the consequence of divine createdness. When I ask him how he draws a connection between his relationship with God and his current 'changes', meaning his increasing masculinisation due to ongoing Gender-Affirming Hormone Therapy, he offers an interconnecting strategy.

First, Aarone appeals to the Qur'ān to support his scripturally based belief that he is to 'take responsibility [for his] actions'. Although he is uncertain of the location of a singular verse in scripture to support this belief, it is probable that Aarone actually has in mind several sacred verses that speak of personal responsibility. For instance, the Sūrah Fuṣṣilat proclaims that 'whoever works righteousness benefits [their] own soul; whoever works evil, it is against [their] own soul' (Qur'ān 41.46). Moreover, the Sūrah al-Isrā' states that they 'who receiveth guidance, receiveth it for [their] own benefit' (Qur'ān 17.15). Aarone thus subscribes to a deeply personal, scripturally inspired drive to be proactive, undergo the necessary 'changes' and become who he is meant to be in life as a trans man. His insight and experience augment Meredith B. McGuire's suggestion that the living out of spirituality is an embodied practice of 'postures, movements, [and] ways of focusing [one's] attention' (2003, 3). For this Muslim trans man, the doing of spirituality is parsed as a scripturally mandated embodied ambition to be the best human being that he can be.

Second, Aarone appeals to the *adhān*[6] or the Muslim call to mandatory daily prayer. According to Isaac A. Weiner, the *adhān* 'invests Islamic space with meaning, regulates the rhythms of daily life, and orients Muslims in relation to God and to each other' (2014). Aarone specifically picks up on one verse from the *adhān* prayers—'*ha ya 'alal falah*'—which can be loosely translated as 'hurry' or 'rush to success' to buttress his gender identity. For him, to become a trans man is to participate actively in the realisation of a successful, meaningful life in accordance with an Islamic injunction. Aarone may have drawn on the *adhān* primarily as a familiar cultural artefact that provides him with a sense of security. Yet, I contend that the *adhān* also serves as a significant method with which he connects to God and the greater Muslim *ummah* or community without relinquishing his gender identity. As both cisgender

[6]This term is commonly spelled and pronounced as '*azan*' in Malaysia.

and transgender Muslims are obliged to respond to the same *adhān*, he heeds a personal directive to be 'successful' as a man without abandoning a relationship with God and solidarity with fellow Muslims.

When I ask Axman, a Christian, on how he understands the role of God in his life, he first responds in terms of the divine bestowal of human freedom in everyday realities:

> In my gender ... He's already answered me in what I get day to day ... I mean as long as you're getting on ... You do your best that you can ... I think you're okay already lah ... God allows each of us to be our own person. And he's given us that liberty to be our own person. And of course if that own person means you go around and whack people and you know, cheat people, I'm sure God does not approve of that ... I think God gave me the liberty to be my own person that with his grace and mercy ... be the best person I can be to everyone who comes across to me.

Axman describes a two-pronged insight into the relationship between his faith and self-affirmed gender identity. First, and unlike Superman, Axman does not merely rest on divine createdness to authenticate his existence as a trans man. Akin to Aarone, he provides a more proactive stance in which the living out of gender identity is a project of human self-realisation 'to be [his] own person' in collaboration with God.

That he mentions God's permission and freedom for him 'to be [his] own person' four times in succession suggests that Axman wholeheartedly perceives gender identity as a divine gift of gender democratisation in which both the trans man and God share a common goal of human fulfilment, but one in which Axman ultimately holds the prerogative of deciding his gender identity as a 'creature-in-process ... a unity of body-mind that is continually shaped by discourses' (Lowe 2017, 31). As Justin Edward Tanis eloquently describes it,

> Trans bodies also speak of a collaboration between God and humanity in co-creating what our bodies are and what they become ... while God set in motion the process that led to our evolution, conception, and birth, we who are these bodies make choices about ... how we will treat our bodies, how we move our bodies – and all of these actions play a role in shaping our bodies, literally and figuratively. (2003, 166)

Additionally, the association between faith and gender identity for Axman is concomitantly the imperative to fulfil the 'day to day' obligations of life. By 'getting on' and 'do[ing the] best that [he] can', he receives a daily dose of divine endorsement even if such quotidian activities do not seemingly correlate to his subjectivity in a direct way. The ability to live life as a trans man, is to experience divine presence and validation.

Nevertheless, this project is built on the premise of an ethical interpersonal relationship, a topic I will discuss in greater detail later in this chapter. Axman is cognisant that he is not to 'go around and whack [and] cheat people'. Instead, the permission and freedom that he receives from God 'to be [his] own person' is contingent on his ability to 'be the best person [he] can be to everyone' and reflect God's 'grace and mercy'. It is only then that he becomes 'okay already' or meets the approval of God to become the person that he is. For Axman, the 'pull of this identity is a sacred process' (Tanis 2003, 26) as it is a process in which he cooperates with God.

Gaining Spiritual Independence

Spiritual independence refers to deliberate and conscious efforts on the part of trans men to make informed decisions about matters of faith in their lives. I have discovered that for many Malaysian trans women or *mak nyah*, such efforts frequently entail reconfigurations of ideas of God and reimaginings of the relationship between God and the human person (Goh 2012c). Spiritual independence is also 'rooted in life-as-lived, as well as affecting how life is lived', in which transgender and queer people feel more inclined 'to respond to and emphasise the personal … rather than the doctrinal and organizational' (Sweasey 1997, 12–13). On varying levels, and depending on personal contexts and circumstances, personal spirituality both resonates with and outrightly contravenes the teachings of official religious hierarchies.

'Fulfilments from the Inner Side': Formulating Independent Insights

Two techniques that trans men employ towards spiritual independence include conceptualising spiritual insights that can complement or substitute transphobic religious discourses, and reinterpreting religious texts to support their gender identities. As the following narrative demonstrates, Superman distinguishes between his 'religious faith' and 'spiritual base':

Goh: Okay, so let's talk about your religion. What's your religion, what's your faith? How is it related to your identity as a man, or a trans man?

Superman: My religious faith is Catholicism. Normal Catholicism. That I think everybody recognises. My spiritual base is love. Light and love. Erm, it is my, because of my spirituality that I found my, I started finding my way back to myself. My identity. Because my spirituality er, focused and is centred on the base of love. So basically I have to do everything, to centre my life … For a long time I didn't realise I didn't love myself. I have to value me, over others first.

Upon asking Superman how his 'religion' or 'faith' are connected to his self-affirmed gender identity, he provides a layered response that demonstrates a bricolage of Christianity and other contributing elements. 'Light and love' are biblical imageries, such as those found in the Christian gospels of Luke (8.16) and John (8.12; 15.12–15), which may suggest that Superman sees himself as being the recipient and channel of divine guidance and love that form the foundations of 'normal Catholicism' for him. The 'normalcy' of Catholicism in this context alludes to popular doings of religiosity which 'everybody recognises', and which thus remain on the level of anticipated and acceptable performances of Christianity. Despite appropriating this religious label for himself, he mentions it fleetingly as though to suggest that this label comes with facile religious recognisability but little else.

Superman contrasts and augments this seeming banality of Roman Catholicism with his 'spiritual base'. Notions of 'light and love' are not abstract and ethereal formulations of otherworldliness but life principles that enable him to come into intimate contact with his gender identity. Superman's spirituality acts as the impetus for him to 'centre [his] life', or the act of 'striving towards integration [and] overcom[ing] fragmentations that … challenge the development of [transgender] identities' (Goh 2014a, 134). In this sense, 'light and love' are cherished gifts of enlightenment, awareness, self-prioritisation and self-acceptance that confront and banish self-doubt. Gary Bouma's assertion that 'what is held protectively in the heart is sacred' (2006, 2) points to the fact that the knowledge and values which have been gleaned from exercises of deep interiority hold immense spiritual value for a person. Spirituality assists the trans man in being finally cognisant of the need to 'love [and] value [himself]' as a trans man after a spell of allowing his self-worth to be gauged by cisnormative and cissexist appraisals of his gender identity.

Like Superman, Warp formulates his own spiritual vistas, and predicates his constructions of God on the idea of diversity:

> I think the basic tenet that most religions have is that God is … omniscient … right? … Christians have this thing like God works in mysterious ways … who are you to say that you understand what God is actually doing here? And if you see the diversity in the world, who are you to say that God only made men and women? Everybody is a different colour, everybody is a different height, build, eye colour, lives, experiences. Why can't we have different genders and different sexualities? The way of nature is diversity, not binary. Binary is the way of man. If you look at Hinduism, Hinduism is SO (raises voice) grey. There's no black and white … gods can be evil, demons can be good.

Warp currently adheres to a hybrid spirituality that weaves Hinduism with personal spiritual concepts. His impression that all religions subscribe to the 'basic tenet' of an all-knowing God divulges his notion that all religious adherents admit to the unbounded wisdom of God in permitting and determining various forms of human 'diversity in the world' in terms of ethnicity, physicality and lived reality.

His attribution of the popular anecdote that 'God works in mysterious ways' to Christianity is based on popular culture rather than official doctrine or scriptural sources, but still reveals a certitude that divine 'omniscience', understood in a sense as 'God's all-knowing certainty about one's "true" gender' (Burke 2014, 5) lies beyond the grasp of the human intellect. Nonetheless, religions that propound the ineffability of the divine also lay claim to an unequivocal 'understand[ing of] what God is actually doing' in matters of gender. For him therefore, the God of mystery has been reduced to a predictable deity who takes the side of vitriolic transphobic Christians.

Susannah Cornwall (2009) draws a parallel between a God who refuses to be bound by the limits of human imagination and is ultimately shrouded in 'unknowingness', and the transgender person whose identity is dynamically open to unpredictable possibilities. I suggest that Warp's idea of a 'God [who] works in mysterious ways' resonates with Cornwall's insights of divine ineffability which is mirrored in the fluidity and enigma of human identities. Warp deploys the notion of divine mystery against know-it-all religions that dismiss the possibility and permissibility of 'different genders and different sexualities'. He rebuffs their arrogant attitudes by holding God responsible for acting outside dichotomous boundaries and creating diversity in 'nature'.

Moreover, Warp proposes that both human and divine beings cannot be taxonomised according to clear, neat 'binary' and unambiguous categories. To buttress his point, Warp emphasises the 'grey[ness]' or blurred boundaries of Hinduism alongside a reminder that benign 'gods' can act in the interest of 'evil' and malignant 'demons' can perform 'good'. The 'grey[ness]' of which he speaks corresponds to Serena Nanda's observations of a diversity within

> the Hindu sex/gender system, the interchange of male and female qualities, transformations of sex and gender, the incorporation of male and female within one person … alternative sex and gender roles, among deities and humans, are meaningful and positive themes in mythology, ritual, and art. (2002, 138)

In unsettling the binary of 'good gods' and 'bad demons', Warp constructs a platform from whence to interrogate cisnormative assumptions of divine identities and disrupt ideas of cisnormativity as the sole divinely mandated destiny for human beings.

Trans activist Dorian Wilde mentions the worship of 'a specific god[dess who] is dedicated to trans people … called Bahuchara Mata', and that there are cultural spaces, rituals, traditions and religious festivals that cater to transgender Hindus throughout Malaysia (Appendix 2: Interviewing Dorian Wilde, para. 39; [see also Taparia 2011]). Yet, in stark contrast with Nanda's and Wilde's seemingly idealistic portrayals of Hinduism as unequivocally open and affirming towards gender and sexual heterogeneity, many lesbian, gay and transgender Indian friends have intimated to me horrific tales of explicit family rejection. Born into a Hindu family, Wilde himself identifies with many who 'left home because [they were] disowned, and kicked out' (Appendix 2: Interviewing Dorian Wilde, para. 4).

Class and economic status also play a major part in the ill-treatment of transgender people in Malaysian Indian-Hindu communities. Wilde discloses how these communities relegate transgender people to 'the lower echelons of society' by default, and how 'middle class people [are] generally supposed to disassociate [from] people who are trans … because they are in a different caste' (Appendix 2: Interviewing Dorian Wilde, para. 32). Here, the rejection of transgender identity is coupled with class and caste differences. The inclusivity of Hinduism and the powerful patronage of the mother goddess Bachura Mata are apparently no match for stigma, shame and caste strictures, and the violence, humiliation and repudiation that assail those who depart from culturally defined norms in Malaysia.

'Between You and God': Bracketing and Challenging Mainstream Religiosity

The personal performance of spirituality occasionally necessitates a forceful rebuttal of mainstream religious ideologies. By bracketing and challenging hierarchically and socioculturally sanctioned religiosities that affect gender and sexuality issues, a more affirming profile of spirituality is allowed to emerge (see Goh 2016b; Yip with Khalid 2010; Yip 1997). Axman provides an interesting insight into his personal spirituality when he insists that he is still a Christian despite encountering problems with church hierarchy due to his gender identity:

> *Goh*: But you still consider yourself a Christian?
> *Axman*: Yeah.
> *Goh*: Why do you hang on to your faith when you know that your faith can turn around and bite you?
> *Axman*: You see, there is a separation, I mean, I've come to realise, I mean, it's my own experience, there is a separation between church and God himself. Church is, you know, they interpret the bible as their own interpretation. But what I experience with God is my own personal thing. And nobody can actually come in between that. I mean, I believe lah, what I can get so far, how I managed to pull through and pay my bills or whatever, that is God's grace and mercy. Church will tell me, oh you know, you do like this is sin or whatever. You're not going to get your blessing or whatever shit. I don't want to listen to that.

Despite being cognisant of the fact that Christianity has, and can continue to 'bite' him or cause him consternation, Axman continues to 'hang on to [his] faith' due to 'experience[s] with God' that are deeply personal. His acute recognition of the presence of God as 'grace and mercy' in his life is premised on concrete material experiences of God, such as the ability to 'pay [his] bills'. For Axman, God is not encountered in ecclesiastical doctrine or law, or in ethereal episodes, but in practical, quotidian realities (refer also to Goh 2019a).

I believe that this awareness of the role that God plays in his life is as much fuelled by personal life events as it is by the strategy of distinguishing and separating church from God. Like many other transgender and queer Christians, Axman possesses an aptitude for delineating hierarchical religiosity from inclusive, personal spirituality (Aune 2015; Shallenberger 1996), even if these two entities are inextricably interwoven for him. I suggest that the designation of the ecclesiastical system as an entity that upholds a myopic interpretation of scripture against transgender people also exposes their role in manufacturing the corrosive poison of transnegativity and 'the venom of homonegativity' (Yip 2010, 37). Such pronouncements that declare his gender identity as 'sin' and thus ineligible for 'blessing' refute 'an inclusive Christian gospel that trumps heterosexism [and cisnormativity] in favor of celebrating the diversity of God's creation' (Childs 2009, 39).

The contradiction between a God who unconditionally accepts him in everyday life and a condemnatory church that purports to represent this God becomes glaringly obvious. When Axman is able to recognise this 'shit'—or nonsensical rhetoric that accuses him of sinfulness and excludes him from God's benedictions—and not 'listen to [it]', he develops a heightened sensitivity to the palpable workings of God in his life.

Aarone's experiences of God echo those of Axman's, albeit from a Muslim perspective that refutes popular expectations of a 'valid' Malaysian Islam. In a process of code-switching between English and Malay, he explains how he lives as *both* a Muslim *and* a trans man, which contravenes popular Islamic expectations:

Goh: Can you explain, what Islam means to you, in terms of your gender identity?

Aarone: Okay. Islam is all about who you are, and you and God. That's about it. You know? Er, you male or female is between you and God. And er, so, after I made, I find, I found peace with myself, er, and I've prayed and begun to pray as who I really am, so I find it, I find peace in, in saying my prayers so, er, I guess er, I don't really, I don't really see what is the problem between me and God. Because if you believe that, He listens … it says in the Qur'ān … That's how you, that's how I talk to God … No doubt you see there are lots of people who go to the *masjid* (mosque), they have all this facial hair, *janggut* all *panjang-panjang* (long beards) … this mark on the forehead … it doesn't reflect you or them, as being the true Muslim. The true Muslim is being, is between, is what's in your heart.

At my prompting, Aarone emphatically proclaims that Islam is fundamentally a religion 'about who [he is], and [about him] and God'.

Hence, he interprets Islam as a deeply personal exercise of faith which may be incongruent with normative expectations of Islamic knowledge, appearance and practice. Aarone provides a series of stereotypical images associated with popular Malaysian Islamic male piety which include 'people who go to the mosque' and show off lengthy 'beard[s]', and whose foreheads are bruised and darkened in one spot due to long and frequent periods of prayer. Many local Muslims see this 'mark on the forehead' or *zabība* as the ultimate sign of Islamic male piety. Such individuals are stereotypically acclaimed in Malaysia as 'true [male] Muslim[s]' that parallel 'overt displays of Muslim piety such as the wearing of the veil' (Lee 2010b, 28) by Muslim women in the country.[7] Seemingly superficial and exterior semiotics, as such, become incontestably indicative of authentically devout and perfect interior cis male Islamic practice.

I suspect that Aarone may have gone through a period of time in his life when he saw himself positioned at the periphery of ideal Muslim manliness because he neither sported a beard nor displayed a *zabība* as hallmarks of Muslim piety. He may have felt inadequate as a Muslim due to his embodiment as a person who was assigned female at birth but who now wished to worship God as a man. It is possible however, that at the time of our meeting, these issues were no longer as formidable or pressing to Aarone as they might have been before. His comment that being 'male or female is between [oneself] and God' could be evidence of a steadily growing sense of clarity and conviction with which he continues to address the complexities of being a Muslim trans man in Malaysia.

Therefore, rather than complying with a normative image of Muslim maleness, Aarone constructs himself as a 'true Muslim' on his own terms through a specific form of 'piety-trumping' (Liow 2009, 15) in which he concentrates on 'what's in [his] heart', or a willingness to prostrate himself in obedience to God who is 'conscience, or … Creator, or the joyous integration of both, known as integrity' (Manji 2011, xxv). The rejection of popular exterior Muslim male piety is, I submit, a concomitant rejection of cis masculinity as the singularly legitimate embodiment of Malay-Muslim manliness.

Consequently, the coupling of a self-affirmed gender identity that is ultimately 'between [him] and God' and a careful preservation of 'the spiritual core of religion – the most important of which is one's personal

[7] Refer to my analysis of Hadi's experiences in 'Engaging Society'.

relationship with God' (Yip 2005a, 280) enables Aarone to '[find] peace with [him]self', or to attain some serenity upon realising that there is no 'problem between [him] and God' as a trans man. It is only within this peaceful relationship with God that he is able 'to pray as who [he] really [is]', in accordance with a Qur'ānic-based conviction that God 'listens' to him as one who is 'proximate, not distant' (Kelly 2010, 238).

Spiritual independence is thus an exercise of constructing personal insights that defy hierarchical religious stipulations and relegate them to lesser significance. God is perceived as the creator of human and non-human diversity within actual lived experiences, rather than bound by religious policies and regulations. Doings of faith which are deeply personalised evince 'an emancipatory logic' (Yip 2005a, 278) that assist trans men in the sense-making of their subjectivities.

Constructing Ethics

In general terms, 'ethics' refers to frequently highly volatile debates surrounding what is 'wrong' and 'right' in human relationships. A perspective of Margaret Farley's idea of sexual ethics as the 'need to assess human actions and possibilities, asking about discernible contradictions or harms, looking for patterns of relationship that promote individual and social well-being' (2008, 15) is helpful in teasing out the nuances of ethical living among Malaysian trans men.

As heteronormative and cisnormative ethical ideals are often unproblematically imposed on transgender and queer people (Cheng 2013; Goh 2016a), in which they are often branded as unethical, some of them find it necessary to create their own ethical principles. In fact, all my research participants disclose an assortment of ways in which they integrate ethical values into their becomings. This section showcases a few examples of how some trans men turn to humanistic principles as the basis of their ethical outlook while others appeal to, and draw on official religiosity.

'Be Good to Others': Treating Others Well

For some trans men, the conceptualisation of ethics revolves primarily around the notion of treating people in a warm-hearted and kindly manner. Ray's living out of a specific 'life principle' allows him to exercise benevolence in social interaction:

Goh: Do you have any life principles or spirituality or life philosophy that you live by?

Ray: I guess the easiest way to say is that for me is that, I would treat people as I would treat myself, which means with love and kindness. I would treat them as I expect them to treat me. So I treat them with respect, with understanding, compassion, kindness, I try to treat them that way lah. Although I am a little bit of an arsehole sometimes (laughs) depending on my mood. So the thing is that, for me is that, I do try to be understanding and kind and compassionate as far as I am personally able to …

Goh: Are there any ways in which your life principles are connected to your gender identity?

Ray: I guess I would say so a little bit because, me being part of what is called a marginalised community or marginalised identity, I know how it feels like to be treated like shit. So it's like, it's not a nice feeling, I don't want people to be treated that way. Especially those who are, whether they're treated unfairly because of their race, or their gender, or their sexuality, or their … disability. Because I try to be … as kind and compassionate a person as I possibly can.

Ray's 'life principles' are built loosely or 'a little bit' on his own gender identity within 'a marginalised community or … identity'. As a self-identified transmasculine individual, he is keenly aware of 'be[ing] treated like shit', or negative experiences of gender identity. In musing over such incidents as 'not a nice feeling' and thus 'bringing *consciousness* and *intentionality* to the issue of embodiment' (Horn et al. 2005, 97; original emphasis), he is determined to avoid inflicting any pain on others in his interpersonal relationships. Subsequently, Ray appropriates a personal manifesto of 'treat[ing] people as [he] would treat [him]self', namely with 'love … respect … understanding, compassion [and] kindness'. Such people include those who experience unjust treatment due to identities of 'race' or ethnicity, 'gender', 'sexuality' and 'disability'.

Ray's personal experiences of being 'treated unfairly' due to his gender identity is transformed into a resolution to treat others fairly. Ethics, which 'involves the self in relation with some other and indeed is more profoundly relational than it is individual' (Bouma 2006, 12–13), becomes for Ray a concrete embodiment of his transmasculinity. This vision is, however, not totally altruistic as he also 'expect[s others] to treat' him in a similar fashion. Neither has Ray achieved perfection in this regard, as he can occasionally be 'a little bit of an arsehole' or cause irritation, anger and/or anguish to others. The performance of ethics is thus a series of interminable ventures with sporadic failures, rather than a successful and absolute point of arrival.

While Ray confesses to a minimal connection between gender identity and ethics, Michael states that his principle 'to be good as possible to everyone' is completely devoid of any gender or godly influences. His desire to live ethically has been embedded in him in 'all [his] life', even prior to transitioning:

> *Goh*: How would you describe yourself in terms of your religion?
>
> *Michael*: I don't believe in God, that's to be honest, I don't believe in God, because like not … experienced anything with God's presence in my life … but for now, what I believe in is like just do good and be good, that's it. You know, you don't have to like be a God-fearing person … as long as you know what you're doing, as long as … you're in the right direction, go ahead … be good to people, and … just accept them for … who they are …
>
> *Goh*: Alright, the principles … how are they connected to your life as a trans man?
>
> *Michael*: No, I kind of, I kinda like been this all my life, like if you do good, you just do good and, you know, like, I, I know I'm not that good kind of person, but I've done so many other things like bad things and stuff, but, but, that's what I think, like just be as good as you can … I know sometimes I've done bad things … but it's just that, I don't like mean it kind of thing, and what I mean, like, it's not like I've been good my whole life, it's just like, just, I just try to be good as possible to everyone … Because it's not like I chose to be this way, ever since I transitioned, but I've been like this my whole life, so yeah, it's been there.

Michael '[does not] believe in God' as he has 'not … experienced anything [of] God's presence in [his] life'. His scepticism lies in polarity with Axman's experiences of God who helps 'pay [his] bills'. Michael substitutes this disbelief with the principles of 'just do[ing] good and be[ing] good', which he applies both to others and himself. Not unlike Axman however, a concrete performance of ethical principles for Michael is twofold, as it involves both the self and others. First, ethics is executed through 'be[ing] good to people' by 'accept[ing] them for … who they are'. Second, these ethical principles are channelled through 'know[ing] what [he is] doing' and remaining 'in the right direction', which I understand as a sort of 'embodied cognition [or] congruity of body-mind' (Lowe 2017, 34) that enables him to deepen the self-understanding of his subjectivity in everyday life.

Although Michael's claims that his self-affirmed gender identity is completely detached from his sense of ethics, my interpretation of his narrative offers the possibility that they may in fact be deeply intertwined. His belief in 'accept[ing others] for … who they are' may in reality be a reflection of his personal desire to be accepted for who he is as a trans man. Although he may have 'been like this [his] whole life', I propose that his sense of personal ethics would inevitably have heightened 'since [he] transitioned'. There is very likely a synergy between the yearning to be treated well and accepted as a trans man and the incitement to treat others well and accept them for who they are irrespective of their gender identities.

Michael's retort that he is 'not that good [a] person' is actually a confession that he is not as ethical as he would like to be, as he has 'done so many … bad things' even if he '[didn't] mean it'. Despite this clear cognisance of wrongdoing and not having been 'good [his] whole life', which is similar to Ray's idea of being the occasional 'arsehole', Michael strives to 'just do good' and to 'be as good as [he] can'. Hence, to be ethical as a trans man is to recognise the proclivity for faltering as an imperfect human being without losing sight of the aspiration to 'do good and be good' in all circumstances.

'I Can't Lie to Me': Giving Life and Being Truthful to Oneself

The performance of ethics, as articulated earlier by Ray and Michael, involves respectful and benign attitudes towards both the self and others. I now focus on the idea of prioritising one's own physical, emotional and mental wellbeing as a personal ethical exercise. For this purpose, I look to the narrative of Schulz who foregrounds the idea of 'giving life to [him]self'. This perspective, I suggest, is demonstrative of an ethics of self-care:

Goh: And you, you don't think God has any problems with you as a … trans man?

Schulz: I solely believe not. I'm very affirmed with that belief, that I don't think he has a problem with me being a trans man … Teachings … written theories in the Catholic faith that has caused people to pinpoint

> and say … the transgender community is going against the church teachings. But what are we doing that is going against the church teachings? … Unless, me being a trans man, I have done, you know, a killing … To take away a life or, or anything in that sense. Then yes, it's very prominent because it's going against the main teaching of the church which is love. If you're killing a life, you're taking away life. But I'm giving life to myself. I'm choosing to be happy. And that gives me life to live every single day in a much more happier way.

Schulz's declaration that '[he does not] think that [God] has a problem' with his self-affirmed gender identity echoes an earlier account of Aarone's belief that '[he does not] really see … the problem between [him] and God'. Schulz addresses the problem of Roman Catholic 'teachings [and] written theories' as destructive elements that contribute to the detriment of 'the transgender community'. Akin to Axman who spoke out against ecclesiastical denouncements of his gender identity as sinful, and invalidations of his concomitant identity of gender and faith, Schulz recognises the insidious agendas of 'church teachings' that can be injurious to transgender people and which are evidently 'incompatible with the Creator's law of love and compassion' (Yip 2010, 37). He takes the church to task for the lack of inclusivity, as 'the inclusivity of the gospel … creates a mandate for the church as the body of Christ to reflect that inclusivity' (Childs 2009, 35) without any form of discrimination and exclusion.

In raising the question of what transgender people are 'doing that is against church teachings', Schulz debunks an automatic conflation of transgender identities with a sinfully unethical state of being that breaches ecclesiastical regulations. Instead, it is a transgender person's actions that constitute the meaning of ethics, such as the act of 'killing' which 'go[es] against the main teaching of the church which is love'.[8] He then argues that instead of 'taking away life', he is 'giving life to [him]self' by living truthfully as a trans man. Schulz seems to imply that a trans man's personal decision in 'choosing to be happy' through a self-affirmed gender identity is life-giving just as the Church's condemnation of his gender identity is tantamount to 'killing a life' and thus death-dealing to him.

[8] See a similar discussion on gay men and sexual ethics in Goh (2016a).

Furthermore, if the act of 'taking life' constitutes a violation of 'church teachings' and the antithesis of love, Schulz's gender identity and 'giv[ing himself] life to live every single day in a much … happier way' must somehow be compliant with 'church teachings' and translate as the manifestation of love. By providing contrasting imageries of killing and living, of contravening and complying with ecclesiastical law, and of infringing and upholding the mandate to love, Schulz disarms the condemnatory demeanour of the Church as the 'stigmatizer' (Yip 1998, 43) while affirming his gender identity.

For SR, speaking truth to self is a personal ethical principle that he resolutely upholds:

> I just … be like me. What you see me now, I just, this is how I represent myself, my appearance to people. So whenever they talk to me, oh, there is some of the people which is uhm… typical Malay … They start judging … I hate that. Because I never judge people. Because for me, my happiness is within myself. And I don't, I don't care about other people. They can say something to me, I might take it, I might not. Only me know about that. So, but, things I hate the most is when they start, you know, advising me in the wrong way, like you know, God, this and that … I hate negative people, because I'm being positive at all time. Because for me, what matters the most, is myself. This is myself. This is what I want the most. I can't lie to me. I can't lie to everyone. I can't wear *baju kurung* if, in the sake of, people to like me. No, I'm not gonna do that. I just wanna be myself…

SR's endeavour to be true to himself is constantly interrupted by 'other people' who '[judge]' and '[advise him] in the wrong way' in terms of his subjectivity. What he particularly loathes is the way in which 'typical Malay[-Muslims]' manipulate the person of 'God' as an invective against him. Norani Othman's comment that it is near impossible 'to identify easily which values emanate from religion and which originate from a society's culture' (1995, 1) seemingly speaks to SR's situation. Nonetheless, I am not completely convinced that religious and cultural beliefs and practices are necessarily or always distinct or distinguishable, particularly in the case of Malays who are constitutionally codified as Muslims whereby Islam serves as 'a marker of Malay identity' (Lee 2010a, 19; see also Martin 2012). Religious beliefs and practices are, I propose, inevitably encapsulated in sociocultural performances, even if these performances are borrowed and/or adapted. There is no such thing as culture-free, 'pure' religiosity. My reiterated argument here is that Malaysianness, Malayness and Muslimness are indivisibly united, and that it is more accurate to speak of a Malaysian Islam rather than simply 'Islam' in the country.

As I see it, SR feels conflicted due to two contradictory manifestations of Malaysian Malay-Islam in his life. The first is a non-judgemental form to which SR subscribes as it allows him to be true to himself and be happy. SR's quip, 'what you see me now', refers to how he 'represent[ed]' himself to me during our conversation. His hairstyle, clothes and mannerisms were those that are usually associated with popular representations of manness. By using these signifiers to perform masculinity, SR's goal is to 'be [him]self'. Akin to Aarone, he recognises that 'what matters the most [to him] is [him]self', or the imperative to flourish in his gender identity. Consequently, the project of becoming a trans man is of paramount importance to him in order to avoid having to 'lie to [himself and] everyone' about his gender identity.

Christopher Grant Kelly posits that 'while Islam has its own theological narrative based upon official traditions, it can take on different valences – different situated meanings – in the contexts of other relational settings and other narratives' (2010, 239–45). Democratisation of Islam can enable a Muslim trans man to live freely, truthfully and ethically as a trans man without censorious feedback from fellow Muslims, but I am doubtful that it will materialise any time soon due to a prevalent judgemental manifestation of Malaysian Islam. SR's insistence that he will not wear the '*baju kurung*',[9] a traditional loose-fitting Malay dress worn mainly by Malay women, is noteworthy. It is possible that the 'typical Malay[s]' he meets feel obliged to deploy a fusion of theological and cultural rhetoric against him for his dissidence in being un-feminine, un-Malay, un-Muslim and un-Malaysian.

SR knows that to dress as a woman would elicit their approval, but it would be to 'lie to [himself and] everyone' and thus be incompatible with his conscience. In a country where nationalistic zeal, ethnic pride and unchallenged religious superiority amalgamate to appraise, adjudicate and condemn 'what is and what is not *Malaysian*, *Malay*, *Muslim*, *male* and *properly sexual*' (Goh 2015a, 16; original emphasis), the only available option to live ethically as a Malay-Muslim trans man in this

[9]The *baju kurung* is first mentioned in by SR in 'Engaging with Society'.

instance is to defy oppressive political, cultural and pietistic ideologies of gender in order to live freely and be true to himself.

Hence, for trans men, to act ethically towards others is to communicate attitudes that uphold human dignity towards others, both as a mark of humanism and in recognition of a divine approval of gender identity. Second, to be ethical is to recognise the importance of thriving as a trans man, which may necessitate the fracturing of sociocultural norms and the risk of incurring public disapproval.

Conclusion

Many Malaysian trans men enlist performances of faith in the construction of their self-affirmed gender identities. These beliefs are often the consequence of a dialectic between gender identity and official religious pronouncements, which allow for the emergence of personalised faith systems that affirm, inform and nurture their gender embodiments. For many trans men who were brought up in official religious beliefs, specific traits of faith linger as inextricable components of their subjectivities. In some cases, the construction of faith entails an explicit contradiction of religious hierarchies. In others, faith is a combination of specific official tenets and personal discernment that muddy and trouble the 'official' religiosity–'unofficial' spirituality distinction. In others still, a moral standpoint is constituted by the optimal living out of humanness. This chapter has been 'alert to the social meanings behind such distinctions, because making distinctions involves trying to delineate acceptable from unacceptable beliefs and practices, desirable from denigrated identities and status, and worthy from unworthy ideals and values' (McGuire 2008, 6).

Trans men enlist the creative prowess of a God who fashions them as they are, verifies their existence and prompts them towards holistic self-actualisation. Although such a theological methodology may effectively sacralise and essentialise the gender binary (Burke 2014), meaning that gender identities are seen as preordained by God and thus primordially immutable, it enables trans men to experience divine validation in a particular manner in romantic and familial relationships. Trans men also allow their gender identities to animate their sense of ethics. Their motivation to do good to others is often the consequence of experiencing the sting of marginalisation in their own lives and a subsequent avowal to avoid re-enacting such antagonistic dynamics in the lives of others.

Faith does not endow a comprehensive and perfect sense of subjectivity for trans men as it continues to be a double-edged sword in many instances. Yet, in its contradictions and complexities, faith provides a vital transcendental dimension—a deepening of the meaning of gendered materiality—for the becomings of Malaysian trans men.

Bibliography

Abdullah Yusuf Ali, trans. 2013. *The Holy Qur'an: Original Arabic Text with English Translation & Selected Commentaries.* Kuala Lumpur, Malaysia: Saba Islamic Media.

Agoramoorthy, Govindasamy, and Minna J. Hsu. 2015. 'Living on the Societal Edge: India's Transgender Realities'. *Journal of Religion and Health* 54 (4): 1451–59.

Althaus-Reid, Marcella, and Lisa Isherwood, eds. 2009. *Trans/Formations.* London: SCM Press.

Aune, Kristin. 2015. 'Feminist Spirituality as Lived Religion: How UK Feminists Forge Religio-Spiritual Lives'. *Gender & Society* 29 (1): 122–45.

Beardsley, Christina, and Michelle O'Brien. 2016. *This Is My Body: Hearing the Theology of Transgender Christians.* London: Darton, Longman & Todd.

Bong, Sharon A. 2020. *Becoming Queer and Religious in Malaysia and Singapore.* New York: Bloomsbury Academic.

Bouma, Gary. 2006. *Australian Soul: Religion and Spirituality in the 21st Century.* Leiden, The Netherlands: Cambridge University Press.

Burke, Kelsy. 2014. 'What Makes a Man: Gender and Sexual Boundaries on Evangelical Christian Sexuality Websites'. *Sexualities* 17 (1–2): 3–22.

Burke, Sean D. 2013. *Queering the Ethiopian Eunuch: Strategies of Ambiguity in Acts.* Minneapolis, MN: Fortress Press.

Cheng, Patrick S. 2006. 'Reclaiming Our Traditions, Rituals, and Spaces: Spirituality and the Queer Asian Pacific American Experience'. *Spiritus: A Journal of Christian Spirituality* 6 (2): 234–40.

———. 2013. 'Lesbian, Gay, Bisexual, and Transgender Liberative Ethics'. In *Ethics: A Liberative Approach*, edited by Miguel A. De La Torre, 207–21. Minneapolis, MN: Fortress Press.

Childs, James M. 2009. 'Transsexualism: Some Theological and Ethical Perspectives'. *Dialog* 48 (1): 30–41.

Chim, Ezra. 2012. '"She" Is My BROTHER—Pastor Edmund Smith of Real Love Ministry (RLM) in Malacca'. Christianity Malaysia, 16 October. http://christianitymalaysia.com/wp/she-brother-pastor-edmund-smith-real-love-ministry-rlm-malacca/.

Cornwall, Susannah. 2009. 'Apophasis and Ambiguity: The "Unknowingness" of Transgender'. In *Trans/Formations*, edited by Lisa Isherwood and Marcella Althaus-Reid, 13–40. London: SCM Press.

———. 2012. 'Recognizing the Full Spectrum of Gender? Transgender, Intersex and the Futures of Feminist Theology'. *Feminist Theology* 20 (3): 236–41.

Farley, Margaret A. 2008. *Just Love: A Framework for Christian Sexual Ethics.* London: Continuum.

Geissinger, Aisha. 2012. 'Islam and Discourses of Same-Sex Desire'. In *Queer Religion*, edited by Donald L. Boisvert and Jay Emerson Johnson, 1:1: 69–90. Santa Barbara, CA: Praeger.

Goh, Joseph N. 2012a. 'Mary and the *Mak Nyahs*: Queer Theological Imaginings of Malaysian Male-to-Female Transsexuals'. *Theology & Sexuality* 18 (3): 215–33.

———. 2012b. '*Mak Nyah* Bodies as Sacred Sites: Uncovering the Queer Body-Sacramentality of Malaysian Male-to-Female Transsexuals'. *CrossCurrents* 62 (4): 512–21.

———. 2012c. '*Nyah*-Islam: The Reconstruction of God and Institutional Islam by Malaysian Male-to-Female Transsexuals'. *in God's image* 31 (2): 33–44.

———. 2013. 'Repent or Believe in the Closet: When Pastoral Care Is Anything But'. *Queer Eye for God's World* (blog), 16 November. http://josephgoh.org/?p=125.

———. 2014a. 'Transgressive Empowerment: Queering the Spiritualities of the *Mak Nyahs* of PT Foundation'. In *Queering Migrations Towards, From, and Beyond Asia*, edited by Hugo Córdova Quero, Joseph N. Goh, and Michael Sepidoza Campos, 123–37. New York: Palgrave Macmillan.

———. 2014b. '"You Must Follow Our Belief or Else You Can't Receive God": Constructing a Sexual Bi/Theology of Eucharist'. *Dialog* 53 (2): 149–58.

———. 2015a. 'Peculiar Politics in Malaysia: A Queer Perspective on Non-Heteronormative Malay-Muslim Men'. In *Ways of Queering, Ways of Seeing*, edited by Jillian E. Cox and Jo Grzelinska, 3–33. Oxford, UK: Inter-Disciplinary Press.

———. 2015b. 'Outing the Self/Outing God: Reimagining the Cross for Christians with Same-Sex Attractions'. *in God's image* 34 (1): 22–31.

———. 2016a. '"Why Is It Wrong?": Conceptualisations of Sexual Wrongdoing and Sexual Ethics among Gay-Identifying Malaysian Men'. In *Doing Asian Theological Ethics in a Cross-Cultural and an Interreligious Context*, edited by Yiu Sing Lúcás Chan, James F. Keenan, and Shaji George Kochuthara, 347–60. Bengaluru, India: Dharmaram Publications.

———. 2016b. 'Imaginative Assemblages of Transcendent/Desire: Non-Heteronormative Malaysian Men Speak Up and Talk Back'. *Critical Research on Religion* 4 (2): 125–40.

———. 2018. *Living Out Sexuality and Faith: Body Admissions of Malaysian Gay and Bisexual Men*. London: Routledge.

———. 2019a. 'Untying Tongues: Negotiations and Innovations of Faith and Gender Among Malaysian Christian Trans Men'. *Culture and Religion* 20 (1): 1–20.

———. 2019b. 'God>Cursing>Shaming>Blessing>Pride'. *TSQ: Transgender Studies Quarterly* 6 (3): 435–41.

Harper, Susan. 2010. '"All Cool Women Should Be Bisexual": Female Bisexual Identity in an American NeoPagan Community'. *Journal of Bisexuality* 10 (1–2): 79–107.

Hendricks, Muhsin. 2011. 'Diversity of Sexuality in Islam: Interview with Imam Muhsin Hendricks'. *CrossCurrents* 61 (4): 496–501.

Hero, Jakob. 2012. 'Toward a Queer Theology of Flourishing: Transsexual Embodiment, Subjectivity, and Moral Agency'. In *Queer Religion*, edited by Donald L. Boisvert and Jay Emerson Johnson, 2:2: 143–65. Santa Barbara, CA: Praeger.

Hipsher, B. K. 2009. 'God Is a Many Gendered Thing: An Apophatic Journey to Pastoral Diversity'. In *Trans/Formations*, edited by Lisa Isherwood and Marcella Althaus-Reid, 92–104. London: SCM Press.

Horn, Martha, Ralph Piedmont, Geraldine Fialkowski, Robert Wicks, and Mary Hunt. 2005. 'Sexuality and Spirituality: The Embodied Spirituality Scale'. *Theology & Sexuality* 12 (1): 81–101.

Hornsby, Teresa J., and Deryn Guest. 2016. *Transgender, Intersex and Biblical Interpretation*. Atlanta, GA: Society of Biblical Literature.

Hossain, Adnan. 2012. 'Beyond Emasculation: Being Muslim and Becoming *Hijra* in South Asia'. *Asian Studies Review* 36 (4): 495–513.

Jabatan Mufti Kerajaan Negeri Sembilan. 2008. 'Hukum Wanita Menyerupai Lelaki (Pengkid)'. Keputusan Mesyuarat Fatwa. http://www.muftins.gov.my/index.php/arkib2/himpunan-fatwa/171-keputusan-mesyuarat-fatwa/729-hukum-wanita-menyerupai-lelaki-pengkid.

Kalthom Abdullah, Noraini M. Noor, and Saodah Wok. 2008. 'The Perceptions of Women's Roles and Progress: A Study of Malay Women'. *Social Indicators Research* 89 (3): 439–55.

Kamali, Mohammad Hashim. 2009. 'Transgenders, from Islam's Perspective'. International Institute of Advanced Academic Studies (IAIS) Malaysia. http://www.iais.org.my/e/publications/articles/item/download/55.html.

———. 2011. 'Transgenders and Justice in Islam'. International Institute of Advanced Academic Studies (IAIS) Malaysia. http://www.iais.org.my/e/index.php/publications-sp-1447159098/articles/item/81-transgenders-and-justice-in-islam.html.

Kelly, Christopher Grant. 2010. 'The Social Construction of Religious Realities by Queer Muslims'. In *Islam and Homosexuality*, edited by Samar Habib, 2: 223–45. Santa Barbara, CA: Praeger.

Khartini Slamah. 2005. 'The Struggle to Be Ourselves, Neither Men Nor Women: *Mak Nyahs* in Malaysia'. In *Sexuality, Gender and Rights: Exploring Theory and Practice in South and Southeast Asia*, edited by Geetanjali Misra and Radhika Chandiramani, 98–111. London: Sage.

Kolakowski, Victoria S. 1997. 'Toward a Christian Ethical Response to Transsexual Persons'. *Theology & Sexuality* 3 (6): 10–31.

Kugle, Scott Siraj al-Haqq. 2010. *Homosexuality in Islam: Critical Reflection on Gay, Lesbian, and Transgender Muslims*. Oxford, UK: Oneworld Publications.

Lee, Julian C. H. 2010a. *Islamization and Activism in Malaysia*. Singapore: Institute of Southeast Asian Studies.

———. 2010b. 'Oversanctification, Autonomy and Islam in Malaysia'. *Totalitarian Movements and Political Religions* 11 (1): 27–46.

Li, Yu-Chen. 2007. 'Reconstructing Buddhist Perspectives on Homosexuality: Enlightenment from the Study of the Body'. In *Heterosexism in Contemporary World Religion: Problem and Prospect*, edited by Marvin Mahan Ellison and Judith Plaskow. Cleveland, OH: Pilgrim Press.

Liow, Joseph Chinyong. 2009. *Piety and Politics: Islamism in Contemporary Malaysia*. New York: Oxford University Press.

Lowe, Mary Elise. 2017. 'From the Same Spirit: Receiving the Theological Gifts of Transgender Christians'. *Dialog* 56 (1): 28–37.

Luk, Small. 2015. 'God Loves Intersex People'. *in God's image* 34 (2): 5–13.

Maggard, Thea Rae. 2014. 'Queering Trans(Theo)Phobia: A Comparative Analysis between Jōdo Shinshū Buddhism and Roman Catholicism on Transgender Issues'. *Religión e Incidencia Pública*, no. 2: 109–36.

Manji, Irshad. 2011. *Allah, Liberty and Love: The Courage to Reconcile Faith and Freedom*. New York: Free Press.

Martin, Dahlia. 2012. 'Redefining "Malayness": Expectations of Young-Adult Malaysian Muslims'. In *Thinking Through Malaysia: Culture and Identity in the 21st Century*, edited by Julian Hopkins and Julian C. H. Lee, 31–49. Selangor, Malaysia: Strategic Information and Research Development Centre.

McGuire, Meredith B. 2003. 'Why Bodies Matter: A Sociological Reflection on Spirituality and Materiality'. *Spiritus: A Journal of Christian Spirituality* 3 (1): 1–18.

———. 2008. *Lived Religion: Faith and Practice in Everyday Life*. New York: Oxford University Press.

Muzaffar, Chandra. 2011. *Exploring Religion in Our Time*. Penang, Malaysia: Universiti Sains Malaysia.

Naim, M. Khairul, Syed M. Hilmi, S. Che Zarrina, S. Nurul Salikin, Khadijah M. Hambali, Wan Adli, Azmil Z. Abidin, M. Anuar Mamat, Joni T. Borhan, Faizuri A. Latif, Ali G. Saged, M. Hazim Azhar, Rohaida M. Dawam. 2016. 'Understanding the Concept of Al-Ibtila' (Trial) in Personality Development: The Muslim Flood Victims' Experience'. *International Review of Management and Marketing* 6 (7S): 133–40.

Nanda, Serena. 2002. 'The Hijras: An Alternative Gender in Indian Culture'. In *Religion and Sexuality in Cross-Cultural Perspective*, edited by Stephen Ellingson and M. Christian Green, 137–63. New York: Routledge.

Norani Othman. 1995. 'Gender Inequality, Culture and the Historicity of Religious Interpretation'. In *Gender, Culture and Religion*, edited by Norani Othman and Cecilia Ng, 1–12. Kuala Lumpur, Malaysia: Persatuan Sains Sosial Malaysia.

Norani Othman, and Cecilia Ng, eds. 1995. *Gender, Culture and Religion*. Kuala Lumpur, Malaysia: Persatuan Sains Sosial Malaysia.

Pembroke, N. 2008. 'Narratives of Silence: Availability in a Spirituality of Fathering'. *Journal of Men, Masculinities and Spirituality* 2 (2): 82–94.

Reay, Lewis. 2009. 'Towards a Transgender Theology: Que(e)Rying the Eunuchs'. In *Trans/Formations*, edited by Lisa Isherwood and Marcella Althaus-Reid, 148–67. London: SCM Press.

Reddy, Gayatri. 2005. *With Respect to Sex: Negotiating* Hijra *Identity in South India*. Chicago, IL: University of Chicago Press.

Robinson, Margaret. 2017. 'Two-Spirit and Bisexual People: Different Umbrella, Same Rain'. *Journal of Bisexuality* 17 (1): 7–29.

See, Jade. 2019. 'What It Means to Suffer in Silence: Challenges to Mental Health Access Among LGBT People (Policy For Action No. 2/ 2019)'. Galen Centre for Health and Social Policy. https://galencentre.org/2019/04/22/conversion-therapy-is-a-form-of-violence/.

Shallenberger, David. 1996. 'Reclaiming the Spirit: The Journeys of Gay Men and Lesbian Women Toward Integration'. *Qualitative Sociology* 19 (2): 195–215.

Sweasey, Peter. 1997. *From Queer to Eternity: Spirituality in the Lives of Lesbian, Gay, and Bisexual People*. London: Cassell.

Tanis, Justin Edward. 2003. *Trans-Gendered: Theology, Ministry, and Communities of Faith*. Cleveland, OH: Pilgrim Press.

Taparia, Swadha. 2011. 'Emasculated Bodies of *Hijras*: Sites of Imposed, Resisted and Negotiated Identities'. *Indian Journal of Gender Studies* 18 (2): 167–84.

Teh, Yik Koon. 2008. 'Politics and Islam: Factors Determining Identity and the Status of Male-to-Female Transsexuals in Malaysia'. In *AsiaPacifiQueer: Rethinking Genders and Sexualities*, edited by Fran Martin, Peter A. Jackson, Mark McLelland, and Audrey Yue, 85–98. Urbana, IL: University of Illinois Press.

Tham, Jia Vern. 2018. 'Here's How Malaysia "Cures" LGBTs with Conversion Therapy'. *SAYS.Com*, 20 December. https://says.com/my/news/here-s-how-malaysia-cures-lgbts-with-conversion-therapy.

Vanita, Ruth. 2012. 'Hinduism and Homosexuality'. In *Queer Religion*, edited by Donald L. Boisvert and Jay Emerson Johnson, 1: 1–23. Santa Barbara, CA: Praeger.

Weeks, Jeffrey, Brian Heaphy, and Catherine Donovan. 2001. *Same Sex Intimacies: Families of Choice and Other Life Experiments.* London: Routledge.

Weiner, Isaac A. 2014. 'Calling Everyone to Pray: Pluralism, Secularism, and the Adhān in Hamtramck, Michigan'. *Anthropological Quarterly* 87 (4): 1049–77.

Whitehead, James D., and Evelyn Eaton Whitehead. 2014. 'Transgender Lives: From Bewilderment to God's Extravagance'. *Pastoral Psychology* 63 (2): 171–84.

Wu, Rose. 2000. *Liberating the Church from Fear: The Story of Hong Kong's Sexual Minorities.* Kowloon, Hong Kong: Hong Kong Women Christian Council.

Yip, Andrew K. T. 1997. 'Attacking the Attacker: Gay Christians Talk Back'. *The British Journal of Sociology* 48 (1): 113–27.

———. 1998. 'Gay Male Christians' Perceptions of the Christian Community in Relation to Their Sexuality'. *Theology & Sexuality* 1998 (8): 40–51.

———. 2005a. 'Religion and the Politics of Spirituality/Sexuality'. *Fieldwork in Religion* 1 (3): 271–89.

———. 2005b. 'Queering Religious Texts: An Exploration of British Non-Heterosexual Christians' and Muslims' Strategy of Constructing Sexuality-Affirming Hermeneutics'. *Sociology* 39 (1): 47–65.

———. 2010. 'Coming Home from the Wilderness: An Overview of Recent Scholarly Research on LGBTQI Religiosity/Spirituality in the West'. In *Queer Spiritual Spaces: Sexuality and Sacred Places*, edited by Kath Browne, Sally Munt, and Andrew K. T. Yip, 35–50. Surrey, UK: Ashgate.

Yip, Andrew K. T., and Michael Keenan. 2009. 'Transgendering Christianity: Gender-Variant Christians as Visionaries'. In *Contemporary Christianity and LGBT Sexualities*, edited by Stephen Hunt, 87–101. Surrey, UK: Ashgate.

Yip, Andrew K. T., with Amna Khalid. 2010. 'Looking for Allah: Spiritual Quests of Queer Muslims'. In *Queer Spiritual Spaces: Sexuality and Sacred Places*, edited by Kath Browne, Sally Munt, and Andrew K. T. Yip, 81–109. Surrey, UK: Ashgate.

CHAPTER 7

Epilogue

'We're not an "ism", Joseph, we're trans men, we're men who happen to be trans!' Uttered by trans activist Dorian Wilde in a casual conversation with him prior to commencing fieldwork, these words left a deep impression on me, and steered the tone and trajectory of my research project thereafter. My initial research proposal was peppered with the term 'transgenderism', which I thought would be a worthy equivalent to homosexuality and bisexuality, and even queerness. What did not emerge at the forefront of my consciousness then was that a long history of transgender (and transsexual) pathologisation had transformed the 'ism' from an innocuous medical classification to a badge of abnormality, 'psychopathology, a sexual fetish, or perversion' (Pfeffer 2017, 21). The 'dominant discursive fields that authorize identities but do not represent lived experiences' (Cromwell 1999, 11) frequently reduce transgender people to case studies of mental disorder and gross deviance. My conversation with Wilde led me to forsake a detached investigation of 'isms' for a more profound and meaningful unveiling of real people with real flesh and blood and sweat and tears.

Therefore, I pen this monograph about people who 'see themselves as being normal rather than pathological and therefore challenge knowledge-validation processes of gender constructions and critique the view that their gendered ways of being constitute mental illness' (Cromwell 1999, 10). I write about men who happen to be transgender, not about a species called 'trans men'. I write about fellow human

J. N. Goh, *Becoming a Malaysian Trans Man*,
Gender, Sexualities and Culture in Asia,
https://doi.org/10.1007/978-981-15-4534-4_7

beings and citizens who are deserving of privacy, autonomy, equality, respect, dignity and protection, but find themselves forced to confront daily disqualifications due to their subjectivities. My primary task in the research project which birthed this monograph has been to interpret the meaning-makings of trans men within a particular sociocultural and political ethos. Within spaces of confidentiality and trust during fieldwork, my research participants and I have been able to co-interpret and co-articulate the sense-making of real lives.[1]

My main argument in this book is that self-selected gender identities, complex interactions with families, friends and colleagues, intense struggles with Gender Dysphoria (GD), precarious navigations in medical transitioning, and intricate negotiations with religiosities and spiritualities are primary contributory factors in the becomings of Malaysian trans men. Within these everyday strategies of gender affirmation, trans men confront the unpredictability of passing in society. They find themselves embroiled in the simultaneous dynamics of concealing and revealing their past and present lives. They are exposed to the harshness of gender policing in spaces such as public toilets that strictly regulate the rules of the gender binary. Trans men discover that deficient medical expertise and precarious healthcare services frequently inhibit any development towards self-affirmed gender identities. Such limitations are further curtailed by monetary issues, even though they may receive moral support and technical counsel from fellow trans men, 'each shaped by intersecting experiences of marginalisation and privilege' (Pearce 2018, 179).

Malaysian trans men reveal a proliferation of self-descriptors, such as 'Female-to-Male (FTM)', 'transmasculine', 'trans man', 'man' and 'male' towards self-comprehension and self-expression, even at times to clarify and justify who they are to themselves and to the world around them. Some are deeply cognisant of female history, while others have never experienced what it is to be a woman. Many take great pains to distance themselves from any semblance to femaleness, womanness, womanliness or female femininity. Very few are comfortable with a greater fluidity in their gender identities and expressions by traversing both culturally dictated norms of masculinity and femininity in their personal lives. Nevertheless, all trans men express a desire to live, be recognised and addressed in accordance with the frameworks of maleness, manness,

[1] See 'Appendix 1: Designing the Research Project' for details of my research methods and methodology.

manliness and male masculinity in varied but meaningful and life-giving ways. The plethora of self-descriptors attests to the pursuit of meaningful identity that the trans man pursues for himself and the society in which he lives.

I recall a brief online conversation I had with Malaysian academic and Learning & Development Practitioner Alwyn Lau on transgender communities some two years back. Perhaps it is more accurate to say that our conversation took the form of alternate postings on my Facebook timeline. Lau asked me how transgender people can possibly dismantle the gender binary, contrary to popular belief, seeing as people who were assigned male at birth want to live as women, and people who were assigned female at birth want to live as men. 'Aren't they simply reinforcing the gender binary? They are abandoning one gender for another, aren't they?' I responded by saying that yes, I agree that many transgender people are colluding with the strictures of the gender dichotomy because they are insistent on being positioned at one end of the gender spectrum or the other, but perhaps subconsciously so and certainly with all sincerity. 'Look at genderqueer or non-binary people', I said, 'the gender nonconforming folks are the ones who shatter the gender binary by refusing to choose one gender over another'.

In hindsight, perhaps my response was a tad too hasty and simplistic. Just because a person is assigned female at birth and wishes to live as a man does not mean that he should necessarily be unproblematically condemned for sinister complicity in the fortification of the gender binary. After all, not everyone is comfortable with living in perpetual interstices that are socioculturally unintelligible. Moreover, one can still choose to upend gender normativities even if one has chosen to locate oneself on one side of the gender binary. While I still stand by my belief that transgender people, like their cisgender counterparts, do uphold the gender binary in many ways—often subconsciously—the dis-concatenation of assigned-at-birth anatomy from gender when assigned-at-birth anatomy and gender are presumed to be infallibly indivisible produces a certain disruption of what 'should be' in the Malaysian sacrosanctum of normative gender, sexual and biological alignments. If this ordinarily uncontested concatenation were not the case, transgender individuals would not be treated with the *kezaliman* (cruelty) that currently plagues them in their own country for being betrayers of the imagined and hagiographised Malaysian ideals of gender, sexuality and sex.

Yet, owing to the possibility of unwanted exposure of (trans)gender identities, particularly a female history for trans men, the disruption which I just mentioned is always fraught with complications. The desire for invisibility as 'unremarkably, men' (Hansbury 2005, 247) is always accompanied by the potential to be 'remarkably, non-man' as the process of blending in always harbours the possibility of being outed. To be like anybody else is to risk not being like anybody else. Many trans men who wish to live anonymous lives, unnoticed and unharassed, avoid any undertaking that can usher in disruption.

Trans men realise that their subjectivities suffer a blow when they are exposed to hostility and mistrust from biological family members, cisgender friends, fellow trans men and colleagues on account of their gender identities. Alternatively, they tend to flourish in more accepting and welcoming environments. Unsurprisingly, social interactions mould and shape the liveabilities of gender. Malaysian trans men find themselves inevitably mired in negotiations of disclosure and non-disclosure of their past and present gender identities, which often prove to be formidable tasks of self-defence and self-justification. As I see it, this predicament stems from the country's compulsion for neat, tamed categories of gender, sexuality and sex as an attempt to incarnate a 'proper' Islam ic modernity and purity, and in response to a perceived tide of decadence that relentlessly assails Malaysia from all directions, seemingly 'threatening to erode the very moral fabric of our society and lay the cultural foundations of society to ruin' (Noor 2010, 136).

Former Malaysian Prime Minister Mahathir Mohamad denigrates the 'West' for their moral corrosion, and pontificates on 'Asian values' which include the preservation of (imagined, universal, timeless and decontextualised) Islamically inflected Malaysian traditions and customs (Mahathir and Ishihara 1995, 71–86). In many ways, 'Asian values', which Farish A. Noor also sees as encompassing 'the values of blind deference to authority, submission to power and the inability to stand up for one's rights' (2002, 258), can easily be imagined as the last bastion against the encroachment of moral decay. Nonetheless, I contend that it is important not to lose sight of the nexus between morality debates and political mileage. Recent remarks from the leader of the former ruling coalition *Pakatan Harapan* (Coalition of Hope) Anwar Ibrahim that the state must not succumb to international pressure over transgender and queer matters because it has its 'own system and leadership that is free to protect the interest of the country and its people' and that it must 'not feel pressured by external reactions' (quoted in Rahimy 2019) suggest that state disapprobation pertaining to transgender and queer concerns is largely driven by issues of state sovereignty that are then manifested in religio-moral conservatism. Moreover, the fact that Malaysian politicians are inundated with claims of sexual scandals (Looi 2018; Walden 2019)—Anwar himself was imprisoned on charges of man-on-man sexual activity—while battling for gender and sexual uprightness reveals the bare truth of frenetic political rat races. Armed with pious rhetoric and innocuous platitudes, the demagogue who appears as the most religiously ethical figure can also appear as the ideal personification of immaculate and thus credible leadership to create an immaculate nation.

Trans men experience public toilets as sites of gender surveillance and deconstruction, as well as sites of affirmation and empowerment. In these scenarios, work colleagues and total strangers serve as agents who regulate the production of docile bodies. In 2010, I attended some events organised by *Seksualiti Merdeka* ('Sexuality Liberation' or 'Sexuality Independence'), a local gender and sexuality rights festival which was supported by concerned individuals, civil society organisations and non-governmental organisations that champion human rights. The three-day festival, which showcased testimonials, storytellings, forums, workshops and film screenings to raise awareness on gender and sexuality issues, burst on the Malaysian scene in 2008. Perceived as 'damaging the moral fabric of society, promoting free sex, promoting sin, increasing the transmission of HIV, and allowing an infiltration of Western influence' (Goh 2012b, 148), it was banned in 2011, much to the chagrin of the Malaysian queer and trans communities (Lee 2013, 2014).

One of the most interesting features of the festival in 2010 was musical entertainment provided by the queercore band *Sshh...Diam!* ('Shhh ... Quiet!' or 'Shhh ... Shut Up!'), comprising transgender individuals, and lesbian and/or masculine-presenting women (Kong 2019). As a prelude to one of their opening numbers, one of the band members recounted an incident in which they were rushing to a public toilet but were halted by a *makcik*[2] (aunty) cleaner who asked them in Malay, '*Awak ni laki ke perempuan*'? ('are you a man or a woman'?). Taken aback, this band member retorted—and much to the amusement and delight of the festival participants who were all ears—'*Makcik, laki*

[2]It is common practice to address a more mature woman whom one perceives to be of similar age to one's mother as '*makcik*'.

perempuan tak penting! Yang penting, nak kencing sekarang'! ('Aunty, it's not important if I'm a man or a woman! What's important now is that I have to wee'!). Evidently, gender identity precedes human identity in many Malaysian spaces.

Trans men invariably reveal a sense of discomfort with the discordance they perceive between their self-affirmed gender identities and their physical bodies which have been socioculturally signified as female and woman. Even research participants who profess to be accepting of, and comfortable with these incongruities consistently allude to their intolerance of this mismatch. Encounters with corporeal lack and excess sometimes proves unbearable. GD, particularly when coupled with intersectional issues such as experiences of sexual abuse as women, can propel trans men towards multifaceted manifestations of illbeing, including suicidal ideations. Gender, as such, is not exclusively social construction as many are wont to say. Gender is even more than a personal embodied truth. The intensity of emotions that can drive trans men to contemplate snuffing out their lives suggests that gender is inexorably connected to the preservation of meaningful corporeal existence in society.

I concur with Judith Butler that gender is reiteratively performative, and this performativity needs to be materially rooted instead of being a 'free-floating artifice' (1999, 10) or a 'set of free-floating attributes' (1999, 33). Nevertheless, the depth and width and breadth of the body's import for meaningful personhood suggests a sort of core, 'beingness' (Cromwell 1999, 42) or 'essential self' (Hines 2007, 60) that is inexorably connected to, draws on, and gives countenance to an embodiment, even if its meaning is constructed. This core, I propose, must be thought of as *experienced* rather than ontological before it can be understood as a dynamic that anchors human persons in practical intelligibility, a 'centre' that is impermanent and contingent and thus can be decentred, but still 'essential' to the human experience in its seeming illogicality. The body may not be 'prior to discourse' (Butler 1999, 164), but particular assemblages of its cultural meanings and lived experiences are constitutive of gender for trans men. In many respects, the body defines what it means for them to live as men. Hence, 'bodies are not mere biological material providing a canvas for the bold strokes of gender to be painted on [but] can be reshaped and modified to embody discourses about sexuality or gender literally' (Cornwall 1994, 114).

It is for this reason that many trans men are willing to bear with the inconvenience and discomfort of binding, device techniques of disassociation, endurance and adaptability, and appeal to numerous configurations of medical transitioning that encompass Gender-Affirming Surgery (GAS) and Gender-Affirming Hormone Therapy (GAHT). My research findings suggest that while GAHT is more accessible and less invasive than GAS, and that medical transitioning is an undertaking that is constantly fraught with unruliness, unpredictability, frustration, fragmentation and incompletion. Financial constraints play a crucial role in the decision-makings of trans men in regard to medical transitioning.

Some time back, I chanced upon Malaysian academic Alicia Izharuddin's blog posting entitled 'The Transmen Community is Still Overshadowed by Phallocentric Logic in Malaysia'. As the title of the entry suggests, she weaves a discursive brocade of how 'the idea of what it means to be a man is reduced to the possession of a penis' (2012), which thus explains how female masculinities, transmasculinities and lesbian subjectivities are undermined and/or annulled by virtue of a missing appendage. Men are men only because they have penises. This scenario, she suggests, is particularly true for the Malaysian trans man who is relatively unknown vis-à-vis the trans woman or *mak nyah*, who adopts the largely Western-groomed term 'trans man', and who holds both non-Malaysian and Malaysian transmasculine icons as role models.

Izharuddin's thoughts, the persistence of GD and a tremendous zeal for bodyscapings through 'top' and 'bottom' surgeries as well as endocrinal treatments lead me to think that trans men may perhaps be themselves the primary repositories and purveyors of this phallocentric logic, this 'rigid, forced conformity to sexual dimorphism' (Hembree et al. 2009, 3133). Not all my research participants see GAHT as indispensable for gender-affirming transitioning. Even fewer consider GAS as imperative for achieving their self-affirmed gender identities, thus bringing to question 'the assumption that transness is the same for most people' (Aizura 2018, 3). Almost every research participant decries the high costs and high health risks attached to 'bottom' surgeries. Yet *all* my research participants express a longing for a sort of penile completeness, particularly if the aforementioned monetary and medical obstacles can somehow be surmounted. In the minds of many Malaysian trans men, biology may not be destiny, but neither does it need to be totally relinquished from the malescaping pursuits of a self-affirmed gender identity.

Similar to an earlier enquiry on the role of trans men in the sedimentation of the gender binary, I ask: are trans men thus in collusion with surgical and endocrinal efforts that promote the idea that biology is indeed destiny, even fabricated and reconstructed biology? Is this a case where 'the demand for surgery may be seen to be an outcome of the social and cultural investment in a gender binary system[?]' (Hines 2007, 65). After all, studies show that 'individuals who referred themselves to a gender binary identity more often declared to have undergone or their wish to undergo GAS in the future' (Vitelli et al. 2017, e50).

Somewhat similar to my response to my initial question is my belief that both collusion and disruption are present, even if subconsciously so. In other words, just because a person was assigned female at birth yearns for a penis as an integral part of his bodily assemblage does not mean that he should be mercilessly tagged as colluding in the notion of biology as destiny. In terms of disruption, I hold that while the tenacious desire to own an actual functioning penis with all its sensory faculties may be present in trans men, the fact that this desire is articulated by men who were assigned female at birth *fractures* and *displaces* the phallocentric logic. *The penis is democratised*, because it is now within the reach of those who wish to live as men, regardless of the anatomy ascribed to them at birth. For trans men, men may be men only because of their penises, but they can also be men without *being born* with penises as well as men with *constructed* penises. A second consideration is that manness can only be accomplished through strategic deployments of limited cultural props that point to man. The penis is one such prop, and to desire this organ is to desire an architecturing of a manly identity which can more recognisably occur with specific architecturings of cultural signifiers of man. As Butler avers, 'identity is asserted through a process of signification' (1999, 183). Yet again the desire to remain invisible renders this fracturing and displacement hidden for the most part.

Another significant finding, and admittedly somewhat anticipated, is the crucial role that faith plays in the becomings of trans men. As a Gender Studies educator at Monash University Malaysia, I teach a variety of classes that often include topics on the intersectionality of gender, sexuality and religion. Occasionally, the matter of how transgender people are 'viewed with disdain as permutations of the transgression of legitimate and divinely sanctioned gender and sexual configurations' (Goh 2012a, 168) becomes a subject of debate. Consequently, I am quizzed by students, that 'if religion is so hostile and unsympathetic towards homosexual and transgender people, why do they still hang on to it?'

This often proves to be a window of opportunity for me to explain, albeit rather tentatively and after eliciting their views, the intricate embeddedness of religious faith in the psyche of many Malaysians, including transgender and queer Malaysians. To relinquish faith is akin to relinquishing family, or ethnicity, or language, or traditions, or any other element of cultural production that anchors a person in recognisability, readability and meaningful belonging. Subsequently, many such individuals construct spaces where they can exercise their faith while being transgressively gendered and sexual. The demand to be *either* transgender and/or queer *or* religious becomes moot for them.

Trans men of faith, as my research findings indicate, often find hierarchical doctrines and dogmas stifling and even destructive to their emotional and mental wellbeing. In response, they create transgender technologies of the spirit that can accommodate both their self-affirmed gender identities and their faith performances and experiences. These personalised spiritualities often conscript an accepting, affirming and supportive God who creates them as they are, and who is as interested in their ethical exercises as much as their gender identities. In a certain sense, while trans men rely on divinity to essentialise their subjectivities, this technique proves to be beneficial for their overall wellbeing. While some have deemed it necessary to completely renounce the religion assigned to them at birth, others continue to straddle both 'official' religiosities and 'unofficial' spiritualities with the latter often dictating the former.

A final thought: The imperative of transnegative and homonegative authorities to create a Malaysia that is devoid of all undesirable 'Western', 'un-Islamic,'—and by extension, irreverent—'un-Asian' and 'un-Malaysian' elements is futile, fruitless and counterintuitive. Such labours manifest a convenient amnesia that turns its back on the kaleidoscope of subjectivities that have always been present in Southeast Asia. Noor insists on

> the urgent need for Malaysians to reclaim the histories, biographies, symbols, tropes and markers that dot the narrative and discursive landscape of Malaysia from the clammy clutches of politicians, ideologues and soap-box orators who would otherwise be inclined to reduce the semiotic repertoire of our public discursive domain to simplified and essentialised totems that stand for a communitarian and divisive politics that is not only historically inaccurate, but politically dangerous. (2010, 12–13)

Noor also uncovers a 'pre-modern, pre-colonial environment' in Southeast Asian societies that accommodated gender and sexual diversities, and that 'homosexuality, lesbian ism and bisexuality were commonplace and normalised, as were transsexuality and ambiguous gender distinctions' (2010, 152). Even 'transgendered courtiers were … a common sight in the royal courts of the archipelago right up to the early 20th century' (Noor 2010, 153).

In addition to 'transgendered priests and courtiers (*sida-sida*) that existed in pre-Islamic Malay kingdoms' (2006, 322), Michael G. Peletz also writes about mid-twentieth-century existence of

> several 'specialized homosexual villages' in or near the capital [of the Malaysian state of Kelantan], Kota Baru, the best-known of which adjoined the sultan's palace [which] were made up entirely of male couples engaged in same-sex sexuality whose 'breadwinners' earned their living as transvestite performers of a dramatic genre known as *mak yong*. (2006, 320)

The conflation of homosexual and gender-diverse subjectivities requires a more critical reading, but Peletz drives home the point that non-normative genders and sexualities were not alien to the country.

Experts also underscore the existence of the *manang bali* or 'transformed' (Graham 1987) shamans among the indigenous Iban of the Malaysian state of Sarawak who are believed to have become extinct by the nineteenth century (Masing 1997). Assigned male at birth, the *manang bali* embodied 'womanness' and femininity, wore female clothes and married male partners in response to a calling from the deity Menjaya Manang Raja to be shamans. While these shamans were lauded for their spiritual prowess, they were also ridiculed for their inability and/or refusal to live up to sociocultural dictates of manness and masculinity (consult Barrett 1993; Sandin 1983; Sutlive 2001). What is noteworthy, I submit, is that ordinarily conservative communities were able to appreciate diversity and live harmoniously with those who did not adhere to the gender binary.

Some terms used by the aforementioned scholars are derived from contemporary categories. It would be wise, therefore, to approach the use of these terms with some measure of criticality, for to do otherwise would be to succumb to the pitfall of anachronism. Nevertheless, the heart of the matter is indisputable. By exposing the 'awkward silences and blind spots in the national historical narrative' (Noor 2002, 21), and thus providing evidence of a colourful past that was not given to religiously and socioculturally inflected fanaticisms of the present day, these scholars recuperate suppressed, hidden, overlooked, forgotten, dismissed and condemned epistemologies which show that *gender and sexual diversities have always been a defining feature of Malaysia*. By reading the past in light of the present and the present in light of the past, it becomes clear that diversity is built into the very fibre of what it means to be Malaysian in Malaysia. The trans man must take his rightful place with pride and honour in the long historical line of this Malaysian heterogeneity.

Bibliography

Aizura, Aren Z. 2018. *Mobile Subjects: Transnational Imaginaries of Gender Reassignment*. Durham, NC: Duke University Press.

Barrett, Robert J. 1993. 'Performance, Effectiveness and the Iban *Manang*'. In *The Seen and the Unseen: Shamanism, Mediumship and Possession in Borneo*, Borneo Research Council Monograph Series; v. 2, edited by Robert L. Winzeler, 235–79. Williamsburg, VA: Borneo Research Council.

Butler, Judith. 1999. *Gender Trouble: Feminism and the Subversion of Identity*. New York: Routledge.

Cornwall, Andrea. 1994. 'Gendered Identities and Gender Ambiguity Among *Travestis* in Salvador, Brazil'. In *Dislocating Masculinity: Comparative Ethnographies*, edited by Andrea Cornwall and Nancy Lindisfarne, 111–32. London: Routledge.

Cromwell, Jason. 1999. *Transmen and FTMs: Identities, Bodies, Genders, and Sexualities*. Urbana, IL: University of Illinois Press.

Goh, Joseph N. 2012a. 'The Homosexual Threat: Appraising Masculinities and Men's Sexualities in Malaysia'. In *Thinking Through Malaysia: Culture and Identity in the 21st Century*, edited by Julian Hopkins and Julian C. H. Lee, 167–86. Selangor, Malaysia: Strategic Information and Research Development Centre.

———. 2012b. 'The Word Was *Not* Made Flesh: Theological Reflections on the Banning of *Seksualiti Merdeka* 2011'. *Dialog* 51 (2): 145–54.

Graham, Penelope. 1987. *Iban Shamanism: An Analysis of the Ethnographic Literature*. Occasional Paper (Australian National University Department of Anthropology). Canberra, Australia: Department of Anthropology, Australian National University.

Hansbury, Griffin. 2005. 'The Middle Men: An Introduction to the Transmasculine Identities'. *Studies in Gender and Sexuality* 6 (3): 241–64.

Hembree, Wylie C., Peggy Cohen-Kettenis, Henriette A. Delemarre-van de Waal, Louis J. Gooren, Walter J. Meyer, Norman P. Spack, Vin Tangpricha, and Victor M. Montori. 2009. 'Endocrine Treatment of Transsexual Persons: An Endocrine Society Clinical Practice Guideline'. *The Journal of Clinical Endocrinology & Metabolism* 94 (9): 3132–54.

Hines, Sally. 2007. *TransForming Gender: Transgender Practices of Identity, Intimacy and Care*. Bristol, UK: Policy Press.

Izharuddin, Alicia. 2012. 'The Transmen Community Is Still Overshadowed by Phallocentric Logic in Malaysia'. London School of Economics and Political Science. *Engenderings* (blog), 15 February 2012. https://blogs.lse.ac.uk/gender/2012/02/15/the_transmen_community_phallocentric_logic_malaysia/.

Kong, Lee Lian. 2019. 'Shh… Diam! Is a Queer Band Fighting to Silence the LGBTQ Hate In Malaysia'. *VICE*, 24 January 2019. https://www.vice.com/en_in/article/d3banw/shh-diam-is-a-queer-band-fighting-to-silence-the-lgbtq-hate-in-malaysia.

Lee, Julian C. H. 2013. 'Sexuality Rights Activism in Malaysia: The Case of Seksualiti Merdeka'. In *Social Activism in Southeast Asia*, edited by Michele Ford, 170–86. New York: Routledge.

———. 2014. 'The Creation of Sexual Dissidence: The Case of Seksualiti Merdeka'. In *The Other Kuala Lumpur: Living in the Shadows of a Globalising Southeast Asian City*, edited by Seng Guan Yeoh, 168–89. New York: Routledge.

Looi, Sylvia. 2018. 'Anwar: Dr M and I Both Oppose Gay Marriage'. *Malay Mail*, 22 September 2018. https://www.malaymail.com/s/1675376/anwar-dr-m-and-i-both-oppose-gay-marriage.

Mahathir Mohamad, and Shintarō Ishihara. 1995. *The Voice of Asia: Two Leaders Discuss the Coming Century*. New York: Kodansha International.

Masing, James Jemut. 1997. *The Coming of the Gods: An Iban Invocatory Chant (Timang Gawai Amat) of the Baleh River Region, Sarawak*. Vol. 1 & 2. Canberra, Australia: Department of Anthropology, Research School of Pacific & Asian Studies, Australian National University.

Noor, Farish A. 2002. *The Other Malaysia*. Kuala Lumpur, Malaysia: Silverfish Books.

———. 2010. *What Your Teacher Didn't Tell You: The Annexe Lectures*. Selangor, Malaysia: Matahari Books.

Pearce, Ruth. 2018. *Understanding Trans Health: Discourse, Power and Possibility*. Bristol, UK: Policy Press.

Peletz, Michael G. 2006. 'Transgenderism and Gender Pluralism in Southeast Asia Since Early Modern Times'. *Current Anthropology* 47 (2): 309–40.

Pfeffer, Carla A. 2017. *Queering Families: The Postmodern Partnerships of Cisgender Women and Transgender Men*. New York: Oxford University Press.

Rahimy Rahim. 2019. 'M'sia Must Not Bow to International Pressure on LGBT Issues, Says Anwar'. *The Star Online*, 15 May 2019. https://www.thestar.com.my/news/nation/2019/05/15/msia-must-not-bow-to-international-pressure-on-lgbt-issues-says-anwar/.

Sandin, Benedict. 1983. 'Mythological Origins of Iban Shamanism'. *The Sarawak Museum Journal* XXXII (53): 235–50.

Sutlive, Vinson H., Jr. 2001. 'The Encyclopaedia of Iban Studies: Iban History, Society and Culture'. In *Manang*, edited by Vinson H. Sutlive Jr. and Joanne Sutlive, 2: H-N:1035–51. Sarawak, Malaysia: Tun Jugah Foundation.

Vitelli, R., C. Scandurra, R. Pacifico, M. S. Selvino, S. Picariello, A. L. Amodeo, P. Valerio, and A. Giami. 2017. 'Trans Identities and Medical Practice in Italy: Self-Positioning Towards Gender Affirmation Surgery'. *Sexologies* 26 (4): e43–51.

Walden, Max. 2019. 'Malaysian Cabinet Minister Allegedly Depicted in Gay Sex Video, Accused of Corruption'. *ABC News*, 12 June 2019. https://www.abc.net.au/news/2019-06-12/gay-sex-video-sparks-scandal-for-malaysian-government/11201834.

Appendix 1: Designing the Research Project

Context

Located in Southeast Asia, Malaysia comprises Peninsular Malaysia between Thailand and Singapore, and the states of Sarawak and Sabah on the island of Borneo. Peninsular Malaysia, which was previously a loose conglomeration of states known as Malaya gained independence from the British in 1957. Prior to British presence which intensified around the late eighteenth century, the Portuguese and Dutch held power in the Malay states in the sixteenth and seventeenth centuries respectively. The Japanese also occupied Malaya briefly in the 1940s. Malaysia came into being when the two Bornean states were incorporated into Malaya in 1963, and now includes the Federal Territories of Kuala Lumpur, Labuan and Putrajaya.

Vestiges of British colonialism are visible in the legal system (Chevallier-Govers 2010), the prevalence of the English language among Malaysians (Mandal 2000) and ethnic taxonomies as 'the politicised and racialised nature of an internalised set of assumptions about the characteristics, demeanours, and ways of life across a group's social, economic, and political life' (Koh 2017, 25). Another British legacy is the retention of sections 377A-C of the Penal Code, which criminalise oral and anal penetrative sex as 'carnal intercourse against the order of nature'

J. N. Goh, *Becoming a Malaysian Trans Man*,
Gender, Sexualities and Culture in Asia,
https://doi.org/10.1007/978-981-15-4534-4

(The Commissioner of Law Revision, Malaysia 1997). Malaysian gay activist Pang Khee Teik has referred to this colonial residue as the cause of 'deep wounds' (cited in Yiswaree 2018) for lesbian, gay, bisexual, transgender, intersex and queer (LGBTIQ) communities.

Today, the Muslim-majority country is steadily growing in renown as a preferred international retirement destination (Wong and Musa 2014), for its progressive Islamic banking (Sulaiman and Joriah 2013), and as an international media and education hub (Malaysia Digital Economy Corporation 2017; Singh and Jack 2018). Malaysia's obsessive desire to portray itself as a pristine, postcolonial state that adheres faithfully to Islam-inflected 'Asian values' propels it to repudiate or retreat from any perceived manifestation of Western moral decadence, such as unrestrained pleasures, sexual permissiveness, unconventional families, individualism, irreligiosity and same-sex behaviour (Mahathir and Ishihara 1995; see also Gatsiounis 2006).

Within an overarching climate of moral conservatism, the state feels obliged to admonish, anathematise and criminalise transgender and queer people as 'Malaysia's Other' (Lee 2011, 107). Ironically, despite its aversion to presumed Western debauchery, the state continues to retain the Penal Code—a legacy of the West—as a means to penalise those whom it accuses of being deceived by the false ideologies of the West.

Personal Location

I bring to these pages the privilege, location and bias that constitute and are constituted by my multiple identities as a masculine-presenting[1] cis gay man, trans ally, educator and researcher in gender and sexuality studies, theological activist, ordained minister and Malaysian citizen of mostly Chinese heritage who is more spiritual than religious. This situation potentially evokes 'a problem in speaking for *others*' as

> where one speaks from affects the meaning and truth of what one says [and] the practice of privileged persons speaking for or on behalf of less privileged persons [can] actually [result] in increasing or reinforcing the oppression of the group spoken for'. (Alcoff 1991, 6–7)

[1]Perhaps a more apt description would be that I am read as more masculine-acting by more feminine-acting men, and as more feminine-acting ('gentle' and 'soft-spoken') by more hypermasculine men.

I am not transgender and thus can never presume to know the lived experiences of trans people as a transgender person. Rather than succumbing to any feelings of disentitlement however, I co-opt Jason Cromwell's opinion that 'one does not have to be ... a transman to understand the nature of ... transman identity (as gender), although that is likely the case in order to understand the depth of feeling' (1999, 42). This book, which showcases trans lives, emerges as a collaborative enterprise of sorts with trans people rather than a solo project. I am also cognisant of, and readily acknowledge my deployment of writing as a theological and political act of social transformation.

Fieldwork

Upon receiving an Internal Research Grant from my university in April 2016, I conducted face-to-face, in-depth interviews using open-ended questions with 15 self-identified trans men in Kuala Lumpur and Selangor on issues pertaining to identity construction, sociopolitical interaction and faith engagement. I allowed myself to be steered by concerns that trans men prioritised in their conversations with me. Interviews ranged between 1.0 and 1.5 hours in duration, mostly in English and interspersed with smatterings of Malay and Chinese languages with varying levels of proficiency. My fieldwork experiences were extremely positive, as research participants readily shared their stories with me. I believe that this situation was facilitated by the very fact that I am not a trans person, and that many of my research participants identified with me as man. I found it helpful at times to share my own struggles in performing and struggling with masculinity, especially when it facilitated conversations.[2]

Most of the members of this 'nonsituated population' (Cromwell 1999, 151) were fluent in English, and all of them were urban dwellers, educated, financially independent, technologically literate and spoke a minimum of two to three languages. I suspect that some research participants may have found my social standing, language proficiencies and level of education appealing, and this could have contributed to a certain degree of social desirability. Hence, any perceptions of privilege may well have worked in my favour, as I would have been perceived as the 'expert' authority on gender and sexuality issues from a reputable university.

[2]Physician and social worker Marcus Greatheart (2013) also experienced an affinity with his trans men participants based on the gender identity of man.

On many occasions however, I found myself learning (more) about (trans)gender issues from my research participants. I did my utmost to ensure self-reflexivity throughout the periods of fieldwork, analysis and writing by constantly interrogating my interpretations of the research findings and through conversations with trans activist Dorian Wilde.

Gatekeeping[3]

Wilde was an indispensable resource person who helped me secure research participants and advised me on my research design. As I had no prior experience of conducting research with trans men, I was initiated into a world that was significantly different from that which informed previous research undertakings on gay and bisexual men, and trans women or *mak nyah* (Goh 2018, 2012). I used Wilde's comments and critiques to refine my research design, and his experiences and insights continue to guide and inform my thoughts throughout this volume. He also gave his blessing for ToM to act as the main gatekeeper of my project, and agreed to an elite interview with me.[4] It was mostly due to Wilde's and ToM's interventions that I was able to meet fifteen men over a period of a year. Their narratives form the bedrock of this monograph.[5]

Method, Methodology and Limitations

Audio recordings of interviews were transcribed, thematically coded and analysed using ATLAS.ti 8.0, a Computer Assisted Qualitative Data Analysis Software. I found Kathy Charmaz's (2001) constructivist grounded theory methodology to be vital in interpreting and theorising stories that unfolded within specific social contexts as it allowed me to

[3]Clinical social worker and trans man Griffin Hansbury (2005) provides an interesting insight into the term 'gatekeeper' as a metonym for the Standards of Care which previously insisted on obligatory psychotherapy prior to gender transitioning. I use this term for Wilde and ToM not in that sense, but in reference to their role in helping me as a cis man to gain access to trans man research participants.

[4]See 'Appendix 2: Interviewing Dorian Wilde'.

[5]Permission to undertake this research project was granted by the Monash University Human Research Ethics Committee (Project No: CF16/1275 - 2016000673) in June 2016.

pay heed to the partiality and situatedness that mark the lives of trans men. While I work on the premise that epistemological pursuits occur from the ground up, this is not a matter of simply 'discovering' and showcasing knowledge that has hitherto been latent. The production of knowledge within a researcher–participant setting is always a labour of co-construction in which the researcher attempts to make meaning of the exchanges in a reflexive manner (Charmaz 1995; 2005), without circumventing or dismissing extant scholarship *from various academic disciplines* as 'sensitizing concepts' (Charmaz 2000, 515). This multi-disciplinary approach resonates with much of transgender studies that is 'interdisciplinary' and 'intertextual' (Hines 2007, 28).

I am neither painting a singular nor an overarching image of the Malaysian trans man with a broad brush. Instead, what I offer are glimpses of their lived realities with which they have graciously provided me. Most of my research participants are also members of ToM, which could account for a strong sense of self-awareness and knowledge of (trans)gender issues among them. Furthermore, I did not have the opportunity to interview trans men from outside Kuala Lumpur and Selangor, or trans men who lived in non-urban settings. What I offer are meaningful *vignettes* of trans men's lives. Moreover, I do not focus on substance use or HIV issues, butch lesbian identities, female partners of trans, sexual orientations, sexual practices, marriage and relationships, reproductive technologies, childbearing, pregnancy or adoption, the reception of trans men in the wider transgender and queer Malaysian community, social movements, laws, citizenship, human rights activism and feminist theorisings of transgender subjectivities.

Research Participants[6]

Aarone

47-year-old Malay-Muslim with an undergraduate degree who works in construction and identifies as man.

[6]These details were furnished by the research participants themselves.

Adam
45-year-old Peranakan[7] Muslim who holds a master's degree, works in the media and identifies as man and male.

Alco
49-year-old Malay-Muslim social worker and community leader with a diploma certificate who identifies as a trans man.

Axman
36-year-old 'Chinese Malaysian' Christian rideshare driver with an undergraduate degree who identifies as male.

Bottle
26-year-old Chinese retailer with an advanced diploma who identifies as male and a freethinker.

Braveheart
57-year-old 'Messianic Christian' of 'borderless' race who works in sales and has an undergraduate degree, and identifies as man and gay.

Hadi
33-year-old Malay-Muslim technician with a diploma who identifies as a trans man.

Jon
46-year-old Chinese-Christian homemaker with an SPM[8] certificate who identifies as a trans man, and as gay, homosexual and bearing the soul of man.

Michael
22-year-old Indian who identifies as Female-To-Male and man, works in the food and beverage industry, professes to be spiritual, an atheist and culturally Roman Catholic, and holds an SPM certificate.

[7]Peranakans are Malaysians who manifest a '"hybrid culture" mixing elements from their Chinese and Malay ancestries' (Lim 2015, 154). They profess various religious beliefs.

[8]SPM or *Sijil Pelajaran Malaysia* refers to the Malaysian Certificate of Education, 'a national examination taken by all fifth-year secondary school students' (Mamun et al. 2016, 390). These students are usually 17-years old.

Pokerface
A 28-year-old professional of Malaysian and Thai-Chinese ancestry who identifies as a trans man and cis man, professes multiple faiths and holds an undergraduate degree.

Ray
28-year-old Chinese with an STPM[9] certificate who identifies as trans-masculine and agnostic, and is engaged in clerical work.

Schulz
28-year-old Indian-Roman Catholic logistician with a diploma certificate who identifies as man.

Superman
33-year-old Peranakan public servant and lawyer with a postgraduate diploma who identifies as man, and believes in Roman Catholicism and Universal Love.

SR
30-year-old Malay-Muslim with an SPM certificate who works in marketing and identifies as man.

Warp
29-year-old Indian Malaysian freelancer of multiple faiths with an undergraduate degree who identifies as a trans man.

Bibliography

Alcoff, Linda. 1991. 'The Problem of Speaking for Others'. *Cultural Critique* 20: 5–32.

Charmaz, Kathy. 1995. 'Grounded Theory'. In *Rethinking Methods in Psychology*, edited by Jonathan A. Smith, Rom Harre, and Luk Van Langenhove, 27–49. London: Sage.

———. 2000. 'Grounded Theory: Objectivist and Constructivist Methods'. In *Handbook of Qualitative Research*, edited by Norman K. Denzin and Yvonna S. Lincoln, 2nd ed., 509–35. London: Sage.

[9]STPM or *Sijil Tinggi Persekolahan Malaysia* is the Malaysian Higher School Certificate, one of several pre-university programmes undertaken 'at the end of 13 years' schooling' (Ong 2010, 94).

———. 2001. 'Qualitative Interviewing and Grounded Theory Analysis'. In *Handbook of Interview Research: Context & Method*, edited by Jaber F. Gubrium and James A. Holstein, 1st ed., 675–94. London: Sage.
———. 2005. 'Grounded Theory in the 21st Century: Applications for Advancing Social Justice Studies'. In *The Sage Handbook of Qualitative Research*, edited by Norman K. Denzin and Yvonna S. Lincoln, 507–35. London: Sage.
Chevallier-Govers, Constance. 2010. 'The Rule of Law and Legal Pluralism in Malaysia'. *Islam and Civilisational Renewal* 2 (1): 90–108.
Cromwell, Jason. 1999. *Transmen and FTMs: Identities, Bodies, Genders, and Sexualities*. Urbana, IL: University of Illinois Press.
Gatsiounis, Ioannis. 2006. 'Islam Hadhari in Malaysia'. *Current Trends in Islamic Ideology* 3: 78–88.
Goh, Joseph N. 2012. 'Mary and the *Mak Nyahs*: Queer Theological Imaginings of Malaysian Male-to-Female Transsexuals'. *Theology & Sexuality* 18 (3): 215–33.
———. 2018. *Living Out Sexuality and Faith: Body Admissions of Malaysian Gay and Bisexual Men*. London: Routledge.
Greatheart, Marcus. 2013. *Transforming Practice: Life Stories of Transgender Men That Change How Health Providers Work*. Toronto, Canada: Ethica Press.
Hansbury, Griffin. 2005. 'The Middle Men: An Introduction to the Transmasculine Identities'. *Studies in Gender and Sexuality* 6 (3): 241–64.
Hines, Sally. 2007. *Transforming Gender: Transgender Practices of Identity, Intimacy and Care*. Bristol, UK: Policy Press.
Koh, Sin Yee. 2017. *Race, Education, and Citizenship: Mobile Malaysians, British Colonial Legacies, and a Culture of Migration*. Migration, Diasporas and Citizenship. New York: Palgrave Macmillan.
Lee, Julian C. H. 2011. *Policing Sexuality: Sex, Society and the State*. London: Zed Books.
Lim, Sep Neo. 2015. 'Essentialising the Convenient Baba-Nyonyas of the Heritage City of Melaka (Malaysia)'. In *Cultural Essentialism in Intercultural Relations*, edited by Fred Dervin and Régis Machart, 153–77. New York: Palgrave Macmillan.
Mahathir Mohamad, and Shintarō Ishihara. 1995. *The Voice of Asia: Two Leaders Discuss the Coming Century*. New York: Kodansha International.
Malaysia Digital Economy Corporation. 2017. 'Bill of Guarantees (BoG)'. Malaysia Digital Economy Corporation. https://www.mdec.my/msc-malaysia/bill-of-guarantees.
Mamun, Abdullah Al, Roselina Ahmad Saufi, and Mohammad Bin Ismail. 2016. 'Human Capital, Credit, and Startup Motives: A Study Among Rural Micro-Enterprises in Malaysia'. *The Journal of Developing Areas* 50 (4): 383–400.

Mandal, Sumit K. 2000. 'Reconsidering Cultural Globalization: The English Language in Malaysia'. *Third World Quarterly* 21 (6): 1001–12.

Ong, Saw Lan. 2010. 'Assessment Profile of Malaysia: High-Stakes External Examinations Dominate'. *Assessment in Education: Principles, Policy & Practice* 17 (1): 91–103.

Singh, Jasvir Kaur Nachatar, and Gavin Jack. 2018. 'The Benefits of Overseas Study for International Postgraduate Students in Malaysia'. *Higher Education* 75 (4): 607–24.

Sulaiman Abdullah Saif Al Nasser, and Joriah Muhammed. 2013. 'Introduction to History of Islamic Banking in Malaysia'. *Humanomics* 29 (2): 80–87.

The Commissioner of Law Revision, Malaysia. 1997. *Malaysian Penal Code*. http://www.agc.gov.my/agcportal/index.php?r=portal2/lom2&id=1687.

Wong, Kee Mun, and Ghazali Musa. 2014. 'Retirement Motivation Among "Malaysia My Second Home" Participants'. *Tourism Management* 40: 141–54.

Yiswaree Palansamy. 2018. 'Thanks for Acknowledging "Deep Wounds" UK Left Malaysia, LGBT Activist Tells Theresa May'. *The Malay Mail Online*, 18 April 2018. https://www.malaymail.com/s/1621696/thanks-for-acknowledging-deep-wounds-uk-left-malaysia-lgbt-activist-tells-t.

Appendix 2: Interviewing Dorian Wilde[10]

On the Population of Trans Men

1. Goh: Do you know how many trans men there are in Malaysia?
   Wilde: No idea. This is also a question that has been posed in other places. And they usually say that it's a number that's lesser than trans women. But … we haven't had the time that trans women and effeminate gay men have had to separate ourselves. So we still exist on this spectrum called transmasculinity. That this spectrum even exists is blurring up the lines.

2. In a way it's a good, because, it's good for, you know, fluidity, but it's also very rooted in patriarchy, that a gender identity and sexual orientation, or gender expression even, of people who have been assigned female at birth, are not as important. Because they are

[10]The actual transcription of my interview with Dorian Wilde that occurred in the afternoon of 4 June 2016, on which this Appendix is based, has been minimally edited and rearranged for better flow and greater ease of reading. The transcription has also been thematised with numbered headings and paragraphs to facilitate in-text referencing of quotes from the interview that appear variously throughout this volume. While the interview was conducted chiefly in English, Wilde and I found ourselves code-switching at various junctures to Bahasa Malaysia (Malay), the official language of the country.

J. N. Goh, *Becoming a Malaysian Trans Man*,
Gender, Sexualities and Culture in Asia,
https://doi.org/10.1007/978-981-15-4534-4

not men. So I think that that's something with that that's still in the process of being worked out, maybe remain in the spectrum, maybe later we will separate ourselves. But in Malaysia, so far from what I've seen from the community itself, like, they want to be separate from butch women, or other forms of identity. Because they know that they are men, not women at all.

3. Goh: Where are trans men located in Malaysia?
   Wilde: Oftentimes, urban centres, so, Penang, KL.[11] Singapore, plenty of Malaysian trans men there. There's quite a huge community there. But they're everywhere. We have numbers from Pahang, Sabah, Sarawak, Kedah, Kelantan,[12] everywhere. But a lot of them have left their original states and come to urban centres, to find work and community and all that.
4. Goh: Are there any other reasons why they migrate?
   Wilde: Sometimes it's due to family unacceptance. Sometimes families don't kick them out, but still don't accept them. So they feel uncomfortable being there. Because they have to conform to certain standards so they leave, and live their own lives. Also for work, for acceptance, you know, a bigger place. Especially you know when you're in a small town. A lot of people like me, left home because we got disowned, and kicked out, and we had to find and live our own lives. When I left, it became a very big news in that area, my sister had to take the brunt of the situation.

On Gender Identity Disclosures of Trans Men

5. Goh: So you started out thinking you were a lesbian?
   Wilde: Yeah. So, a lot of trans guys go through that experience. They start off as butch lesbians, or lesbians in general, and then like slowly, feels weird, and then you finally find out that there's such thing as trans man. It's a light bulb moment. And then you research, and you find out that's exactly you. I mean, they're living the cis life, they're not coming out, I mean, in a way it's a good thing for them,

[11]The acronym for Kuala Lumpur, the Federal Territory of Kuala Lumpur. Penang is a Malaysian state.

[12]These are various Malaysia states.

but they also have a lot of mental trauma from needing to be in the closet and to hide from basically everyone. Er yeah, but stumbling block in the sense that you know, there's no visibility, for the next generation there is no continuous information passing, and there's no community, because so many guys are stealth.

6. I understand why, but it doesn't make it less of a stumbling block, especially for people like me, when I'm looking for a successor, people to expand ToM, like, it's really difficult and I'm running a lot of things by myself. And that also very personally makes me feel, er burnt out so much quicker if I'm the only one doing it rather than a group of people. When it goes to trans women, I guess the persecution, the fact that a lot of them, I mean passing is an issue, so they already used to being in the public eye, so they actually get involved, and there so many people doing it. One of our main stumbling blocks is that a lot of the guys are stealth. So 'stealth' meaning they do not tell anybody that they are trans, only they know by themselves. So everyone just knows them as a regular cis guy. We have people who are in the closet, people who are out and people who are stealth.
7. Goh: You mentioned 'stumbling block'. Can you say more?
   Wilde: Basically because, er number one, visibility, so it's a double-edged sword right, visibility helps us, like, get issues out there, so, because right now when people think trans issues, they mostly think trans women. And so issues affecting trans men just, you know, are not taken into consideration. Also it's very hard to find people who are willing to step up and do something about it, willing to join activism and willing to work on issues, because a lot of people are very comfortable.
8. Goh: Well the thing is that, you know, in our country, not many people can come out.
   Wilde: I completely agree.
   Goh: And for a lot of trans men, to come out means to lose their job, their family support, religious affiliations. So, we can't expect everyone to come out.
   Wilde: For sure. I think this is the issue for everybody, right. I don't blame them at all. I totally understand, which is why the Transmen of Malaysia group, ToM, is basically designed for the

stealth guy, you know, at least to have a community, a group of people who are like them, who understands, and who they can talk to. Because this was my main criteria. The group has to be built in such a way that nobody else can know that they are part of that group.

9. So yeah, people have no clue, even people within the LGBT[13] spectrum, they have no clue about us. We exist in so many different forms, and people just don't get that yet. And when I say I'm the opposite of trans women, some of them go like, oh, oh (gestures in a way to indicate understanding), finally they understand.

On Trans Men and the MyKad

10. Goh: What are your thoughts about our Identity Cards?
Wilde: IC? *MyKad*. It's basically your ID.[14]
Goh: That's right.
Wilde: Once you start transitioning ... you cannot change your ID. There ARE (raises voice) trans guys who have changed their IDs. But before, in the nineties and in the eighties, it was far easier to do that. So they have been people who change their, actually not even that long ago, in the 2000s, there have been people who successfully went and changed their ID. But now you just can't do it anymore. I've asked people to look at different departments, but so far, no. JPN.[15] They actually have a form. The form is actually meant for you to change details on your ID. So when they say details, obviously you should be able to change every detail that is there ... which is why they have the gender part as well.

11. The reason it's there is because of intersex children as well. So if you're, at birth, the doctor says this, that you're born intersex, later on, with the doctor's thing saying that this is so, and that this person wants to have a corrective surgery done, then you can go to court, because you have the doctor's thing to back you up,

[13]Lesbian, gay, bisexual and transgender.

[14]Identity.

[15]An acronym for *Jabatan Pendaftaran Negara* or National Registration Department.

then they'll allow. They need documents attached to that and of the documents these people claim is a court order. But also trans people have been using that, from the eighties, seventies even, and they've been successful.

12. Goh: What names do trans men use in their work places? Birth Certificate names or trans names?
Wilde: We never use 'trans names'. They would prefer to use their real names, which means how they identify themselves. Like me, my real name is 'Dorian'. Among our colleagues, depends on how far the person is into transition, most guys prefer to use nicknames that are quite general, that don't raise questions. While post-op guys who have been on the hormones for some time, they usually and can pass, they usually use their preferred names.
13. Goh: What is the level of importance for a trans man to change his gender, to change his name, that were given to him at birth?
Wilde: It is of such massive importance. Like I cannot even begin to start, this same for trans men and trans women. You basically cannot live your life, probably like everyone else. I can't get married. Let's go to the most basic thing. One of our trans men friends called me and asked me to help him to change his Maybank[16] password. He had to reset it. But he cannot call in to do it, so he sent me a snapshot of his identification card, and he said, 'these are all my security questions, can you get someone to call in and tell them that this is so and so, so that they can reset it'.
14. We had another friend who lost the handphone, he was right here. He couldn't call to the telco. He called, he said 'I've lost my telephone, can you please block the number because it's a post-paid'. And they were like, you are not the main person on this thing. You can only register on your IC right. And if your IC is already carrying say, like 'Felicia' or whatever, and then it's like er, 'sir, you sound like a man. The account belongs to Felicia, we cannot do anything'. So he hung up, a woman friend called. And then when she called, they said 'are you Felicia'?, 'I'm yeah, I'm Felicia'. They were like, 'a man just called about this, so we

[16]A Malaysian bank.

put a bar on the account, until the owner walks in', this was on a Saturday. They open on a Monday. 'So until the owner walks in we cannot block the line'.

15. This has happened to me as well. So I got involved in an accident and the adjustor called me to ask for explanation, about the police report and how the accident happened. He was like, 'I need to speak to [Birth Certificate name]' and I was like, 'yes this is he'. And he was like, 'er but here say female'. And then I, 'yes'. And then, 'no I need to speak to this person'. 'Yes, this is me speaking, can we please go to the accident, this is really not the matter here'. At the end, he was like, 'er, so the police write your IC number wrong'? And I was like, 'it's correct'.

16. Actually one of our friend who managed to change his Identity Card. This is what he did. He brought out a list of all the problems that he went through because of his IC, and at that time he was lucky, that when he submitted, they're like 'these are problems that we didn't think you would have'. And they called him in for an interview just to have a look at him, but this was quite a few years back. He was lucky, and they're like okay. This guy was like one of the last person who managed to change the gender on the IC.

On Trans Men, Medical Transitioning and Health Issues

17. Goh: When you say that trans men appear in many forms, what do you mean?
Wilde: You know, like bigger, physically we exist in so many different forms. There are some who are non-op, non-transition, which means that they don't want to transition. Minority mostly. We don't believe in this pre-op, post-op thing. Because that defines a sort of a designated journey that you need to be on, a start and an end. For a lot of trans people, there is no start and there is no end. The start can be anywhere from, starting with hormone shots or starting by presenting yourself as male. Some people have presented themselves as male since they were young, because their parents were okay with it.

18. Where do you start from? From the first time you expressed yourself, like when does it begin and where does it end, you know,

you have to be on hormones for the rest of your life (chuckles). And for a lot of trans guys they cannot go for bottom surgery because it's really, really expensive. So there is not start, there is no end. It's just a matter of, I not wanting to go for the surgeries, or wanting to take hormones. If you're already comfortable with yourself, then there's no point to taking on these things, because you're still a man regardless of what you look like.

19. Goh: When you say 'transition', what does that mean?
    Wilde: Either starting off on hormones, and/or going for surgery.
    Goh: Is it politically correct to say transitioning and non-transitioning instead of pre-op and post-op?
    Wilde: Er, non-transitioning, transitioning and maybe pre-transitioning. But again, we also have non-operative, post-operativeand pre-operative. But, it's a very dated term because it defines that trans people really need to go for operation. A lot of times people either don't want to, or they just don't have the money to. You don't have to be on hormones, you don't have to be on surgery, as long as you identify as a man, you know yourself. Hormones and surgery is not important to us.

20. Goh: From your experience, are the majority of Malaysian trans men pre-op or post-op?
    Wilde: There are many who haven't started taking testosterone. But the majority have already started testosterone. And a lot of us consider top surgery as the priority, mastectomy. So those of us who can afford have done it, or who have managed to fund raise have done it (chuckles). And then there are some people who cannot afford these surgeries, because they're very, very expensive. And they just got a lot more expensive. But the rough average of surgery right now, top surgery is about 15, 000 ringgit.[17] We also have a place to do oophorectomy and hysterectomy, which is the removal of the internal reproductive organs.

21. So we have secret Facebook page. A secret group that nobody can find, it's not listed anywhere, and the only way you can get access is if I approve it. If I add you to the group, then only you can have access. It's actually a lot of work on my part. So recently

[17]Approximately USD4000.

I started with a board. ToM has a board right now. It started last year, but the board is basically like not working lah. One of the guys, he's very actively involved with, like talking to people and meeting people, which I frankly just don't have the time to do. But he is very keen on that, so he is on the board, so I basically gave him permission to vet through and add people.

22. Goh: What's the information on the secret Facebook page about?
Wilde: Basically any sort of information pertaining to transitioning, or anything to do with the trans man experience, or anything that's going on in the world, really basically anything (laughs). But mostly it is transitioning and access to health and all this. What we've been doing is also like looking for doctors, clinics, and all this then, so one of the things that has been the biggest problem is hormone replacement therapy. Most of the time we self-prescribe and we self-inject, and we self-determine whether it's good or not. So this is very harmful (laughs). You don't know how many doctors I've approached. Most of them, majority of the, ninety-nine percent have no idea what I'm talking about. They don't know how to do it.

23. Goh: When you say that trans men go on hormone therapy, what are the hormones that they use apart from testosterone?
Wilde: That's it. *Satu jer* (just one). But many different brands. And many different properties, different effects.
Goh: Is hormone replacement therapy expensive?
Wilde: It used to be. One of the reasons why I started ToM is also because there were a few senior trans men that were selling hormones for an exorbitant price to guys that they know. It's not that expensive, it's about maximum 15 ringgit[18] per shot. Three weeks once, for the rest of your life.

24. Goh: What about other health issues that trans men go through?
Wilde: Er, anything related to the uterus, ovaries, vagina, that general area is er, a very big question mark, I would say, because trans men would not go for pap smear. Because, can you imagine going to the clinic with a beard, looking like a man and asking for a pap smear?

[18]Approximately USD4.

You know, people are not informed, like, doctors, clinics, I've been to so many clinics where the nurses would be gossiping, and ask you pointed questions about your gender, and even your sex life. The doctors of course will ask lah, but sometimes it's related, sometimes it's not related, and you know you just have to *tahan* (endure). But the worst I think is the *Klinik Kesihatan* (Health Clinic) lah. So trans men in general would not go for medical treatment for anything, even a fever, because then you'll still have to explain yourself.

25. But the middle-class people are different lah, to be honest. Like, those who can afford private clinics, private hospitals, they still go, because they have access to doctors who are a little bit more understanding, and who won't really care because the money is there. A lot of times, trans men generally self-medicate, or only go to hospital when it's absolutely last minute. It's really gotten bad.

26. Goh: So what would be some of the major health risks that trans men go through?
Wilde: Basically anything that natal, females, have. Gynaecological problems. Like cysts and ovarian cancer. Cervical cancer. Even UTI. Oh my God, urinary tract infection is probably the number one problem that we have. Really, no joke, because trans men are very loathed to use public toilets. Because you're so scared, you *tahan* lah. *Tahan sampai balik* (endure until you reach home) lah. I know this trans guy who *tahan* his pee for like 12 to 14 hour every day, so that he *balik rumah* (went home) and pee, and he got kidney stones and all sorts.

On the Ethnicities, Ages, and Class and Economic Status of Trans Men

27. Goh: In ToM, what ethnic groups do trans men belong to?
Wilde: Pretty balanced. Malay, Indian, Chinese, Kadazandusun, everyone. But a lot of English-speaking. We also have a lot of foreign people who are currently living in Malaysia. They are accepted. Or people who have been living in Malaysia for a very long time, so we also accept them as part of the group. *Mat Salleh* (individuals of White European descent), Filipino, Indonesian.

28. Goh: What is the average age of trans men in ToM?
Wilde: Young, very young, twenties, thirties. But we have an increasing amount of middle-age, senior citizen trans guys who have just recently found that there is such a thing as trans man. And they come, and they approach me. Actually we have people who are in their sixties even.

29. Goh: When you talk about culture and trans men, are you talking about the Tamils, or?
Wilde: Indian culture brought from India. But among Tamil people in Malaysia, we're still heavily stigmatised. And we're still heavily marginalised, because it's seen as an embarrassment. Basically, every time you come out, you're an Indian trans person, you come out to your family, the first thing they'll say is 'what will the four people say'. For us, four people means the world lah apparently. Basically what it means is what will everybody say?

30. There's a divide here. So there's the middle upper class Indians who see this as very taboo. And then you have also have the working class Indians who see it as a taboo, but also as a cultural thing. And they believe that trans people exist, and they know that trans people exist. They just see it as a karma, almost. Usually the Malayalees and the Singhalese and all of them, they're usually middle class, or upper middle class, or upper class. Because of the nature of the way Indians came to Malaysia.

31. Goh: What's the difference between middle class and working class Indians in their perception of transgender people as taboo?
Wilde: While the British colonialist mentality that gender diversity, that this is taboo, exists like in both classes, the working class Indians are still more in touch with the cultural side. And also like the transgender community also heavily uses the family system that you get from India. And so a lot of the working class Indians can see that connection very clearly. So while it is still considered taboo, and it is still considered taboo in the middle class, it's just that they don't really care about it, their family system, and it's seen as a working class thing.

32. Because transgender people are supposed to be the lower echelons of society, right, so, erm, middle-class people see transgender people as taboo because you're generally supposed to disassociate

with people who are trans. Because they are in a different caste level altogether. It's all these are remnant ideals and belief lah. Whereas when it comes to working class I guess, because trans people are also in the same society bracket that, they seem to have this accept but don't accept situation, you know, this kind of tolerating kind of situation. So yeah, I mean it has a lot to do with social structure and yeah, the socio-economic status lah.

33. Goh: So what you're saying is that middle-class Indians see transgender people as lower class, and therefore disassociate from them, and then working class Indians see transgender people as er, maybe on the same level, and therefore they sort of accept them in a way, but don't really accept them in another way. Is that what you're saying?
Wilde: Ah yes. Pretty much. But of course this is a gross generalisation lah, so many other, but this is what I'm getting from it.

34. Goh: What about the economic status of trans men that you've come across?
Wilde: Mostly struggling. A lot of working class. Plenty of middle class going towards working class. They're also upper middle class and upper class but they're few and far between.
Goh: In Malaysia there's this stereotype that *mak nyahs* are poor, uneducated, can only do sex work. Are there such stereotypes as well for trans men?
Wilde: Again, they don't know much about us to stereotype lah, but among trans men themselves like, erm, there is a belief that it is very hard to like, go up, increase your socio-economic status.

On Education and Employment among Trans Men

35. Goh: In your dealings with trans men, what is their level of education, generally?
Wilde: Generally, a lot, they have degrees. Either SPM[19] or degree holders.

[19]As previously mentioned, the acronym for *Sijil Pelajaran Malaysia* or Malaysian Certificate of Education, 'a national examination taken by all fifth-year secondary school students' (Mamun et al. 2016, 390), who are ordinarily 17 years of age.

36. Goh: There's this idea that trans women are always involved in make-up, perfume sales, sex work, weddings, which is often not true, because a lot of trans women are doing other kinds of work. But for trans men, what are the kinds of work that trans men do?
Wilde: So many things. We have chemical engineers, we have this one guy who's a professional diver or something like that. There's this guy who owned a gym with another trans guy. They're both personal trainers. And one of them is a dietician. There're teachers, government officials, there are people who work with NGOs (non-governmental organisations), videographer, whatever job you can think of, a trans man is probably doing it (laughs).

37. Goh: The Malaysian public, does it stereotype trans men as doing a particular job?
Wilde: Erm, they don't know much about us. They don't know anything about us. Every time I tell people I'm a trans man I still get like, 'what's that'? Every time I tell them like you know 'I'm a trans man', they're like, 'what's that'? And then I have to like go on this long explanation. By that time I'm already like turned off, especially if there are some stupid questions, 'are you a boy or a girl', these kind of things.

On the Religious Beliefs of Trans Men

38. Goh: Would you say that generally most of the trans men in Malaysia that you have met are religious or spiritual in some way?
Wilde: Yeah. Spirituality is something that we don't talk as much about because in these kinds of spaces we usually talk about hormones and surgeries, transformations and these sorts of things right (chuckles). But there are lots of times when, if the matter comes up it becomes a hot topic. So I guess that there are many who ARE (raises voice) spiritual. I don't know about the majority, I cannot speak for everyone, but I would say there's a lot of very religious people, spiritual people.

39. There are very many who are, not just spiritual, but religious, following, going to mosque and church and all that. Especially Hindu trans men. They become even MORE (raises voice) religious. Because Hinduism, there is a place for trans people. There are gods dedicated to trans people. We actually have a specific god

that is dedicated to trans people, which is called Bahuchara Mata. Her story is very interesting. She gave a boon of being the other gender to a trans man. So even within Hinduism there are stories of trans men. All over the place. Stories of trans women. All over the place. The story is that there was a princess who wanted to be a man, and prayed to Bahuchara Mata. Bahuchara Mata transformed him. And also, there's a place in the culture, and there's a place in rituals and traditions. So I don't know if you've heard of the festival that they have once a year, that is basically for trans people. Everywhere in Malaysia.

40. Goh: What about Buddhists?
Wilde: Buddhists I don't really know, because a lot of the Buddhists that I speak to are very abstract about their beliefs (chuckles). You know, those Abrahamic religions, they're very rites and rituals and specific path, you know. But when it comes to Buddhism and Hinduism, it's basically like umpteen gods (both laugh). I think the Buddhist they don't really necessarily stop believing in God, they just maintain with whatever beliefs that they have from before.

41. Goh: How do their religious institutions view them?
Wilde: I'll start first with Islam. Considering that in three states we have *Syariah* (Islamic) laws against trans men, Pahang, Perlis and Sabah, they come with '*lelaki berpakaian seperti perempuan, atau sebaliknya*' (men who dress like women, or vice versa). But Pahang is special, where they have '*mana-mana perempuan yang berlagak sebagai lelaki*' (any woman who acts like a man). But, it's not enforced in all three states. Perlis is the most severe of all the states, five thousand fine, one year jail. For Islam I would say, they're very against, Christianity very mixed, basically it's whatever those religious institutions believe about trans women, they believe about trans men. Or they have no idea we exist (laughs).

42. From what I've heard from the community itself, from the Malays, a lot of them are afraid to transition because transition is pretty much permanent. It's very effective (laughs). Once the changes happen, it's very hard to change back. So they're worried about that, and they worry that the *kubur tak terima* (literally, 'the grave will not receive', or complications pertaining to burial

rites that are specific to gender identities assigned at birth), so they're worried about dying. We understand as much as we can, but we also try to bring, like these sort of dogmas, we try to like challenge, we give a mixed perspective, we encourage discussion. We maintain that you are free to believe whatever you want, you don't have to transition in order to be a trans man.

On Transmen of Malaysia (ToM)

43. Goh: So do tell me more about the Trans Men of Malaysia. You call it 'ToM' right?
    Wilde: Yes. So, in our community itself there's 172 members, but we know there are so many more, but the problem with trans men in Malaysia or anywhere else to be honest, is that there's not much information out there about trans men. Only recently with Aydian Dowling and all these other people that you actually see trans men coming to the forefront. But not too long ago, even last year, there wasn't much news about trans men, there wasn't much information out there about trans men.
44. And in society, traditionally, you only see trans women. Trans women are visible, but trans men are extremely invisible, you cannot see them, you don't know who they are. And a lot of them have no idea who they are as well. Because like me personally, I had no idea that trans men existed until I was disowned by my father. And left home, went to Singapore to work, and then found out from my girlfriend at that time, six months after we got together.
45. Goh: So far we've been talking about all these things about trans men, are you referring specifically to trans men that you know through ToM?
    Wilde: Pretty much, yes. Because, basically, if he is a trans man, and he is known, then he will be in ToM. Whoever I can find, I just throw them in ToM. For too long, we never had a community. It's good to have a place where everybody is in. At least you can get information about hormone and surgeries, and health information, access to clinics, access to doctors, access to all these things that you generally don't have.

46. Goh: When was ToM established?
    Wilde: 12 September 2011. When I started, I didn't think it was going to be some big deal. I had a YouTube site where I uploaded videos of my transition as a personal record. But so many people found me through there. So many Malaysian trans guys. So they all started adding me on Facebook, and sending messages. I had no idea how to group them, I kept forgetting who they were. So I spoke to a friend, I was like, what if we started this group, yeah it's a good idea, so just started it. Added a few people, and I thought maximum ten people in there. Now 172. I don't think I actually prepared myself for such a thing to happen, so it's basically like, just go with the flow kind of thing. Just wanting to have this group of us who like, share the same experiences, to talk about what we know of. Basically to be friends like that.

47. Goh: How has ToM developed?
    Wilde: It's developed so much to the point where we have 172 members. And we also have members from almost every state. And we have members from all sorts of backgrounds, all sorts of language capacity, basically you know, like just such a variant group, such a diverse group. I'm still surprised to this day there's so much diversity. But there's a lot of silent members as well, in any group. Those who are vocal are very vocal, and that's great.

48. Goh: What are the aims of ToM now?
    Wilde: To create a community of trans men in Malaysia, so basically to have a community that people can turn to, you know, and to share resources, share information, basically as a community-based organisation. So far we don't really aspire to very much other than providing a space for trans guys to come together.

49. Goh: When you say community, do you mean online, offline?
    Wilde: Both.
    Goh: So what are some of the things that have been happening offline and online?
    Wilde: So online a lot of times when we have conversations in the group itself. But offline, a lot of people have found friends like in their areas, so recently there was a trans guy who approached

me and I linked him up to another trans guy who's in Ipoh. So they're both in Ipoh. So they started a friendship, that's pretty nice. And we have many groups of guys who do that as well. And some of them, they have links to the *pengkid* community, and they spread awareness about trans men to the *pengkid* community.[20] We have gatherings, we've only had one gathering, but we might have another this year. It's very hard to do anything without funding.

50. Goh: What would you consider as some of the achievements of ToM?
Wilde: Wow. The fact that we are still here (both laugh). Even though it's a secret group, only available through word of mouth, but they must find me personally and I must have the time to enter, we still have 172 members (laughs). There's probably like a hundred more in my inbox somewhere (laughs). Even though with such limited ways of finding us, they still manage to find us. And also we've managed to find safe hormone replacement therapy methods. We actually found a doctor in [a public hospital], and [a local psychologist][21] is helping with the psychology, so with the writing of the letter. So I wouldn't say it's cheap, it's definitely more expensive than doing it yourself, but at least it's safe. And your levels are being monitored. And funnily I have been doing this for other people but I myself haven't gone to see him.

51. Goh: What do you think are the main challenges of ToM?
Wilde: Er, the fact that we cannot be a more open group, because if we are an open group, there would be so many more people who can find us. But because of the stealth guys, I have to keep it a secret group probably forever. One way we tried to overcome that is having the public page, so that people can message us on the public page and we can just add them there. But em, our public page isn't very popular, because it's not being updated. I think that's our main challenge lah.

[20]See 'Prologue'.

[21]The hospital and individual have been de-identified for privacy, confidentiality and security.

52. The next challenge would be how to develop our group as a real community-based organisation, have like money to conduct events and training, workshops. You know, this sort of gatherings and all these things. And of course our other issue is that Malaysia is not recognised as a developed country, which makes funding even harder to get. And there're so many people vying for funding. And being trans men, we're not openly persecuted, people don't know about us. So when we apply for funding, yes, we're a hot topic, but if you want to compare giving to trans women who are being publicly persecuted, or trans men who are like invisible, hidden.

Bibliography

Mamun, Abdullah Al, Roselina Ahmad Saufi, and Mohammad Bin Ismail. 2016. 'Human Capital, Credit, and Startup Motives: A Study Among Rural Micro-Enterprises in Malaysia'. *The Journal of Developing Areas* 50 (4): 383–400.

Index

J. N. Goh, *Becoming a Malaysian Trans Man*, Gender, Sexualities and Culture in Asia, https://doi.org/10.1007/978-981-15-4534-4

The manufacturer's authorised representative in the EU is Springer Nature Customer Service Centre GmbH, Europaplatz 3, 69115 Heidelberg, Germany. If you have any concerns regarding our products, please contact ProductSafety@springernature.com

Printed and bound by CPI Group (UK) Ltd, Croydon, CR0 4YY

30/09/2026

02225461-0007